D1590181

TREMPER LONGMAN III is the Robert H. Gundry Professor of Biblical Studies at Westmont College, Santa Barbara, California. He has written numerous books and articles for both scholarly and lay audiences. His books include *Literary Approaches to Biblical Interpretation, Fictional Akkadian Autobiography, The Cry of the Soul,* and *An Introduction to the Old Testament.* He is also the author of the volume on Ecclesiastes in the New International Commentary on the Old Testament series.

THE NEW INTERNATIONAL COMMENTARY
ON THE
OLD TESTAMENT

General Editors

R. K. HARRISON
(1968–1993)

ROBERT L. HUBBARD, JR.
(1994–   )

SONG OF SONGS

TREMPER LONGMAN III

WILLIAM B. EERDMANS PUBLISHING COMPANY
GRAND RAPIDS, MICHIGAN / CAMBRIDGE, U.K.

© 2001 Wm. B. Eerdmans Publishing Co.

Wm. B. Eerdmans Publishing Co.
255 Jefferson Ave. S.E., Grand Rapids, Michigan 49503 /
P.O. Box 163, Cambridge CB3 9PU U.K.

Printed in the United States of America

06 05 04 03 02 01   7 6 5 4 3 2 1

Library of Congress Cataloging-in-Publication Data

Longman, Tremper.
Song of songs / Tremper Longman III.
cm.   — (The New International Commentary on the Old Testament)
Includes bibliographical references and index.
ISBN 0-8028-2543-5 (alk. paper)
1. Bible. O.T. Song of Solomon — Commentaries.
I. Title.   II. Series.

BS1485.53 L66   2001
223′.9077 — dc21

2001040347

www.eerdmans.com

To Alice

CONTENTS

TEXT AND COMMENTARY

INDEXES

GENERAL EDITOR'S PREFACE

Long ago St. Paul wrote: "I planted, Apollos watered, but God gave the growth" (1 Cor. 3:6, NRSV). He was right: ministry indeed requires a team effort — the collective labors of many skilled hands and minds. Someone digs up the dirt and drops in seed, while others water the ground to nourish seedlings to growth. The same team effort over time has brought this commentary series to its position of prominence today. Professor E. J. Young "planted" it forty years ago, enlisting its first contributors and himself writing its first published volume. Professor R. K. Harrison "watered" it, signing on other scholars and wisely editing everyone's finished products. As General Editor, I now tend their planting, and, true to Paul's words, through four decades God has indeed graciously "[given] the growth."

Today the New International Commentary on the Old Testament enjoys a wide readership of scholars, priests, pastors, rabbis, and other serious Bible students. Thousands of readers across the religious spectrum and in countless countries consult its volumes in their ongoing preaching, teaching, and research. They warmly welcome the publication of each new volume and eagerly await its eventual transformation from an emerging "series" into a complete commentary "set." But as humanity experiences a new century of history, an era commonly called "postmodern," what kind of commentary series is NICOT? What distinguishes it from other similarly well-established series?

Its volumes aim to publish biblical scholarship of the highest quality. Each contributor writes as an expert, both in the biblical text itself and in the relevant scholarly literature, and each commentary conveys the results of wide reading and careful, mature reflection. Ultimately, its spirit is eclectic, each contributor gleaning interpretive insights from any useful source, whatever its religious or philosophical viewpoint, and integrating them into his or her interpretation of a biblical book. The series draws on recent methodological innovations in biblical scholarship, e.g., canon criticism, the so-called "new literary criticism," reader-response theories, and sensitivity to gender-based and ethnic readings. NICOT volumes also aim to be irenic in tone, summarizing and critiquing influential views with fairness while defending their own. Its list of contributors includes male and female scholars from a number of Christian faith-groups. The diversity of contributors and their freedom to draw on all relevant methodologies give the entire series an exciting and enriching variety.

What truly distinguishes this series, however, is that it speaks from within that interpretive tradition known as evangelicalism. Evangelicalism is an informal movement within Protestantism that cuts across traditional denominational lines. Its heart and soul is the conviction that the Bible is God's inspired Word, written by gifted human writers, through which God calls humanity to enjoy a loving personal relationship with its Creator and Savior. True to that tradition, NICOT volumes do not treat the Old Testament as just an ancient literary artifact on a par with the *Iliad* or the Gilgamesh Epic. They are not literary autopsies of ancient parchment cadavers but rigorous, reverent wrestlings with wonderfully human writings through which the living God speaks his powerful Word. NICOT delicately balances "criticism" (i.e., the use of standard critical methodologies) with humble respect, admiration, and even affection for the biblical text. As an evangelical commentary, it pays particular attention to the text's literary features, theological themes, and implications for the life of faith today.

Ultimately, NICOT aims to serve women and men of faith who desire to hear God's voice afresh through the Old Testament. With gratitude to God for two marvelous gifts — the Scriptures themselves and keen-minded scholars to explain their message — I welcome readers of all kinds to savor the good fruit of this series.

ROBERT L. HUBBARD, JR.

AUTHOR'S PREFACE

Relationship is a wonderful, mysterious, often elusive, sometimes painful part of the human experience. Family, friends, colleagues, and acquaintances are the characters that people the plot of our lives. The most intimate of all human relationships, according to the Bible at least, is that between a husband and a wife. Indeed, as the commentary will later argue, this relationship provides a powerful analogy to that most fundamental of all relationships — God and his people.

It is, thus, not a surprise that there is a book of the Bible that focuses on the experiences and emotions of intimate male-female relationship. Though it has had a long history of repression by interpretation, the Song of Songs is now widely recognized as a poem celebrating human love and sexuality.

The late R. K. Harrison invited me to write this commentary about a dozen years ago. Though it was not the sole object of my professional interests, I started teaching the book regularly since that time. I would like to take this opportunity to thank the many students I have had in courses on the Song, often coupled with Ecclesiastes, at Westminster Theological Seminary, Fuller Theological Seminary, Regent College (Vancouver), Mars Hill Graduate School (Seattle), and Westmont College. Special mention should be given to a small doctoral seminar I gave a Trinity Evangelical Divinity School where the students were both insightful and helpful. It was particularly my years at Westminster, where I taught five doctoral seminars between 1989 and 1999, the last as a Visiting Professor, that played an important role in shaping my ideas about the Song. In particular, I would like to thank three of my doctoral students who chose to write on the Song — George Schwab, Steve Horine, and Phil Roberts. I will show my indebtedness to their work by way of footnotes. Further, I am grateful to my two student assistants, Erik Allen (Philadelphia) and Jake Werley (Santa Barbara), who helped me by tracking down references.

However, my interest in the Song was piqued even before I began my teaching career. I had the distinct pleasure of studying with two teachers in my graduate program at Yale University who also loved and studied the Song. First, my doctoral advisor W. W. Hallo was interested in the way that Mesopotamian material illuminated our understanding of Song of Songs 8:6-7. Second, though I never studied the Song with him, my three years of Ugaritic with Marvin Pope brought me into contact with this monumental thinker about this book. One of the earliest memories of my graduate program was a party at his house celebrating the publication of his new commentary. Unfortunately, I cannot adopt his basic ideas about the Song, but the fact that no work is quoted more often in the following pages demonstrates that his contribution is not dependent on his distinctive approach.

Next, I want to express my heartfelt appreciation to my editor, Robert Hubbard. I benefited greatly from his comments, though of course he is not responsible for any errors or interpretive missteps. In addition, my thanks go to Eerdmans and Allen Myers, the in-house shepherd of this series.

I dedicate this book to my gifted and beautiful wife, Alice. The Song inspires me to sing her praises, but that would only embarrass her. Here, I will just thank her for the love and support that inspires my life and work.

TREMPER LONGMAN III
Robert H. Gundry Professor
of Biblical Studies
Westmont College
New Year's 2001

ABBREVIATIONS

AB	Anchor Bible
ABD	*Anchor Bible Dictionary*
AJSL	*American Journal of Semitic Languages and Literature*
AJT	*American Journal of Theology*
ANET	*Ancient Near Eastern Texts Relating to the Old Testament*
ATR	*Anglican Theological Review*
AUSS	*Andrews University Seminary Studies*
BASOR	*Bulletin of the American Schools of Oriental Research*
BHS	*Biblia hebraica stuttgartensia*
Bib	*Biblica*
BibSac	*Bibliotheca Sacra*
BKAT	Biblischer Kommentar: Altes Testament
BN	*Biblische Notizen*
BR	*Bible Review*
BST	Bible Speaks Today
BTB	*Biblical Theology Bulletin*
BZ	*Biblische Zeitschrift*
CBQ	*Catholic Biblical Quarterly*
CS	The Context of Scripture
EHS	Europäische Hochschulscriften
ETL	*Ephemerides theologicae lovanienses*
ExpT	*Expository Times*
FOTL	Forms of the Old Testament Literature
HAR	*Hebrew Annual Review*
HTR	*Harvard Theological Review*
Interp	*Interpretation*
JAAR	*Journal of the American Academy of Religion*
JANES	*Journal of the Ancient Near Eastern Society of Columbia University*

JAOS	*Journal of the American Oriental Society*
JBL	*Journal of Biblical Literature*
JCS	*Journal of Cuneiform Studies*
JETS	*Journal of the Evangelical Theological Society*
JNES	*Journal of Near Eastern Studies*
JQR	*Jewish Quarterly Review*
JSOT	*Journal for the Study of the Old Testament*
JSOTS	*Journal for the Study of the Old Testament* — Supplement Series
JSS	*Journal of Semitic Studies*
JTS	*Journal of Theological Studies*
NAC	New American Commentary
NICOT	New International Commentary on the Old Testament
NIDOTTE	*New International Dictionary of Old Testament Theology and Exegesis*
NIV	New International Version
NIVAC	New International Version Application Commentary
NLT	New Living Translation
OTE	*Old Testament Essays*
PEQ	*Palestine Exploration Quarterly*
RB	*Revue biblique*
RTR	*Reformed Theological Review*
SJOT	*Scandinavian Journal of the Old Testament*
SR	*Studies in Religion/Sciences Religieuses*
TOTC	Tyndale Old Testament Commentary
TynBul	*Tyndale Bulletin*
TZ	*Theologische Zeitschrift*
VT	*Vetus Testamentum*
WTJ	*Westminster Theological Journal*
ZAW	*Zeitschrift für die alttestamentliche Wissenschaft*

INTRODUCTION[1]

I. TITLE

The title Song of Songs comes from the first two words of the first verse in the Hebrew text *(šîr haššîrîm)*. The most obvious meaning of this phrase follows from a recognition that the syntax (the use of the same word in construct relationship, first in the singular and the second time in the plural) denotes a superlative in Hebrew. This, in other words, is the best song of all. Grammatical analogies include "utterly meaningless" (Eccles. 1:2 and throughout) and "Holy of Holies," in reference to the most holy spot on earth (Exod. 29:37) — see other analogies in Deuteronomy 10:14 ("heaven of heavens") and Genesis 9:25 ("servant of servants"). Origen identified seven songs in Scripture and argued that the Song of Songs was the best.[2] This may be compared with rabbinic assertions, stated in different ways, that the Song was the best of the Solomonic corpus (see below under Authorship). Since Luther, Germans have captured this sense by typically titling the book *Hoheleid,* "the best song."

Though I agree that the title has this superlative sense, I believe it intends to convey more than simply "the best song." When we explain the structure of the book, we will see that there are both centrifugal and centripetal forces at work.[3] We will argue that there is a loose unity to the Song suggested by an occasional refrain and a unity of persona (thus the singular

1. For further discussion, consult R. B. Dillard and T. Longman III, *An Introduction to the Old Testament* (Grand Rapids: Zondervan, 1994), pp. 257-65.

2. M. H. Pope, *Song of Songs,* AB 7C (Garden City, NY: Doubleday, 1977), p. 297.

3. The terms are D. Grossberg's; see his *Centripetal and Centrifugal Structures in Hebrew Poetry* (Atlanta: Scholars Press, 1989).

Song), but that the poems are ultimately independent of one another. The book is something like an erotic psalter (thus Songs).[4]

Though this commentary uses and encourages the title Song of Songs, two other titles are also current in the literature. First, Song of Solomon highlights the connection that the superscription ties between the book and David's son (see commentary on 1:1). However, inasmuch as this title implies Solomonic authorship of the whole, it is misleading (see Authorship). Second, the term Canticles is occasionally used and derives from the name given to the book in the Latin Vulgate (*Canticum canticorum*, which means Song of Songs).

Song of Songs is the fourth book in the third section of the Hebrew Bible (the *Ketubim*). While in the English canon it follows Ecclesiastes, in the Hebrew it precedes it. In the latter, as a result, we have the interesting and surely intentional order of Proverbs, Ruth, and the Song. Proverbs, it will be remembered, concludes with the poem concerning the virtuous woman (31:10-31). Ruth and the Song, then, both present virtuous and assertive women for our contemplation.

The Song of Songs is also a part of the Megillot "Scrolls," five books[5] each of which were associated in postbiblical times with a particular Jewish feast. The Song of Songs was read on the eighth day of Passover, an association that likely arose because the book was read as a historical allegory beginning with the Exodus and ending with the coming of the Messiah (see below under History of Interpretation).

II. AUTHORSHIP

The discussion over the authorship of the Song of Songs begins with the superscription in 1:1:

šîr haššîrîm ᵃšer lišlōmōh

The part of the superscription potentially relevant to the issue of authorship is the subordinate clause formed by the last two words. As mentioned above, this verse functions something like a title page, introducing the work that follows. It seems a reasonable hypothesis to suggest that the superscription was added after the book was composed, and the meager evidence that we have

---

4. See the similar view articulated by R. Gordis, *The Song of Songs and Lamentations: A Study, Modern Translation, and Commentary*, rev. and augmented ed. (New York: KTAV, 1974), pp. 17-18.

5. The others are Ruth, Lamentations, Ecclesiastes, and Esther.

invites the conclusion that the superscription was written by someone not connected with the composition of the poems that follow.[6] Does that mean that it claims that Solomon is its author? Not necessarily if viewed from the perspective of the grammar. The preposition l^e that is prefixed to Solomon's name can theoretically be understood in more than one way in this context:

To Solomon: The book is dedicated to Solomon.
By Solomon: Authorship.
Concerning Solomon: Solomon is the subject matter of the book.
Solomonic: which may mean something like "in the Solomonic/wisdom literary tradition."

Traditionally, there is no doubt but that the book was understood to be written by Solomon, if not also about him (see History of Interpretation). The Midrash Rabbah, for instance, talks of the three main contributions of Solomon — Song of Songs, Proverbs, and Ecclesiastes — as belonging to three phases of his life, with the explanation that "when a man is young he composes songs; when he grows older he makes sententious remarks; and when he becomes an old man he speaks of the vanity of things." Thus, the Song is thought to be composed by Solomon in his youth, not only when his sexual energy was high, but also before his apostasy, which was motivated in large part by illegitimate lust (see below). Furthermore, those who believe that the Song was authored by Solomon suggest that the popular title for the book, Song of Solomon, implicitly identifies Solomon as the author.

Even in the modern period, Solomonic authorship has found its defenders.[7] One common line of defense has to do with the imagery of the Song, which assumes both wealth and an international trade that would make the Israelite author and audience aware of the exotic spices that find mention in the poems (i.e., 4:13-14).[8] Others would add the argument that the most natural way to read the superscription is as an attribution of authorship, and, since there is no reason to question Solomon's ability to write love poems, why should modern scholars question the tradition? In addition, it is felt by many that the *lamed* preposition elsewhere indicates authorship, so why not

6. Most notably the use of the relative pronoun ʾ*ašer* rather than *še* as in the body of the book. However, it is conceivable that this change is determined by the prose-like genre of the superscription and the poetic quality of the poems.

7. A. H. Harman, "Modern Discussion on the Song of Songs," *RTR* 37 (1978): 66, lists the following as arguing for a date during or closely associated with the time of Solomon: M. H. Segal, G. Gerleman, and C. Rabin.

8. G. L. Archer, Jr., *A Survey of Old Testament Introduction* (Chicago: Moody, 1974), pp. 498-99.

here? Such views, of course, have to defend against those who understand the language of the book to be late (see below under Language).

Indeed, the tradition of Solomon as a writer and songster is strong in the prose tradition of the Old Testament. The most relevant passage is that found in 1 Kings 4:29-34:

> God gave Solomon wisdom and very great insight, and a breadth of understanding as measureless as the sand on the seashore. Solomon's wisdom was greater than the wisdom of all the men of the East, and greater than all the wisdom of Egypt. He was wiser than any other man, including Ethan the Ezrahite — wiser than Heman, Calcol and Darda, the sons of Mahol. And his fame spread to all the surrounding nations. He spoke three thousand proverbs and his songs numbered a thousand and five. He described plant life, from the cedar of Lebanon to the hyssop that grows out of walls. He also taught about animals and birds, reptiles and fish. Men of all nations came to listen to Solomon's wisdom, sent by all the kinds of the world, who had heard of his wisdom.

In a word, Solomon was quite a prolific wisdom author. Most relevant to the Song is the statement that he wrote over a thousand songs. Could some of these be the songs of that book of love poetry?

It seems most natural on the basis of this evidence to conclude that the superscription is making the claim that Solomon wrote the Song in its entirety. For those who believe that the Bible speaks authoritatively in such matters, this seems the end of the discussion. All that is left to do is to provide arguments in favor of Solomonic authorship and to answer those objections that are brought against it. However, the situation is not quite so simple. There are significant reasons to question the idea that Solomon wrote the entirety of the Song. As we survey these reasons, we will see that some are indeed ill-founded, while others are persuasive. We will move from the weakest to the strongest claims.

In the first place, we have the question of language. We will deal with the specific evidence concerning language later in the Introduction. For now, I simply want to suggest that language is not a reliable indicator of the date of a book for two reasons. First, our knowledge of the development of the Hebrew language is tenuous, particularly in terms of the influence that other languages had on Hebrew. In the past, the discovery of Aramaisms in the text was considered strong evidence of its lateness. Now, with the relatively recent discovery of Aramaic dated to the eleventh century B.C.[9] (Tell Fekheriye Inscription), it appears that the influence of Aramaic on Hebrew occurred earlier than

---

9. Though this has been questioned; cf. J. Naveh, "Aramaic Script," *ABD,* vol. 1, pp. 342-45.

the exilic period. There is no good reason to deny an early influence since we know that the two language groups had contact as early as David (cf. 2 Sam. 8:5-8). The supposed presence of a single Persian loanword (4:3, *pardēs*) is hardly enough to convince us of a late date. Second, we are ignorant concerning the possible linguistic updating of earlier biblical material. As a matter of fact, it is hard to imagine that there was no updating during the long period that we believe the Bible came into existence; otherwise, later generations would have had a hard time understanding the language. Although editors would have tended to be more conservative with poetry in any such updating due to the demands of literary artifice, nonetheless we must allow for the possibility that the Song of Songs was updated, which would not allow us to use (possibly) later linguistic forms to date the composition of the text.

Second, we might question an essential Solomonic role in the Song due to Solomon's dubious reputation in the area of love. Song extols an exclusive, committed relationship. To these lovers there is only one other person — each other.[10] Yet the historical tradition concerning Solomon does not focus on one woman but many wives and concubines. One of his wives stood out from among others, namely, the daughter of the Pharaoh of Egypt, but that is due to the importance of the military alliance that was formed between Egypt and Israel, not because of a unique love between the two. This is made clear in 1 Kings 11:1: "King Solomon, however, loved many foreign women besides Pharaoh's daughter — Moabites, Ammonites, Edomites, Sidonians and Hittites." Furthermore, the Deuteronomic historian makes no secret of the catastrophe that resulted from these marriages: "They were from nations about which the LORD had told the Israelites, 'You must not intermarry with them, because they will surely turn your hearts after their gods.' Nevertheless, Solomon held fast to them in love." Indeed, he had seven hundred wives "of royal birth." The results were a personal tragedy: "As Solomon grew old, his wives turned his heart after other gods, and his heart was not fully devoted to the LORD his God, as the heart of David his father had been. He followed Ashtoreth, the goddess of the Sidonians, and Molech, the detestable god of the Ammonites. So Solomon did evil in the eyes of the LORD; he did not follow the LORD completely, as David his father had done" (1 Kings 4:4-6). His foreign love affairs also led to a national calamity immediately upon his death. God judged Solomon for his apostasy by splitting the kingdom, united under his rule, into two parts. His son and those who descended from his line would only rule the southern kingdom of Judah, and, sure enough, when Solomon died, one of his subordinates led a rebellion against Reho-

---

10. True, Song of Songs 6:8 mentions sixty queens and eighty concubines, but nothing in the text indicates that these women are the man's wives and concubines. He may simply be comparing his beloved to the "best" women in the land.

boam (1 Kings 12). The Deuteronomic historian, however, was interested in even the more devastating effects of this and other acts of rebellion. The final form of Kings should surely be dated to the exile, where the question that it (along with Samuel) grapples with is: "Why are we in exile?" In the mind of the historian, Solomon's sinful marriages constitute a banner reason why Judah was defeated and the temple destroyed. All of this is to query the likelihood of a book about romantic love being written by Solomon. It seems quite a stretch to suggest, along with the above-quoted rabbinic legend, that the Song was a product of Solomon's pure youth. It seems a better strategy to explore other options of understanding the superscription.

A third consideration that causes us to distance the Song of Songs as a whole from Solomonic authorship is the minimal role that Solomon plays in the text. A mere three passages even mention Solomon at all, and in all three it is clear that Solomon is the object of the poem, not its composer. Some might respond by saying that Solomon plays a much larger role if we recognize that he stands behind every mention of the "king" in the text. However, most recent scholarship has rightly recognized that king, like shepherd, is an epithet of respect and endearment,[11] not a reference to an actual political sovereign and certainly not a cipher for Solomon. Furthermore, the three passages themselves refer to Solomon in different ways. A full discussion of the passages may be found in the commentary below, but here we will offer a few guiding comments. In 1:3 Solomon — if he is mentioned at all[12] — is not referred to as a person; only the dark color of his tents is mentioned. In 3:6-11 (particularly v. 11), Solomon's wedding is more the topic than Solomon the person. The glory of his wedding excites those who are called upon to remember it. It brings honor to the institution of marriage. The passage itself is not saying that Solomon married the woman of the Song. It is simply promoting the wonder of marriage by focusing on all the wonderful and expensive accoutrements of Solomon's wedding. Finally, 8:11-12 paints a negative picture of Solomon as one who tries to buy love but is ridiculed for the attempt. It is doubtful that Solomon would characterize himself this way. In conclusion, we find no support for Solomonic authorship in the texts that mention his name. We should also mention the one passage where a woman is called a Shulammite (7:1 [English 6:13]). As explained in the commentary, this appears to be a feminine form of the name Solomon and suggests that perhaps both names are used for their etymological sense of "peace."

Fourth, important to the significance of Solomon in the superscription is how the name is used in the superscriptions of other books. Proverbs explicitly has his name in the first verse (1:1), and Ecclesiastes strongly implies

---

11. See the discussion under Song of Songs 1:4.
12. It may be a reference to Salma, a nomadic tribe.

6

Solomon (1:1). Yet in both cases, a close examination reveals that neither implies that Solomon wrote the whole book. Indeed, as argued in an earlier work, I suggest that Solomon did not write the book of Ecclesiastes but rather provided the fictional background for Qohelet.[13] The book of Proverbs shows signs of multiple authorship, more an anthology composed of a number of texts from different authors and time periods. Frequently, the sections are marked by captions that indicate authorship. They cite a group called "the wise" (22:17; 24:23), Agur (30:1), King Lemuel (31:1), and Solomon (1:1; 10:1; 25:1) as sources of the wisdom of the book. Only Proverbs 1:8–8:18 and 31:10-31 are without an explicit authorship attribution. Proverbs 1:1-7 serves as an extended superscription and introduction to the book that connects authorship to Solomon but does not claim it for the section itself.[14]

In our opinion, the *lišlōmōh* in the Song of Songs is most like the mention of Solomon in the superscription of the book of Proverbs. Below, in the sections on structure and genre, we will describe the Song as an anthology of love poems. There is nothing inconceivable about the idea that Solomon wrote one or more of the poems. However, there is also nothing that indisputably connects the book with Solomon. Fortunately, little is at stake in terms of authorship of these poems. The one thing that is clear is that it is not telling a story about Solomon. To posit such a reading involves excessive eisegesis to make it work. Our translation of the preposition in the superscription (The Song of Songs, which *concerns* Solomon) is purposively ambiguous in terms of Solomon's relationship to the Song.

A WOMAN POET?

One school of thought suggests that a woman poet may have written the Song of Songs. These scholars point out that the woman's voice dominates the book. A. Brenner, for instance, indicates that out of one hundred and seventeen verses, the woman speaks sixty-one and a half of them.[15] She is fully aware that mere quantity does not argue the case for a woman's authorship; indeed, a male can imitate a woman's voice at least to a certain extent. She also understands that the Song is a collection and so can come from a variety of different time periods and authors. However, Brenner still suspects that

---

13. The argument may be found in T. Longman III, *The Book of Ecclesiastes,* NICOT (Grand Rapids: Eerdmans, 1998), pp. 2-9.

14. For further discussion of Proverbs, see Dillard and Longman, *An Introduction to the Old Testament,* pp. 236-37.

15. A. Brenner, "Women Poets and Authors," in *A Feminine Companion to the Song of Songs,* ed. A. Brenner (Sheffield: JSOT Press, 1993), p. 88.

certain poems — she mentions in particular 1:2-6; 3:1-4; 5:1-7; 5:10-16 — "are so essentially feminine that a male could hardly imitate their tone and texture successfully."[16] The thesis of J. Bekkenkamp and F. van Dijk further supports Brenner's thesis. They argue that the Song is part of an extensive tradition of women who sang songs. They survey references to women singing in the Bible (2 Sam. 1:20, 24; Jer. 9:17, 20; Ezek. 32:16) as well as quotations of their songs (Judges 5; 1 Sam. 18:6-7). From this evidence they conclude that "it is very likely that we are dealing with women's poetry in the Song of Songs."[17] S. D. Goiten is even more specific. Following the lead of M. H. Segal,[18] she situates the Song in the time of Solomon. Detecting a woman's voice in the book, she posits a particular woman as the author: "The Song was composed in honour of King Solomon by a young woman, daughter of a nobleman (ndyb), who was brought to his court in order to adorn his parties by her singing. . . . What would be more natural than for Solomon, the great woman-lover, to ask one of the female singers of his court to gather for him the best of current Israelite love poetry?"[19]

It is not just women scholars who argue for this position; they are joined also by F. Landy and A. LaCocque. Indeed, the latter quotes the former as he states his opinion that "the author of the Song was a female poet who intended to 'cock a snook at all Puritans.'"[20] In other words, according to both these commentators, the Song was written by a woman who was resisting social norms, including the idea that women should be receivers not initiators of love.

Against the rising tide supporting the idea of female authorship of the Song comes D. J. A. Clines, always reading "against the grain." In a nutshell, his opinion is that the woman of the Song is the perfect woman from a male perspective, the ideal dream of most men, and thus a fabrication by men.[21] He believes the book was written by men in order to meet the need "of a male public for erotic literature."[22]

16. Brenner, "Women Poets and Authors," pp. 90-91.

17. J. Bekkenkamp and F. van Dijk, "The Canon of the Old Testament and Women's Cultural Traditions," in *A Feminine Companion to the Song of Songs,* ed. A. Brenner (Sheffield: JSOT Press, 1993), p. 79.

18. M. H. Segal, "The Song of Songs," *VT* 12 (1962): 470-90.

19. S. D. Goiten, "The Song of Songs: A Female Composition," in *A Feminine Companion to the Song of Songs,* ed. A. Brenner (Sheffield: JSOT Press, 1993), p. 65.

20. A. LaCocque, *Romance She Wrote: A Hermeneutical Essay on Song of Songs* (Harrisburg, PA: Trinity, 1998), p. xi, citing F. Landy, *Paradoxes of Paradise: Identity and Difference in the Song of Songs* (Sheffield: Almond, 1983), p. 17.

21. His views are found in D. J. A. Clines, "Why Is There a Song of Songs and What Does It Do to You If You Read It?" *Jin Dao* 1 (1994): 1-27.

22. Clines, "Why Is There a Song of Songs?" p. 6.

The discussions of the gender of the author of the Song reveals more about us as commentators than it does about the Song. It relies on a theory of literature and of gender that believes that women and men are typecast in the way that they write. The irony is that the arguments on both sides are not coming from social conservatives, but they certainly feed the agendas of those conservatives. The most honest appraisal is that we do not know for certain who wrote the songs of the Song, a man or a woman, and in any case it is a collection of love poetry, whether by men, or women, or both. It strikes me, though, that Clines is the most egregious of these commentators since his view relies on the supposition that no woman would have the interest in the kind of love that the beloved articulates.

III. LITERARY STYLE

READING THE POETRY OF THE SONG

The Song bears all the characteristics of what we recognize as Hebrew poetry: terseness, parallelism, imagery, and secondary poetical devices.[23] Accordingly, it was one of three poetical books given special accents in the Masoretic tradition *(te'amin)*. Unfortunately, though, we have no native description of the conventions of Hebrew poetry, so we will here give a brief description of the major ones with an emphasis on their manifestation in the Song.

Terseness

Terseness simply describes the fact that Hebrew poetry is distinguished from prose by the brevity of its clauses. Prose is constructed of sentences that form paragraphs that build longer discourses; poetry is made up of short cola that form parallel lines (see below) that may build stanzas or simply longer poems. The colon is short, on average three major words, occasionally four, and rarely more. The second colon of a parallel line is almost always shorter than the first. A significant factor in this is ellipsis, which results when the second

23. For more detail on the nature of Hebrew poetry, see especially W. G. E. Watson, *Classical Hebrew Poetry,* JSOTS 26 (Sheffield: JSOT Press, 1984); R. Alter, *The Art of Biblical Poetry* (New York: Basic Books, 1985); J. Kugel, *The Idea of Biblical Poetry* (New Haven: Yale University Press, 1981); A. Berlin, *The Dynamics of Biblical Parallelism* (Bloomington: Indiana University Press, 1985); as well as my "Biblical Poetry," in *A Complete Literary Guide to the Bible,* ed. L. Ryken and T. Longman III (Grand Rapids: Zondervan, 1993), pp. 80-91.

colon omits a part of the first colon with the understanding that the omitted part of the first colon is to be read into the second. Song of Songs 8:6a provides a banner example with the omission of the verb in the second colon:

> Set me like a seal on your heart,
>> like a seal on your arm.

Another reason for terseness is the relative lack of conjunctions in Hebrew poetry. Conjunctions are brief words (in English "and," "but," "therefore," "however," and the like) but significant in that they make clear to the reader precisely how the clauses relate to one another. They are not completely lacking in poetry, nor in the poetry of the Song, as we see in the first few verses:

> Let him kiss me with the kisses of his mouth,
>> for your love is better than wine.
> How wonderful is the scent of your oils;
>> your name is poured out oil.
> Therefore, the young women love you. (Song of Songs 1:2-3)

Here we see the use of two conjunctions that are explicit in the Hebrew: "for" *(ki)* and "therefore" *('al-kēn)*. More typical is the verse that follows (1:4), which completely lacks conjunctions, raising questions concerning the relationship of the clauses.

> Draw me after you; let's run!
>> The king has brought me into his bedroom.

> We will rejoice and feel happy for you!
>> We will praise your love more than wine!

The terseness of poetry, manifested in part by ellipsis and the lack of conjunctions (as well as the lack of other morphemic markers like the indicator of the direct object [*'et*]), is a prime reason why poetry lacks semantic precision. We will see that both parallelism and especially imagery only deepen the ambiguity of poetry. However, poets relish this intentional ambiguity that results in an emotional richness.

Parallelism

Parallelism is perhaps the most widely recognized device of Hebrew poetry, but even it is not pervasive throughout the literature. Not every line of a Hebrew poem is parallelistic. Furthermore, there are gradations of parallelism, from very strong parallel structures to extremely weak ones. Nonetheless, as a widely used characteristic of Hebrew poetry, and one that appears quite extensively in the Song of Songs, it is important to have a basic understanding of it in anticipation of a commentary on the book.

Parallelism is the common term for the long-observed near repetition that characterizes the poetic line in Hebrew poetry. It was named parallelism by Robert Lowth in the eighteenth century, a term borrowed from geometry to describe what he called "a certain conformation of the sentences" in which "equals refer to equals, and opposites to opposites. . . ."[24]

Since Lowth, parallelism has been recognized as the most telltale feature of biblical poetry. Also since Lowth, literary and biblical scholars have emphasized the equivalence between the related cola of a poetic line. This may be illustrated by C. S. Lewis's statement that parallelism is "the practice of saying the same thing twice in different words."[25] While Lewis did understand the parallel line to operate according to the principle "the same in the other," his emphasis was on coherence of the cola, and handbooks on biblical poetry presented an even less balanced statement on the relationship between the cola than he did.

Parallelism has received intense scrutiny over the past few years from biblical and literary scholars.[26] The emerging consensus is that the parallel line is a more subtle literary device than previously thought. The present paradigm for understanding parallelism is development rather than equivalence. The biblical poet is doing more than saying the same thing twice. The second part always nuances the first part in some way. J. Kugel rightly refuses to replace Lowth's traditional three categories of parallelism (synonymous, antithetic, synthetic) with others. He simply argues that the second colon always contributes to the thought of the first colon, as suggested by his formula "a, what's more b."

The fact that the parallel line is much more subtle than the old traditional formula of equivalence is clearly seen in the Song, where the parallelism is often quite subtle and rarely even close to synonymous. Here are two examples from different sections of the Song.

24. Lecture III of *De Sacra poesi Hebraeorum* (1753), quoted in Berlin, *The Dynamics of Biblical Parallelism,* p. 1.

25. C. S. Lewis, *Reflections on the Psalms* (New York: Harcourt Brace, 1961), p. 11.

26. Berlin, *The Dynamics of Biblical Parallelism;* Kugel, *The Idea of Biblical Poetry;* Alter, *The Art of Biblical Poetry;* M. O'Connor, *Hebrew Verse Structure* (Winona Lake, IN: Eisenbrauns, 1980); M. Geller, *Parallelism in Early Hebrew Poetry* (Missoula, MT: Scholars Press, 1979).

My head is full of dew;
    my locks with the drizzle of the night. (Song of Songs 5:2c)

In this bicolon we have what appears to be nearly synonymous parallelism. Part of our difficulty may be knowing the various nuances of words like "dew" and "drizzle" in the original, not only semantic differences but emotional overtones. Nonetheless, we can see the specification that is achieved as we move from colon a to colon b when we note that "head" is replaced by "hair." More importantly, the mood is enriched and the scene becomes much clearer by the specification of "night" found only in the second colon. Balance is achieved in the line in spite of the additional element, we will note, by the ellipsis of the verb in colon b.

Our second example comes from the descriptive song *(wasf)* of chapter 4. Here we see examples of a parallelism where colon A creates a metaphor for a body part, which is extended in colon b. This particular type of "A, what's more B" construction may be illustrated by simply translating Song of Songs 4:3:

Your "navel" is a rounded bowl,
    which does not lack mixed wine.
Your "belly" is a heap of wheat,
    bordered with lilies.

We should also be aware that parallelism operates on more than the semantic level, as described above. Space does not allow a detailed description, but recent studies have enlarged our understanding to include grammatical and even phonological parallelism.[27]

In the following commentary, the above understanding of parallelism underlies the interpretation but will only be made explicit when it is particularly striking or relevant to the meaning of the verse under consideration.

Imagery

The third trait of Hebrew poetry is imagery and figurative language. Imagery is not the exclusive province of poetry, but the frequency and intensity of imagery is heightened in discourse that we normally recognize as poetic. It is, after all, another way to write compactly, as well as to increase the emotional impact of a passage. The subject matter of the Song, love, calls for a rich use of imagery, and when we turn to the text, we will not be disappointed. Indeed, the Song presents us with perhaps the largest concentration of imagery

27. Berlin, *The Dynamics of Biblical Parallelism;* A. Cooper, "Biblical Poetics: A Linguistic Approach," Ph.D. dissertation, Yale University, 1976.

anywhere in the Bible, and its images are also among the most suggestive and, at times, enigmatic.

As M. H. Abrams points out, imagery is an "ambiguous term."[28] He goes on to quote C. Day Lewis, who speaks of imagery as "a picture made out of words." Such pictures are often the result of comparison, the two most common types being metaphor and simile. Simile, on the one level, is not even figurative language; it is capable of being understood on a literal level. A simile is a comparison between two things and is marked by the use of "like" or "as." Song of Songs 4:1b is a clear example:

> Your hair is like a flock of goats
> descending from Mount Gilead.

Metaphor has long been considered the master image or even the essence of poetry by literary scholars since the time of Aristotle. Metaphor presents a stronger connection between the two objects of comparison and is truly figurative language, as in Song of Songs 4:1a:

> Your eyes behind your veil are doves.

Metaphor catches our attention by the disparity between the two objects and the daring suggestion of similarity. Readers must ponder and reflect on the point of the similarity and, by so doing, explore multiple levels of meaning and experience the emotional overtones of the metaphor.

The commentary proper will note some special characteristics of the imagery of the Song. For one thing, the Song's imagery will exploit comparisons, not only of sight but of all the senses, including taste, touch, smell, and sound. Love excites all the senses, and the poet reflects this through figurative language. Further, the love of the Song is an intimate, sensual, even erotic passion. The subject calls for an evocative language but one that does not offend or expose in an unseemly way.[29] Again, in the commentary below we will note the use of double entendre, imagery that suggests an erotic meaning behind the surface meaning of the text.

The language of love invites images from certain spheres of life more than others. J. M. Munro, in her excellent study of the images of the Song, names four major areas from which the imagery of the Song is drawn: courtly imagery, imagery of family life, nature imagery, and images of space

---

28. M. H. Abrams, *A Glossary of Literary Terms,* 4th ed. (New York: Holt, Rinehart and Winston, 1981), p. 78.

29. Of course, every culture and every individual has different standards of what is acceptable and what is offensive.

and time. It is my opinion that she missed one other major area: military images (e.g., the text and commentary at Song of Songs 1:9; 4:4; 6:4, 10).[30]

It is of the nature of imagery to be controversial in interpretation. Figurative language is not concerned with precision of content. Indeed, imagery both reveals and conceals the object of comparison. To say that the woman's eyes are like doves raises all sorts of questions that are difficult to answer, not just because we lack the ancient context but also because of the nature of imagery.[31] In what way are her eyes like doves? First we go extremely far in unpacking the image, and then we start to question whether or not we have gone too far. It is here that we will find the most disagreement about the interpretation of the images. Some of my readers, especially my professional colleagues, will judge me as taking the images too far; my guess is that far more will say the opposite, that I have been reticent in my analysis of the images. I feel, however, that in the interpretation of some scholars (Landy, Brenner, and Goulder[32] come immediately to mind) free association with the images of the Song is so prevalent that we learn far more about the interpreters than we do about the text. However, since the interpretation of images involves an artistic sense more than a scientific mind-set, the readers of this commentary will have to form that judgment for themselves.[33]

SECONDARY POETIC DEVICES

Besides parallelism and imagery, a number of other ornamental devices appear in Hebrew poetry. While parallelism and imagery are very frequent

---

30. J. M. Munro, *Spikenard and Saffron: A Study in the Poetic Language of the Song of Songs* (Sheffield: Sheffield Academic Press, 1995).

31. As pointed out by M. V. Fox, *The Song of Songs and the Ancient Egyptian Love Songs* (Madison: University of Wisconsin Press, 1985), p. 298: "Readers (of imagery), like young lovers, have a problem of knowing how far to go; but if we sometimes go too far, that is part of the fun."

32. Landy, *Paradoxes of Paradise;* A. Brenner, "'Come Back, Come Back the Shulammite' (Song of Songs 7:1-10): A Parody of the *wasf* Genre," in *On Humour and the Comic in the Hebrew Bible,* ed. A. Brenner and Y. T. Radday (Sheffield: Almond, 1990), pp. 251-76; M. Goulder, *The Song of Fourteen Songs,* JSOTS 36 (Sheffield; JSOT Press, 1986). This said, however, I will also acknowledge that all three of these authors have stimulated my thinking in positive ways.

33. At one point in the study of Hebrew poetry, it was presupposed that it was characterized by meter. Today, there is a rough consensus either that meter does not exist in Hebrew poetry or that it is irrecoverable due to changes in the language over time. For my criticism of the quest for Hebrew meter, see T. Longman III, "A Critique of Two Recent Metrical Systems," *Bib* 63 (1982): 230-54.

in Old Testament poetry, the others are secondary in that they appear less regularly.

Ancient Hebrew poets "beautified" and enhanced their poetic creations in many different ways. Many have been studied, given technical names, and categorized by scholars. This introduction is not the place to introduce even those devices that are used in the Song,[34] but devices like inclusio, merism, and chiasm will be indicated and discussed in the commentary below as they are encountered in the text of the Song.

CHARACTERIZATION

The Song speaks through its characters. There is no narrator, and we will argue below that there is no overarching narrative or plot. However, the characters whom we hear in the Song have a consistency of persona, and we will here briefly present an overview of their function within the Song:

The Woman

We begin with the woman because she is by far the most dominant presence in the Song. She speaks more frequently than the man, and, when the latter speaks, he often speaks of her (see in particular chapter 4). The age of the woman, as well as of the man, is not explicitly mentioned, but we should probably envision them as young, just coming to maturity. In some of the poems the couple is not married, or they are newly married, and M. V. Fox reminds us that the best guess based on the evidence we have is that marriage took place in the early or mid-teens in ancient Israel.[35]

The woman not only speaks more often but also initiates the relationship and pursues it. She frequently expresses her desire for the man; she even overcomes threats and obstacles to be with him (3:1-5; 5:2-8). Her view of herself is modest (1:5-6; 2:1), but as we see her through the eyes of the man she is magnificent (see in particular the *wasf*s in 4:1-7, 10-15; 7:1-6). He calls her "most beautiful of women" (1:8), darling (1:9, 15; 2:2, 10, 13; 4:1, 7; 5:2), his bride (4:8, 9, 10, 11, 12; 5:1); his sister (4:12; 5:1, 2), his dove (5:2).

The Man

We learn about the man not only from his own speech but also from the woman's speech to him. We are introduced to him first by the latter as she

34. The best handbook is Watson, *Classical Hebrew Poetry.*
35. Fox, *The Song of Songs,* p. xii.

describes him as desirable (1:2-4).[36] In this first speech, she also refers to him as king (1:4; see also 1:12 and perhaps 7:5). This fueled interpretive speculation that the man is Solomon and should be understood as such throughout the poem. However, she also refers to him as a shepherd (1:7). Those who wish to preserve the identification of the man with Solomon argue either that the shepherd image is not incompatible with the royal image or that the figures should be divided and two men are described in the Song. However, the approach taken in this commentary is to understand both king and shepherd as figurative terms, wherein the woman endows the man with metaphorical roles to express her respect and desire for him. He is desired to be sure, but he also desires her. She pursues him, but he also pursues her (2:8-14; 5:2-4).

The Women

Throughout the Song we hear from a group of women who are variously identified as "daughters of Jerusalem" (e.g., 1:5), "daughters of Zion" (e.g., 3:11), or simply "young women" (e.g., 1:3). Indeed, in some contexts, they are assumed to be the audience for the woman's addresses without being explicitly mentioned (1:5-6). It is intriguing to suggest that these references apply to the same group of women. While we state this, however, we must be careful also to safeguard against the idea that these are real women. Like the woman and the man of the Song, the women are a literary device, and the question is not so much who are they as what is their function within the poems. However, it is possible to suggest that they have a distinct character, which is signaled in 1:5 by their association with Jerusalem. In a word, they are city girls, young and naïve, inexperienced in matters of love. It is here that they find their functions as a sounding board, a contrast, and students of the woman.

(1) Sounding board: In some poems the women serve as a backdrop to the speeches of the woman, asking her questions that stir longer speeches or reacting to her comments. A good example of this function is found in 5:9, where the young women ask the woman to describe her man, inspiring her moving description of him in 5:10-16. At times the women go beyond mere sounding board in their reaction to the woman and her actions. In 1:4, e.g., they confirm the woman's choice of the man, and in 5:1b they provide an outside witness to the joy of the union between the two. (2) Contrast: The women are associated with Jerusalem, the leading city of Israel. As such, they stand in contrast with the woman, who is identified with country settings

---

36. Also, note that her most common epithet for the man is lover (*dōdî:* 1:2, 4; 4:10; 5:1; 7:13).

— vineyard, orchard, nut grove. It seems that her defensive response to the fact that she has been darkened by the sun in 1:5-6 may be in reaction to the softness of city girls. (3) Sometimes, however, the woman, experienced in love, instructs the young women to be careful not to easily enter into this potentially dangerous relationship (see commentary at 2:7; 3:5; 8:4).[37]

Mother, Brother, Father

The woman's family play a role in the Song, and most interesting is the role of the brothers. They appear in two places, the beginning (1:5-6) and the end (8:8-9), in the Song. She talks about her brothers in 1:5-6, and they speak in 8:8-9. From other stories in the Bible, we understand that brothers play a role in protecting their sister's sexuality and even in marriage negotiations. The brothers thus represent the control of sexuality and societal norms, and both the passages in which they appear bear out this purpose.[38] It is interesting that the woman resists these norms as she pursues her true love.

Perhaps the brothers play a large role because of the absence of the father. This is also underlined by the mention of the woman's mother in 3:4, 11; 6:9; 8:1. Why the father is not mentioned in the Song is a matter of speculation. The theme is the resistance of social norms in the pursuit of true love, and this is well communicated by the use of brothers. Perhaps it would have been unrealistic, considering the ancient context, to have the woman ignore the advice or the guidance of her father. The mother is mentioned in contexts that have to do with sexuality.

IV. LANGUAGE

Language, words, and syntax have been used in biblical studies to try to date the composition of individual books or parts of books. However, such use of language has many pitfalls. First, as some of the debates over specific words in the commentary proper will convincingly demonstrate, there is much flexibility in how we understand the origin and history of the Hebrew language, not to speak of the other languages that supposedly influenced the

37. Fox (*The Song of Songs,* p. 300) describes this role more broadly for all the secondary characters, including the women, in the following way: "Lovers at times find family and others in their immediate vicinity interfering nuisances, but they also look to others for recognition of the legitimacy of their love and for confirmation that they have found true love."

38. With even more malice, the role of the social control of sexuality is played by the watchmen in 3:1-5 and 5:7.

development of Hebrew.[39] Second, we cannot be sure whether the biblical books were themselves updated linguistically. Again, as stated above, the period of transmission even within the Old Testament time period was so long that someone living at the end of that time period may have had difficulty understanding an earlier form of Hebrew. A counter argument might be made that we are dealing with poetry, which has more stringent linguistic demands than prose, when we are reading the Song of Songs. Would a linguistic updating damage the poetic quality of the Song and therefore be discouraged? Perhaps, but Hebrew poetry has no demonstrable meter that would be particularly affected by changes in word length and so forth. My argument is not to prove that dating by language is ineffective, but to point out the pitfalls in order that we might take these arguments with an appropriate grain of salt.

It is notable that the poems of the Song of Songs, for instance, use *še* rather than *'ašer* as a relative pronoun.[40] At one time it was thought that the use of *še* indicated a late date for a biblical book since it occurs in late postbiblical Hebrew, but then occurrences of *še* in texts that are largely thought to be early (like Judg. 5:7) might point to the fact that the difference is dialectical or perhaps geared to genre. We can infer nothing about date from the use of the relative pronoun.

Much discussion swirls around the appearance of terminology pertaining to exotic spices. The Israeli scholar Chaim Rabin[41] has argued that words like *kōper, nērd, karkōm, qāneh, qinnāmôn,* and *'ahālôt* demonstrate a Tamil influence on the Song of Songs. He further argues that this would point to a time when there was trade between Israel and India (perhaps through southern Arabia). The reign of Solomon, he concludes, was such a time. However, this line of evidence, though perhaps enticing for a conservative scholar, has to be tempered by the fact that, as Brenner points out, there were other times when the Near East had trade contacts with India.[42] Furthermore, other etymologies or alternative evidence can be cited for some of these words. A. Harman, e.g., indicates that *kōper* occurs in Ugaritic texts.[43]

39. Part of the problem can be illustrated by W. F. Albright, "Archaic Survivals in the Text of Canticles," in *Hebrew and Semitic Studies Presented to Godfrey Rolles Driver,* ed. D. Winton Thomas and W. D. McHardy (Oxford: Clarendon, 1963), pp. 1-7. In this article, he asserts that the Song is late, though it has a number of early linguistic traits. The latter he simply dismisses as archaisms.

40. For the interesting occurrence of *'ašer* in the superscription, see the commentary at Song 1:1.

41. C. Rabin, "The Song of Songs and Tamil Poetry," *SR* 3 (1973): 205-19.

42. She indicates the neo-Babylonian and Persian period as such a time; see A. Brenner, "Aromatics and Perfumes in the Song of Songs," *JSOT* 25 (1983): 75-81.

43. Harman, "Modern Discussion on the Song of Songs," p. 66.

Arguments may be found on both sides for words that supposedly have Aramaic, Persian, or Greek etymologies, which are said to indicate a late date. Examples of supposed Aramaic influence include *berôt* (for normal Hebrew *berôš;* see 1:17), *nāṭar* (for *nāṣar* in 1:6), and *setāw* (2:11) for "winter." Archer disputes these,[44] and in any case Aramaic loanwords are now less frequently considered an indication of a late date as they once were. A supposed late Greek word (*appiryôn* in 3:9) may have come from India and not Greece, and the same may be said of the frequently noted *pardēs* in 4:13, which is often said to be a late Persian loanword. We cannot be certain about the way these words came into the Hebrew language.

V. DATE

Our observations of the language as well as the authorship of the book lead us to an agnostic stand on the issue of date. Indeed, we have already observed that the Song is a collection much like the books of Psalms and Proverbs. Thus, like those books, it may contain poetic compositions that derive from different time periods. Perhaps some of the poems are Solomonic, but, if so, we must also admit that others are later. We agree with R. Gordis that "being lyrical in character, with no historical allusions, most of the songs are undatable."[45] Gordis, thus, rightly pinpoints the timeless quality of these poems. Fortunately, nothing is at stake in the interpretation of the Song, and thus we will avoid unnecessary speculation.

VI. THE TEXT

The Hebrew text (MT) of the Song of Songs is without major problems, is strongly supported by the versions, and is the basis of the following translation and commentary. The difficulties encountered in the text have to do with the unusual number of rare words, the rich poetry, and the genre rather than with any problems with the text's transmission.

44. Archer, *A Survey of Old Testament Introduction,* p. 498, and see the arguments of D. Fredericks, *Qohelet's Language: Re-evaluating Its Nature and Date* (Lewiston, NY; Queenston, Ontario: Edwin Mellon, 1988). While Fredericks is concerned with the book of Ecclesiastes, his arguments on using Aramaic as a linguistic criterion of date are relevant for the Song as well.

45. Gordis, *The Song of Songs,* p. 23, quoted approvingly by I. Provan, *Ecclesiastes and Song of Songs,* NIVAC (Grand Rapids: Zondervan, 2001), p. 335.

Other ancient witnesses to the text of Ecclesiastes include the Greek, Syriac, Latin, and Aramaic versions. There were four manuscripts of the Song discovered at the Dead Sea.[46] They all came from the Herodian period, between 30 B.C. and A.D. 70. Three were found in Cave 4, and two of these (4QCant[a] and 4QCant[b]) witness to large portions of the text (3:4-5, 7-11; 6:11-12; 7:1-7 and 2:9-17; 3:1-2, 5, 9-10; 4:1-3, 8-11, 14-16; 5:1, respectively). M. Abegg, Jr., P. Flint, and E. Ulrich speculate that 4QCant[a] is missing 4:7–6:11 intentionally because of its erotic nature, but that seems unlikely considering that the scroll contains other passages that are more than a little sensuous. The fourth text was found in Cave 6 (6QCant) and is not a substantial witness to the text.

The Septuagint, Peshitta,[47] and Latin provide only occasional variations from the Masoretic Text and even rarer attestations of superior readings. The commentary below will discuss the individual variants. Lastly, the Aramaic text of the Song is less a textual version than an indication of the early history of interpretation, and thus we reserve comment until the following section.[48]

VII. HISTORY OF INTERPRETATION

Whoever sings the Song of Songs with a tremulous voice in a banquet hall and (so) treats it as a sort of ditty has no share in the world to come.[49]

These words are attributed to Rabbi Aqiba, who flourished around A.D. 100,[50] and are one of our earliest recorded witnesses to the interpretation of the Song of Songs. What is most interesting about his statement is that it reflects a debate over the book's interpretation. Those who were singing it in the banquet hall surely had a sense of the erotic nature of the book, while

---

46. For the information that follows, see M. Abegg, Jr., P. Flint, and E. Ulrich, *The Dead Sea Scrolls Bible* (San Francisco: HarperSanFrancisco, 1999), pp. 611-22.

47. G. Gerleman (*Ruth, Das Hohelied,* BKAT 18 [Neukirchen-Vluyn: Neukirchener, 1965], pp. 82-83) looks closely at the Peshitta and concludes that it, like the Septuagint, follows the Hebrew text closely. He discusses significant variants. See also W. Baars, "The Peshitta Text of Song of Songs in Barhebraeus' Ausur Raze," *VT* 18 (1968): 281-89.

48. The Slavonic version of the Song is outside of the interest of this commentary, but discussion may be found in A. A. Alexeev, "The Song of Songs in the Slavonic Bible Tradition," *The Bible Translator* 47 (1996): 119-25.

49. Quote taken from R. E. Murphy, *The Song of Songs,* Hermeneia (Minneapolis: Fortress, 1990), p. 13.

50. As preserved in *t. Sanh.* 12:10.

Aqiba's prohibition of such a use and understanding is explained in another famous quotation of his concerning the Song. In disputing the idea that the Song had no authoritative status, Aqiba exclaimed: "God forbid! — no man in Israel ever disputed about the Song of Songs [that he should say] that it does not render the hands unclean, for all the ages are not worth the day on which the Song of Songs was given to Israel; for all the Writings are holy, but the Song of Songs is the Holy of Holies."[51] It appears that the lines were drawn early over the question whether the surface meaning of the text had to do with human sexuality or the relationship between God and humanity.

It is our purpose in the present section to trace the history of the debate over the interpretation of the Song from its earliest evidence down to the present. The story of the interpretation of the book is a particularly interesting one, and it is tightly connected to the question of genre identification. What kind of book is the Song of Songs? Thus, our discussion of the Song's history of interpretation will set up the next section concerning genre identification. In other words, the shape of our present discussion is part of the argument for our identification of the genre of the Song. Since our decision about genre will determine the direction of our interpretation of individual passages, the following two sections are crucial. The great rabbinic sage Saadia famously stated, "Know, my brother, that you will find great differences in interpretation of the Song of Songs. In truth they differ because the Song of Songs resembles locks to which the keys have been lost."[52] This statement makes abundant sense, particularly if we imagine that the keys are genre identification. Proper genre identification unlocks the proper interpretation of the book. It is for this reason that we devote considerable space to this issue.[53]

It would be pretentious to suggest, however, that our discussion of history of interpretation will be exhaustive; it would take more than a single volume to approach that goal. In any case, our intention and needs are more modest. We are interested in showing interpretive trajectories and options to aid us in our own discovery of the genre of the Song. Of course, genre identification arises from interaction with the text itself in a kind of hermeneutical spiral (see below under Genre), but we can learn from the wrong turns and successful decisions of the past.

The following survey will move from one interpretive option to an-

51. So quoted in Murphy, *The Song of Songs*, p. 6. See further discussion of this quotation under "Canon."

52. Quoted in Pope, *Song of Songs*, p. 89.

53. It is interesting to note the tendency toward length of the introductions to Song of Songs commentaries when compared with other books of the Bible. This highlights the importance of the decisions about genre in the interpretation of individual passages as well as the convoluted history of the interpretation of the book.

other. We will begin with those that were favored in the early history of interpretation, though we will encounter modern advocates, and move toward the interpretations favored at the beginning of the twenty-first century, though we will note ancient precursors. Furthermore, while we can describe a broad consensus today, there are significant differences in detail. In any case, there are two major interpretive questions that will also shape the following section: (1) Is the Song allegory or natural love poetry? (2) Does the Song have a plot? We will answer these questions by examining the following interpretive options: allegory, love poetry, drama, cultic poetry, psychological poetry, and wisdom. These are not all mutually exclusive categories, and thus we must remain open to the possibility of combining some of them in our final genre identification.

BEFORE AQIBA

We have only the scantiest and most indirect evidence before the turn from B.C. to A.D., which means that a number of centuries passed before we get an inkling of how people read the book. We concluded above (under Date) that we could not precisely date the book, but it almost certainly was the Persian period or before. Thus, we do not have any evidence for how the "original audience" understood the book. By the time of Aqiba it is possible, actually highly likely, that the official interpretive community represented by Aqiba already had imposed a foreign meaning on the text.

It is often pointed out that the Septuagint of the Song shows no sign of allegorizing the text.[54] Unfortunately, we do not know when to date the translation of this book precisely. Furthermore, it may be just a good literal translation of the text that avoided embedding any interpretation into it. In other words, the translator may have understood the book allegorically, but he simply represented the surface meaning of the Hebrew text into Greek.

Allegorical Interpretations

Aqiba's statement that the Song is the "Holy of Holies" strongly implies that he held to an allegorical interpretation of the book. As we will see, this strategy of interpretation was dominant and almost exclusive from the beginning

---

54. It has been suggested by some that the Septuagint translates 4:8 "from the top of Amana" *(mērôš 'amānâ)* as "from the beginning of righteousness" *(apo archēs pisteōs)* and that this points to an allegorical understanding of the text. However, it is more likely that the Septuagint translator simply does not understand that this is a geographical reference and does the best he can with the text that he has.

of our evidence until the middle of the nineteenth century. Indeed, as we will comment below, the allegorical interpretation is enjoying something of a renaissance today in certain circles. We will divide our discussion of allegorical strategies of interpretation into two major parts: Jewish and Christian interpretations. The latter almost certainly took its clue from the former, but its different theology leads to a different understanding of the book.

However, before beginning our survey of Jewish and Christian allegories, we need to define our terms. We need to make a distinction between an allegorical piece of literature and an allegorical interpretive strategy. The former is an intentional piece of writing: an author intends the reader to take the surface meaning of his text as symbolic of another level of meaning. In the words of *The Princeton Encyclopedia of Poetry and Poetics,* "We have allegory when the events of a narrative obviously and continuously refer to another simultaneous structure of events or ideas, whether historical events, moral or philosophical ideas, or natural phenomena."[55] A key aspect of this interpretation is the adverb "obviously." A good example of an allegory is the still-popular work *Pilgrim's Progress* by John Bunyan. That this work is an allegory is blatantly obvious. The main character is named Christian, and he is on a journey to the Celestial City. On his journey, he encounters obstacles like the Slough of Despond. It would be impossible for even the average reader to avoid the below-the-surface meaning, because it is not too far below the surface.

The Bible does contain allegories. In Judges 9 Abimelech had his brothers murdered in order to clear his way to the throne. However, the youngest brother Jotham escaped and then returned after Abimelech proclaimed himself king. Jotham told a story about how the trees chose a king for themselves. The trees went to the most productive and most dignified of their fellow trees first, trees like the olive, the fig, and the vine, but they all rejected the idea. They were too busy being productive. Finally they went to the thornbush and asked that useless plant to rule over them, and it accepted. Not only did it accept, but it began to display qualities and powers well beyond its nature. It would provide shade for all the other trees, and it threatened even the mighty cedar with fire. Jotham's allegory is a clear and consistent allegory that satirized Abimelech and the office of the king.

Though allegory does appear in the Hebrew Bible, it is clear from our definition and example that the Song of Songs is not an allegory. The book itself has no signals that it is to be read in any other way than as a love song. No one can dispute this fact. However, this observation does not end the discussion. Even though the Song is not an allegory as such, it has been the ob-

---

55. N. Frye, "Allegory," in *The Princeton Encyclopedia of Poetry and Poetics,* ed. A. Preminger (Princeton: Princeton University Press, 1965), p. 12.

ject of an allegorical interpretation from the very beginning of recorded commentary on the book.

Allegory as a strategy of interpretation began with Greek myths. The Greek gods were capricious and often capable of what most would regard as immoral actions. As such, the theology of Homer was ridiculed by Plato and others. An attempt was made to salvage Homer by allegory, and so allegorical commentaries on Greek myth rose up with the intention of "the defense of the sobriety and profundity of religious myths which appeared, on the face of it, to ascribe capriciousness or indecency to the gods."[56]

With this background, we will now turn to examples of Jewish allegorization of the Song, and then to Christian ones. After the survey, we will critically interact with this strategy of interpretation.

JEWISH ALLEGORIES

Historical Allegories

Early Jewish interpretations are predominantly allegorical, though we will observe variety among the different allegories proposed. However, most Jewish allegorical interpretations begin with the idea that the man in the Song is God and the woman is Israel. The Song of Songs, then, is not about what it seems to be about on the surface, the sensual love between a man and a woman. It is actually about the love that God has for Israel.

Though Aqiba was an early voice for this approach to the Song, we do not have more than his isolated statements. A longer example is the Targum to the Song, written between ca. A.D. 700 and 900.[57] The Targum will be our prime source for the Jewish allegorical approach that reads the Song as essentially a redemptive history of God's chosen people, Israel.[58]

---

56. Frye, "Allegory," p. 13.

57. A translation of a neo-Aramaic version of the Targum is presented in Y. Sabar, *An Old Neo-Aramaic Version of the Targum on Song of Songs* (Wiesbaden: Otto Harrassowitz, 1991). R. Loewe ("Apologetic Motifs in the Targum to the Song of Songs," in *Biblical Motifs: Origins and Transformations,* ed. A. Altmann [Cambridge, MA: Harvard University Press, 1966], pp. 163-69) argues this convincingly based on internal considerations. T. H. Gaster ("What 'The Song of Songs' Means: The Time of Singing Has Come," *Commentary* 13 [1952]: 317) asserts a sixth-century date, but this is superseded by Loewe's arguments.

58. Similar interpretations of the Song may also be found in the Talmud, the Midrash Rabbah, and certain important medieval Jewish commentators like Saadia, Rashi, and Ibn Ezra (though, as we will observe below, he also read it as a three-character drama). See Pope, *Song of Songs,* p. 89.

The introduction to the Targum situates the Song within Ten Songs that "were uttered in this world."[59] These songs begin with Adam's in Psalm 92 and culminate with Isaiah 20:29, a song for the release of the exiles. Song of Songs is the ninth one in the list. It is referred to as the "best of them all" and is connected with Solomon, who "uttered [it] by the Holy Spirit before the Lord of all the World."

The Targum itself reads the Song as a redemptive history that begins with the Exodus and ends with a section on the description of the Messianic period (7:14–8:7), but with two "flashbacks" (8:8-10 and 8:11-14) to the days before the consummation of history. R. Loewe argues that the Targum plays down the Messiah and his reign as part of an anti-Christian polemic.[60] By this time, Christians have appropriated a distinctive type of allegorical interpretation of the Song, and Loewe notes swipes at it as well as implicit criticisms of Jewish mystical interpretations of the Song, both of which are described below.

The Targum is too detailed and complex to give any kind of running description of its content. We will satisfy our intentions by paraphrasing the Targum's interpretation of the opening section (1:2-9). The woman, Israel, begins by begging the man, God, to kiss her. Israel desires relationship with God. She praises his reputation and asks him to take her into his private room. The bedroom is Palestine, the promised land. This opening unit then refers to the Exodus from Egypt. The kissing itself is the giving of the Law and therefore refers to the revelation of God at Sinai. However, in the wilderness they also sinned by worshipping the golden calf. The girl's confession of blackness is an acknowledgment of this sin of idolatry. Verses 7-8 describes Moses' concern about Israel's future fidelity to the Lord and his warning to them. Verse 9, the reference to the woman as similar to Pharaoh's mare, brings to mind the crossing of the Red Sea.

In this manner the Targum, our example of Jewish historical allegorical interpretation, continues through the redemptive history of the Old Testament. Since there is little substantial connection between the words of the Song and the interpretation, other historical allegories, though similar, are not identical.[61] However, we are interested in simply surveying and under-

59. From the translation of the Targum provided in Pope, *Song of Songs*, p. 296. Pope provides a running translation and commentary of the Targum in an excursus that occurs at the end of every one of his verse notes in his commentary. All further citations of the Targum in this section will be from his translation and may be found at the appropriate verse in the commentary.

60. He also sees an anti-Christian polemic in the Targum's exaltation of the Torah, since Christians tended to downplay the significance of the Law in their theology; cf. Loewe, "Apologetic Motifs," p. 180.

61. Maimonides (twelfth century) in the Mishnah Torah and the Guide to the Per-

standing the different major approaches to the Song, and so we pass on now
to Jewish philosophical/mystical interpretations.

Philosophical/Mystical Allegories

Its fair to describe the historical allegorical approach as mainstream among
early Jewish interpretations, but reading the Song as the story of God's people from Exodus to the Messiah is not the sole attested interpretive strategy.
Many Jewish sages thought the Song was about the union between God and
the individual soul. Again, I will comment only on a couple of representative
examples.

Earlier, we, following the work of Loewe,[62] observed that the Targum
had evidence of an anti-mystical tendenz. It appears that the Targum was, in
part, offering a reading that displaced certain Jewish readings it regarded as
wrong or even dangerous. Specifically, Loewe describes the early traditions
connected to the Shi'ur Qomah (translated "Measure of the Body" in reference to God's body; see below) and cites the work of S. Lieberman, who
"had recently demonstrated that the description, in fantastically exaggerated
physical terms, of the mystical 'body' of the Deity that goes under the name
of Shi'ur Qomah was originally a midrash, intended for esoteric circulation,
on the catalogue of her lover's physical charms given by the maiden in the
Song of Songs (5:10-16)."[63] From this text we learn that the mystical approach to the Song was early.[64]

However, we have more evidence of this approach from the medieval
period, particularly among those rabbis who followed the work of Maimonides. We will focus on the work of one such rabbinic scholar,[65] Levi ben
Gershom (also known as Gersonides), since he is the subject of a new study

---

plexed was the first to argue that the Song is a poem about the love between God and the
individual human soul, not corporate Israel. So M. Kellner, *Commentary on Song of
Songs: Levi ben Gershom (Gersonides)* (New Haven: Yale University Press, 1998), p. xvi.
As we will see in the next section, Maimonides' ideas are at the root of the philosophical/
mystical approach to the Song.

62. Loewe, "Apologetic Motifs."

63. Loewe, "Apologetic Motifs," pp. 184-85.

64. The Shi'ur Qomah is thought to be the product of the Tannaitic period (A.D.
10-220); cf. "Shi'ur Komah," in the *Encyclopedia Judaica* (Jerusalem: MacMillan, 1971),
p. 1418.

65. Other medieval rabbis from the thirteenth and early fourteenth centuries
A.D. who share this approach to the Song include Samuel ibn Tibbon, Jacob Anatoli,
Moses ibn Tibbon, Immanuel ben Solomon of Rome, and Joseph ibn Kaspi, for a num-
ber of which see Pope, *Song of Songs*, pp. 105-10. Pope just briefly mentions Levi ben
Gershon.

by M. Kellner.[66] Levi ben Gershom was an Aristotelian[67] who distinguished between the material intellect, the acquired intellect, and the Active Intellect. The last stands for God, and the first is the capacity for God's creatures to learn. The acquired intellect is knowledge that is accumulated through life. Levi reads the Song as an allegory on two levels.[68] The man represents the Active Intellect and the woman the material intellect; the Song shows them in dialogue, and their union is "a human being's highest perfection and greatest felicity."[69] The second level concerns discussion of the relationship between the faculties of the soul and the material intellect. "In any event, the main thrust of these discussions relates to the overwhelming desire of the material intellect to approach the Active Intellect and its attempts to enlist the (willing) aid of the other faculties of the soul in this quest."[70]

Besides the main characters of the man (Active Intellect) and the woman (material intellect), Gersonides also identifies the minor characters in this drama of epistemological/mystical union. Jerusalem is a human being, and so the daughters of Jerusalem are the faculties of the soul. Zion is the pinnacle of Jerusalem, and so the daughters of Zion specify those faculties that are closest to the intellect. These identifications betray Gersonides' approach to the Song.

Perhaps this is the proper place to mention the interesting twist to interpretation provided by Don Isaac Abravanel (sixteenth century).[71] In his reading, the man is Solomon and the woman stands for wisdom. Thus, their union represents Solomon's divinely given wisdom.

We have thus observed two main lines of ancient Jewish interpretation of the Song of Songs, the allegorical and the philosophical/mystical. The Targum and Levi ben Gershom were our leading examples, though we readily admit that there were many variations on the themes that they represented. Two conclusions are notable for our further explorations. First, we observe the remarkable repression of the "literal" or "natural" reading of the Song. Besides those, chided by Aqiba, singing at the taverns, no one affirms a reading of the Song that promotes an erotic understanding of the relationship between the man and the woman.[72] Second, early Christian interpreta-

---

66. Kellner, *Commentary on the Song of Songs*. Our description here follows his research very closely.

67. Indeed, Aristotle is quoted over forty times in his commentary, far more than any single Jewish source.

68. Kellner, *Commentary on the Song of Songs*, p. xxi.

69. Kellner, *Commentary on the Song of Songs*, p. xxi.

70. Kellner, *Commentary on the Song of Songs*, p. xxi.

71. And discussed at greater length by Pope, *Song of Songs*, pp. 110-11.

72. Loewe ("Apologetic Motifs," pp. 161-62) notes two early rabbis (Samuel and R. Shesheth), who apparently quote the Song (2:14 and 6:5) as a warning to men to "be

tion follows Jewish interpretation *(mutatis mutandi)* very closely, a topic to which we now turn.

CHRISTIAN ALLEGORICAL INTERPRETATION

Hippolytus (ca. A.D. 200) provides us with the first example of Christian exegesis of the Song, and, though we have only fragments of his work, he clearly allegorized its message. For instance, he understands the two breasts of the woman in 4:5 to refer to the Old and New Testaments.[73] Since he was the first attested Christian interpreter of the Song, we do not know the influences on Hippolytus that led him to his conclusions, but we can speculate. We know that at least one hundred years before him Jewish interpreters understood the book to speak of God's love for Israel (see above and in particular the quote from Aqiba). The Christian community grew out of the Jewish community, and it would have been natural for them to adopt the same allegorical approach to the Song but to transform the referents of the symbols from God and Israel to Jesus and the Church. Once this general equation is made, there is still ample room for variations since, as we will point out below, allegorical interpretation is quite arbitrary in its assignment of symbolic value to the text. O. Keel rightly stated that "if two allegorizers ever agree on the interpretation of a verse it is only because one has copied another."[74] As it turns out, particularly after our next example of Christian allegorical exegesis, Christian interpreters did depend on previous tradition to understand the verses of the Song.[75]

Indeed, no one had a larger and longer influence on Christian interpretation of the Song than Origen (A.D. 185-253/54). Origen was born in Alexandria to wealthy Christian parents, though when his father was martyred

---

circumspect" as they encounter the beauty of women. Loewe, though, goes on to argue that these rabbis are not an exception to the rule; they too would understand the primary meaning of the text to be a historical allegory. However, that they could see some application to the relationship between actual men and women is a step toward the literal meaning that we will discuss below.

73. So Pope, *Song of Songs,* p. 114. Note that later commentators took the two breasts of 1:13 in the same way and understood the sachet of myrrh to refer to Christ who transcends the Testaments, an odd expression of what today we would call biblical theology! See O. Keel, *The Song of Songs,* A Continental Commentary (Minneapolis: Fortress, 1994), pp. 7-8, who cites Philo Carpasius and Cyril of Alexandria.

74. Keel, *The Song of Songs,* p. 8.

75. For an interesting study of the early Christian allegorical interpretation as applied to Song of Songs 1:2, 7, see G. Chappuzeau, "Die Exegese von Hohelied 1,2a.b und 7 bei den Kirchenvätern von Hippolyt bis Bernard," *Jahrbuch für Antike und Christentum* 18 (1975): 91-143.

during a persecution, the family lost everything. A wealthy patron helped Origen finish his education, which was in the Greco-Roman tradition, but at a certain point in his life he adopted a radically ascetic lifestyle that included disowning, at least explicitly, pagan intellectual influence. On a practical level, he felt that Christian spirituality entailed a denigration of fleshly concerns, most notably sexuality, a viewpoint that obviously would impact his understanding of the Song of Songs. Indeed, his views on sexuality were so strong that it appears that they moved Origen to undergo castration, and what Origen did to his own body, he did, via allegorical interpretation, to the Song of Songs — he "desexed" it.[76]

However, as R. E. Murphy and others are correct to point out, Origen certainly understood that the form of the Song had to do with human marriage.[77] Indeed, he called the Song an epithalamium, or "wedding song," a song sung before reaching the marriage bed. Yet the "Bridegroom" and the "Bride" in the Song are immediately spiritualized in Origen's conception of the book; they are identified, respectively, with Jesus Christ and the Church or, at least occasionally, the individual human soul. He quickly passes over the "literal" level of the Song because, as he puts it, "these things seem to me to afford no profit to the reader as far as the story goes; nor do they maintain any continuous narrative such as we find in other Scripture stories. It is necessary, therefore, rather to give them all a spiritual meaning."[78]

Surprisingly, at least at first thought, Origen certainly devoted much attention to this book that on a surface reading communicated so little spiritual profit. We know he wrote ten volumes of commentary on the Song as well as a number of homilies.[79] This focus on the Song continues through the Middle Ages with its strong stand on celibacy. It is understandable why some may find this near obsession as an expression of unnatural repression, but it may also be generated by an understandable fear that the Song may be "misunderstood" by those not initiated into the proper interpretive method and may suffer from such a misunderstanding. This indeed is Origen's express intention in his commentary on the Song.

Origen, heavily influenced by Neoplatonism and Gnostic speculation (see below), held that the body and the soul were two separate entities. Both

---

76. Pope, *Song of Songs*, p. 115.

77. As noted by P. C. Miller, "'Pleasure of the Text, Text of Pleasure': Eros and Language in Origen's Commentary on the Song of Songs," *JAAR* 54 (1986): 242.

78. Translation from Murphy, *The Song of Songs*, pp. 18-19.

79. The commentary was written between A.D. 240 and 245. We have only a few fragments of the original Greek, transmitted in quotation in other early commentaries. We have the first three volumes in a Latin translation by Rufinus and Jerome's citation of two homilies. For references see J. P. Tanner, "The History of the Interpretation of the Song of Songs," *BibSac* 154 (1997): 27-28.

were created by God, but the body secondarily and as a kind of repository of the soul. To promote the soul, the body needed to be subjugated and eventually eliminated in death. The Song is so explicitly about the pleasures of the body on the surface that it could not mean what it appeared to mean, and allegorical interpretation was the perfect vehicle for eradicating that surface meaning.

Origen was likely influenced in his interpretation by two sources. First, we know that he was aware of Hippolytus, even visiting the older churchman in Rome in the year 215. Second, and perhaps more important, he was acquainted with Jewish allegorical interpretation because of his relationship with various rabbis, including R. Hillel, who taught him Hebrew.[80] Indeed, Origen lived much of his later life in the coastal city of Caesarea. R. Kimelman notes not only an influence but an implicit debate in the writings of Origen and the rabbis of his day, particularly R. Yohanan, as they argue for different referents for the symbols of the Song of Songs as allegory. For instance, Kimelman cites their comments on 1:2, which in the Masoretic tradition says that the woman prefers the man's love to wine. The Septuagint, on the contrary, mentions breasts instead of wine. It might be a conundrum why Yohanan interprets the Septuagint version rather than the Masoretic tradition, since Jewish interpreters favored the latter, until we recognize that he is purposively and polemically interacting with Origen here, who, as most Christian interpreters of the day, would prefer the Septuagint. The debate is not about which text is adopted but the meaning of breasts. Origen identified the wine as the good teaching of the Law and Prophets, but the even better milk from the breasts as the teaching of the Bridegroom, namely, Jesus. Yohanan, likely implicitly disputing this, rather identifies the wine as the written Torah and the milk from the breasts as the oral Torah.[81] Thus the debate continued.

Origen's influence was immense. His understanding of the Song of Songs in particular endured through the ages. Indeed, E. Kallas notes how popular the Song was during the Middle Ages. He comments that in the Patrologia Latina thirty-two commentaries on the Song are listed between the fourth and eleventh centuries, while there are only six on Galatians and nine

---

80. For his relationship with Hillel as well as other rabbinic authorities of the day, see R. Kimelman, "Rabbi Yohanan and Origen on the Song of Songs: A Third-Century Jewish-Christian Disputation," *HTR* 73 (1980): 569. See also the comments of D. Boyarin ("The Song of Songs: Lock or Key? Intertextuality, Allegory and Midrash," in *The Book and the Text: The Bible and Literary Theory,* ed. R. Schwartz [Oxford: Blackwell, 1990], p. 224), who argues that the difference between Origen and the midrashic interpreters is that the former's interpretation is a move from the concrete to the abstract, while the latter's is the opposite.

81. Kimelman, "Rabbi Yohanan," pp. 589-91.

on Romans![82] Space permits us to comment only on two other prominent early interpreters of the Song: Jerome and Bernard of Clairvaux.

Jerome's significance was that he introduced and popularized Origen's allegorical approach into the Western Church.[83] Jerome lived from A.D. 331-420 and is best known for his work on the Latin Vulgate, but he was an extremely influential theologian and biblical interpreter as well. Jerome embraced the ascetic lifestyle thought to be the expression of highest spirituality during the time. That is, he renounced the desires of the flesh to fan the fires of the soul. It is said that Jerome used to throw himself into thornbushes when he felt the onset of sexual arousal as a youth. After even that didn't work, he took up the study of Hebrew to calm his concupiscence! Jerome, like Origen, learned his Hebrew from rabbis and moved to Bethlehem, where he did much of his work at the end of his life.

Nothing expresses his attitude toward sexuality and toward the Song of Songs better than a letter he wrote to his disciple Paula concerning the course of biblical study that he suggests for her daughter Paula. It is worth quoting at length:

> Let her treasures be not silk or gems but manuscripts of the holy scriptures; and in these let her think less of gilding, and Babylonian parchment, and arabesque patterns, than of correctness and accurate punctuation. Let her begin by learning the psalter, and then let her gather rules of life out of the Proverbs of Solomon. From the Preacher let her gain the habit of despising the world and its vanities. Let her follow the example set in Job of virtue and of patience. Then let her pass on to the gospels never to be laid aside once they have been taken in hand. Let her also drink in with a willing heart the Acts of the Apostles and the Epistles. As soon as she has enriched the storehouse of her mind with these treasures, let her commit to memory the prophets, the heptateuch, the Books of Kings and of Chronicles, the rolls also of Ezra and Esther. When she has done all these she may safely read the Song of Songs but not before: for, were she to read it at the beginning, she would fail to perceive that, though it is written in fleshly words, it is a marriage song of a spiritual bridal. And not understanding this she would suffer from it.[84]

---

82. E. Kalas, "Martin Luther as Expositor of the Song of Songs," *Lutheran Quarterly* 2 (1988): 323.

83. Jerome's famous near contemporary Augustine also held to the view that the Song concerned the love of Christ for the Church; so M. Dove, "Sex, Allegory and Censorship: A Reconsideration of Medieval Commentaries on the Song of Songs," *Literature and Theology* 10 (1996): 219-20.

84. This quote is taken from Pope (*Song of Songs*, p. 119), who is quoting it from *The Nicene and Post-Nicene Fathers*, VI, Letter cvii, p. 194.

After looking at this proposed program of study, I think it is safe to say that she would never read the Song, and that may well be Jerome's intention.

Bernard of Clairvaux (twelfth century) is our example of a late medieval interpreter who continues in the allegorical tradition of Hippolytus, Origen, and Jerome. Bernard was the abbot of the Cistercian monastery at Clairvaux and was a key leader in the rapid expansion of the order throughout Europe. He was concerned to promote the contemplative ideal among Christians of his day, and his treatment of the Song of Songs demonstrates the fervor of his desire.

Bernard wrote eighty-six sermons on the Song between 1135 and his death in 1153. Even so, he covered only through 3:1, thus averaging over two sermons per verse! In his first sermon, Bernard lays the basic strategy for his approach to the Song.[85] We note that he considers the Song the epitome of biblical teaching. Thus, he addresses his sermons to the spiritually mature, his fellow monks, and not the masses. He suggests that people cannot benefit from the Song until they have mastered the two other Solomonic books of Ecclesiastes and Proverbs, in order to despise the world and the self. The Song provides the more constructive lesson of building up one's mystical union with God. After all, the bride is the individual soul who desires God, and the groom is God. Their union is the desired mystical union between the two.

The literal meaning is the "outer husk of the 'dead letter' of the writing,"[86] and a good example is his understanding of Song 1:10, which in our translation is rendered:

> Your cheeks are lovely between earrings;
> your neck, with a necklace.

Bernard comments: "The heavenly goldsmiths, to whom this task is committed, promise that they will fashion resplendent tokens of truth and insert them in the soul's inward ears. I cannot see what this may mean if not the construction of certain spiritual images in order to bring the purest intuitions of divine wisdom before the eyes of the soul that contemplates, to enable it to perceive, as though in a puzzling mirror what it cannot yet gaze on face to face. . . ."[87]

W. E. Phipps has made the persuasive case that Bernard's avoidance of sexuality and concomitant allegorical approach to the Song are the result not only of a tradition of interpretation but also of his "contempt for the flesh

---

85. For an edition of the first sermon as well as a commentary on it, see D. Robertson, "The Experience of Reading: Bernard of Clairvaux's *Sermons on the Song of Songs,* 1," *Religion and Literature* 19 (1987): 1-20.

86. Robertson, "The Experience of Reading," p. 3.

87. Quoted in Robertson, "The Experience of Reading," p. 9.

and for females."[88] The dark side of his sublimation of sexuality comes out in his violent reaction toward enemies of the faith. Nowhere is this illustrated more vividly than in his determination to see Peter Abelard removed from the Church and even erased from life itself because of his different views on love and women. Bernard becomes a timely reminder that the unnatural suppression of sexual love can lead to frightful consequences.[89]

However, this tendency is true not only of celibate monks but of married ministers and theologians in the later Protestant movement as well.[90] We can observe the exact same interpretive strategy among many different Protestant traditions, though the particular shape of the application of the strategy may differ from person to person.

Kallas has not persuaded me that Luther had moved from an allegorical interpretation of the text.[91] While it is true that Luther does take the historical context into account, he utilizes it to develop yet another allegorical interpretation. He explicitly rejects Origen, to be sure, but he just changes the referents of the figurative language of the Song. Instead of God and the Church, or the individual soul, Luther suggests that the relationship between the man and the woman describes the relationship between God and Solomon and is in essence a political allegory.

Luther exposited the Song in a series of lectures at Wittenberg during 1530. In the preface, he rejects the allegorical approach of Origen as well as the literal interpretation of Theodore of Mopsuestia (below). He takes his clue from a document written by the emperor, "The Dangers and Adventures of the Famous Hero and Knight Sir Teuerdank." Behind the story of Teuerdank and Lady Ehrenreich was the true life love of Maximilian toward Mary of Burgundy. According to Kallas, Luther thought that this illustrated the custom of nobility through time, to talk about personal matters in highly figurative literature. So in the Song, Solomon is talking about his intimate relationship with God and its effect on his reign over God's people through poetic imagery. Kallas quotes Luther's own statement of Solomon's intention in the Song as a composition in which he "commends his own government to us

---

88. W. E. Phipps, "The Plight of the Song of Songs," *JAAR* 42 (1974): 91, though M. S. Burrows ("Foundations for an Erotic Christology: Bernard of Clairvaux on Jesus as 'Tender Lover,'" *ATR* 80 [1998]: 478) argues that this criticism is a modern construct.

89. For reasons of space, we will not treat at length the position that the Song is an allegory of the relationship between Mary and Jesus, for which see R. Fulton, "Mimetic Devotion, Marian Exegesis, and the Historical Sense of the Song of Songs," *Viator: Medieval and Renaissance Studies* 27 (1996): 85-116.

90. Below we will document the exceptions to the rule of allegorizing among medieval theologians (Theodore of Mopsuestia) as well as Protestant scholars (Castellio, Calvin).

91. Kallas, "Martin Luther."

and composes a sort of encomium of peace and the present state of the realm. In it he gives thanks for God for the highest blessing, external peace."[92]

Seventeenth-century Reformed theology provides many examples of allegorical interpretations of the Song. Thomas Brightman and Johannes Cocceius both read the Song as a historical allegory beginning from the old dispensation through Christ and up to the consummation of history. They even found connections to the Reformation and Calvin in particular. According to Alexander, Brightman in particular influenced other prominent Reformed exegetes in the succeeding generations, including John Cotton, Nathanael Homes, John Davenport, George Wither, Caspar Heunisch, as well as Cocceius.[93] The Westminster Assembly, which produced the classic Reformed confession *The Westminster Confession of Faith,* condemned those who understood the Song of Songs as "a hot carnal pamphlet formed by some loose Apollo or Cupid."[94]

This kind of historical allegory fell out of favor after the seventeenth century, but a general allegorical approach that understood the man and the woman of the Song to represent God and his people persisted both in and outside of Reformed theological circles. John Wesley (1703-91) represents the perspective that continues to find the literal or natural reading of the Song wrong, even repulsive:

> The description of this bridegroom and bride is such as could not with decency be used or meant concerning Solomon and Pharaoh's daughter; that many expressions and descriptions, if applied to them, would be absurd and monstrous; and that it therefore follows that this book is to be understood allegorically concerning that spiritual love and marriage, which is between Christ and his church.[95]

The allegorical approach has been on the wane in academic circles since the middle of the nineteenth century for reasons that we will turn to in a moment.[96] It is still commonly encountered in popular teaching and preach-

92. Kallas, "Martin Luther," p. 334.

93. P. S. Alexander, "The Song of Songs as Historical Allegory: Notes on the Development of an Exegetical Tradition," in *Targumic and Cognate Studies: Essays in Honour of Martin McNamara,* ed. K. J. Cathcart and M. Maher (Sheffield: Sheffield Academic Press, 1996), p. 18.

94. Westminster Assembly, *Annotations upon All the Books of the Old and New Testaments* (London, 1951), quoted in R. M. Davidson, "Theology of Sexuality in the Song of Songs: Return to Eden," *AUSS* 27 (1989): 3.

95. John Wesley, *Explanatory Notes upon the Old Testament* (Bristol, England, 1765), quoted in Davidson, "Theology of Sexuality," p. 4.

96. Just before publication I received a copy of I. J. Cainion, "An Analogy of the Song of Songs and Genesis Chapters Two and Three," *SJOT* 14 (2000): 219-59, which presents a rather bizarre twist on the allegorical approach. He combines his allegorical reading,

ing in the Church. Though not as popular, a group of Catholic scholars in the twentieth century have exploited their literary insights into offering something very similar to a traditional allegorical approach. The most well-known examples of Catholic allegorical interpretation in the twentieth century are those by A. Feuillet, A. Robert, and R. Tournay.[97] These recent examples are exceptions to the rule. The allegorical approach has gone from being the dominant approach to the interpretation to the Song to almost a kind of eccentric archaism.[98] We will now explore the reasons for this definite shift.

THE REJECTION OF THE ALLEGORICAL APPROACH

The Song of Songs is an interesting study in terms of the history of interpretation because no other biblical book witnesses to such a definite and universally recognized shift in genre identification. Until the nineteenth century the Song was unquestioningly treated as some type of allegory (the rare exceptions will be treated below), and after the nineteenth century we are hardpressed to find supporters of the allegorical approach, at least among scholars. This move has taken place among most Catholics,[99] Jewish scholars, and Protestants, both liberal and evangelical. Why was there such a shift?

---

though he calls it analogical, with a three-character dramatic approach. He takes the king as Satan, the woman as Adam and Eve, and the rustic lover to be God. He then reads the story of Genesis 2–3 into the imagery of the Song. The connections are general and arbitrary, and I only mention this article here to demonstrate the tenaciousness of the allegorical approach.

97. A. Feuillet, *Le Cantique des Cantiques* (Paris: Les Editions du Cerf, 1953); idem, "La double insertion du Cantique des Cantiques dans la vie de la communauté chrétienne et dans la tradition religieuse de l'Ancient Testament," *Divinitas* 35 (1991): 5-18; A. Robert, R. Tournay, and A. Feuillet, *Le Cantique des Cantiques: Traduction et commentaire* (Paris: Gabalda, 1963); R. Tournay, *Le Cantique des Cantiques* (Paris: Les Editions du Cerf, 1967).

98. As a matter of fact, even with authors like Feuillet, Tournay, and Robert there is a fine line between what we have been calling an allegorical approach and what we will later approve of as a proper canonical reading of the text. In *Word of God, Song of Love* (New York and Mahwah, NJ: Paulist, 1988), Tournay consciously backed down from an exclusive allegorical approach and tried to merge what he calls the two traditional lines of interpretation. LaCocque *(Romance She Wrote)*, E. Davis ("Romance of the Land in the Song of Songs," *ATR* 80 [1998]: 533-47), and R. W. Corney ("What Does 'Literal Meaning' Mean? Some Commentaries on the Song of Songs," *ATR* 80 [1998]: 494-516) are further examples of scholars who affirm the literal, sexual meaning of the Song but do not think it is the only or (and here is where I would part company with them) the primary meaning of the text. The latter, for them, is the spiritual meaning of the Song.

99. The exceptions among Catholics are listed in n. 97. See O. Loretz, "Zum Problem des Eros im Hohelied," *BZ* 8 (1964): 191-216, for a defense of a literal reading of the Song of Songs in the Catholic community.

In part the shift may be explained as a result of a larger cultural transformation as Western society moved from a premodern to a modern worldview. In other words, the Enlightenment, often rightly vilified by evangelical Christians as robbing us of a sense of the supernatural, may have been a help to proper interpretation of the Song of Songs.[100]

We begin our account with a reminder of the Church and synagogue's early views on the body and sexuality. Scholars have made the case that the view that reads the Bible as pitting the spiritual over against the physical was the result of the influence of Platonic philosophy.[101] If the physical was inherently evil, then a book like the Song of Songs could be treated in one of two ways. Theoretically, it could have been rejected or removed from the canon. It is likely that the book was already firmly ensconced in the canon, so another strategy of repression had to be adopted. The allegorical method provided a handy means of making a text say something different from what it says on the surface.

An allegorical approach was developed by later Greek philosophers who had moral difficulties with the capricious gods and goddesses as described by Hesiod and Homer. As a result, they assigned symbolic value to the deities and their actions that allowed them to salvage something they considered good from the ridiculously childish conception of the gods passed down from the earlier generations. They made the myths teach something different from what they seemed to say on the surface.[102] It is this method that early Jewish and Christian interpreters adopted, in good faith to be sure. They sincerely felt that the Song's explicit sexuality was at odds with the rest of the Bible, and so they used allegorical interpretation to change the surface meaning into conformity with what they thought the rest of the Bible taught.

However, there is absolutely nothing in the Song of Songs itself that hints of a meaning different from the sexual meaning. As a result, the assignment of spiritual meaning to the text assumes an incredibly arbitrary character. Unless one commentator is simply following in the tradition of another,

---

100. For an excellent study of the relationship between exegesis, hermeneutics, and philosophical-cultural shifts, see C. Bartholomew, *Reading Ecclesiastes: Old Testament Exegesis and Hermeneutical Theory* (Rome: Editrice Pontificio Istituto Biblico, 1998).

101. Davidson, "Theology of Sexuality," p. 2. See D. M. Carr ("Gender and the Shaping of Desire in the Song of Songs and Its Interpretation," *JBL* 119 [2000]: 221-48), who argues that much modern interpretation misconstrues early scholarship on the Song by viewing it through a "myth of repression." Though it is interesting and well argued, I remain unconvinced of his main thesis, although the article came out too late for me to fully assimilate it. However, below it will become clear that I fully agree with his conclusion that "for the ancient Israelites, the jump from human male-female gender to divine-human gender was smaller than it is for us" (p. 247).

102. Phipps, "The Plight," pp. 86-87.

there are virtually unlimited possibilities for interpretation. "The bride's two breasts in 4:5 and 7:8 have been variously interpreted as 'the church from which we feed; the two testaments, Old and New; the twin precepts of love of God and neighbor; and the Blood and the Water. Gregory of Nyssa found in them the outer and the inner man, united in one sentient being.'"[103]

In a premodern cultural environment, this sort of unsubstantiated interpretation could be handed down from one generation to another with little questioning, especially when it was backed by the authority of the Church and its official exegetes. The Renaissance-Enlightenment, however, with its heavy influence on the Reformation, insisted on a return to the sources and reasons for interpretation. If an interpreter suggested that the two breasts of the woman in 4:5 refer to the Old and New Testaments, the critic would demand a basis, which could not be provided. In short, the allegorical approach ran out of steam in large measure because of its *ad hoc* nature.[104]

An Enlightenment insistence that an interpretation be established by a literary argument rather than simple traditional fiat is the first reason for the failure of the allegorical approach to the Song.

The second is probably also to be seen as a part of the ethos of the modern world, namely, the archeology of the Near East, which grew serious during the nineteenth and twentieth centuries. Not only were large architectural structures explored, but the ground yielded tens and even hundreds of thousands of ancient written documents. Among these documents were love poems from Egypt, Mesopotamia, and Ugarit bearing similarities with the Song of Songs (which we will survey in a forthcoming section). These texts, with their familiar epithets, formulas, and phrases, were clearly intended to speak of human love. In the light of these discoveries, it became increasingly difficult to read the Song in a strictly allegorical fashion. As a result, the literal or natural interpretation grew in dominance.

Third, similarities were noticed, not just with ancient literature, but with modern Middle Eastern practice. There was a strong European presence in the Middle East during the nineteenth century, and on occasion Westerners would observe something that would remind them of biblical customs. Perhaps the most notable instance of this, certainly as regards the Song of Songs, is the case of J. G. Wetzstein, who was German consul to Syria in the middle

103. Tanner, "The History of Interpretation," p. 30, quoting D. F. Kinlaw, "Song of Songs," in *The Expositor's Bible Commentary,* vol. 5 (Grand Rapids: Zondervan, 1991), p. 1203.

104. This is not just true of the interpretation of the Song of Songs, though the latter might be its most dramatic example. As M. Silva (*Has the Church Misread the Bible?* [Grand Rapids: Zondervan, 1987], p. 52) states it: "We would not be exaggerating greatly if we described the progress of biblical exegesis as the gradual abandonment of allegorical interpretation."

of the nineteenth century. As German consul, he was witness to many Arab customs, including wedding customs, and in them he saw similarities with the Song.[105] Perhaps most notable, and certainly the most lasting insight that he communicated, concerned the *wasf*. As part of a wedding ceremony, a song would be sung that was "a description of the personal perfections and beauty of the two," that is, the bride and the groom.[106] The similarities between modern Arab wedding customs and the Song bolstered the position that the Song was itself focused on human love.

Fourth, there is a new appreciation for the body in our culture and even in religious circles. There remain, indeed, large disagreements about the exact relationship between the soul and the body, but few today would out-and-out denigrate the body in the interests of the soul. Many, including myself, would affirm that the soul is not a separate substance apart from the body and also would acknowledge that the human body itself is part of what it means to be created in the image of God. Indeed, both male and female gender are connected to image language in Genesis 1:27:

> So God created people in his own image;
>   God patterned them after himself;
>   male and female he created them. (NLT)

THE LITERAL/NATURAL INTERPRETATION OF THE SONG

The literal/natural reading of the Song resists the idea that the Song is a code, saying something different than the words imply. There is no need for a special key to unlock the code, but rather the interpreter applies the same principles to the Song as he or she would to any other comparable writing. It is necessary, though, to point out immediately that literal does not mean a flat or plain interpretation. A natural reading affirms the presence of rich poetry with all the ambiguity and mystery inherent in that poetry. Important precursors to the modern preference for a literal reading of the Song may be seen in Theodore of Mopsuestia, Sebastian Castellio, and John Calvin.

Theodore (A.D. 350-428) was one of the most interesting figures of early church history, frequently taking minority positions that got him in ecclesiastical trouble, but often winning the day in the long run. One such view

---

105. J. G. Wetzstein wrote about his observations in an article "Die Syrische Dreschtafel," *Zeitschrift für Ethnologie* 5 (1873): 270-302, and he communicated with F. Delitzsch, who included an extensive appendix by Wetzstein in his commentary, *Proverbs, Ecclesiastes, Song of Solomon*, trans. M. G. Easton (Grand Rapids: Eerdmans, 1975 [1885]), pp. 162-76.

106. Delitzsch, *Proverbs, Ecclesiastes, Song of Solomon*, p. 172.

was the interpretation of the Song of Songs that he took simply as a passionate love poem between Solomon and the Egyptian princess whom he married. While his interpretive intuitions were valid, his theological conclusions could be and were questioned. He said that such a love poem should not appear in the Holy Scripture. It is probably more for the latter view that he found himself criticized even by his student Theodoret, who judged his teacher's literal interpretation as "not fitting the mouth of a crazy woman."[107] Later, he was condemned, in part for his views on the Song, by the Second Council of Constantinople (A.D. 553).[108]

During the Reformation, John Calvin and Sebastian Castellio disagreed regarding the nature and value of the Song of Songs. The latter revived both aspects of Theodore of Mopsuestia's opinion about the Song, that is, that it was a love poem and also unworthy of the canon. Calvin found this objectionable to the extreme, and M. Pope quotes him in a way that implies that he found the literal meaning intolerable: "Our principal dispute concerns the Song of Songs. He considers it a lascivious and obscene poem, in which Solomon has described his love affair."[109] However, Phipps responds that this is not the case. Calvin believed that the Song concerned physical love, but should be in the canon. The Reformer "did not think it improper to associate the marriage bed celebration with the deepest divine manifestation of love."[110] Calvin did use his considerable influence to see that his former student never was ordained and was eventually exiled from Geneva.

As mentioned, it is fair to say that the literal/natural approach to interpretation has replaced the allegorical approach as the standard way of understanding the intention of the poem. However, that is just the first part of the question. Among those who agree that the Song is a poem about love, there are disagreements about precisely what type of love the poem represents. We will now turn to a discussion of the main schools of thought among those who believe it concerns human love under the following topics: (1) the dramatic approach (two character and three character) and (2) the anthological approach.

The Dramatic Approach

It may be a bit misleading to label this interpretive strategy the dramatic approach because it gives the misimpression that its advocates believe that the Song was connected with the theater and thus was a staged production.[111]

---

107. Davidson, "Theology of Sexuality," p. 3.
108. Kallas, "Martin Luther," p. 324.
109. Pope, *Song of Songs*, p. 127.
110. Phipps, "The Plight," p. 96.
111. Delitzsch, *Proverbs, Ecclesiastes, Song of Solomon*, p. 9.

This is clearly not the case. We have retained the name to describe this strategy, however, on the grounds that it has been used for over a century. What unites the interpretations that, in spite of their differences, we call the dramatic approach is their construction of a plot. They argue, against the allegorical approach, that the Song is about human love, but they also believe it tells a story. We will use leading examples to describe the two most common types of dramatic approach, the two-character drama and the three-character drama.

Two Characters

The two-character approach may well go back to Theodore of Mopsuestia, whom we have seen bucked the nearly universal trend of allegorizing the Song in his day and asserted that the Song was about Solomon and his Egyptian love. Origen apparently also understood that the Song had this historical meaning. However, neither of them thought that such a story was befitting the canon. While the former simply expelled it from his canon, the latter interpreted it in what he thought was the eminently precious allegorical meaning of the text.

We will use the commentary of the conservative Lutheran exegete Franz Delitzsch as our example of a two-character dramatic approach to the text. We do this in large part because Delitzsch's commentary series (written along with C. F. Keil) still finds wide use particularly by ministers and laypeople. Delitzsch asserts that the Song is a love poem, but one that tells a story.[112] The main characters are Solomon — and he defends the traditional Solomonic origins of the Song — and the Shulammite. He believes that the Shulammite is an actual historical figure, but, unlike many before and after him, he does not think she is the Egyptian princess or any prominent woman but rather "a country maiden of humble rank, who, by her beauty and by the purity of her soul, filled Solomon with a love for her which drew him away from the wantonness of polygamy, and made for him the primitive idea of marriage, as it is described in Gen. ii 23ff., a self-experienced reality."[113]

Delitzsch cannot speak highly enough of this rustic country lass, contrasted with the sophisticated city girls known as the daughters of Jerusalem. Her description and also the narrative of their relationship lead him to rhapsodize about how the Song is more about character than sex. Shulammite is a paragon of virtue: "Her words and her silence, her doing and suffering, her enjoyment and self-denial, her conduct as betrothed, as a bride, and as a wife, her

112. The following is a summary paraphrase of Delitzsch's understanding of the Song as described in *Proverbs, Ecclesiastes, Song of Solomon*, pp. 1-12.
113. Delitzsch, *Proverbs, Ecclesiastes, Song of Solomon*, p. 3.

behaviour towards her mother, her younger sister, and her brothers — all this gives the impression of a beautiful soul in a body formed as it were from the dust of flowers."[114] This humble woman humbles the king: "Solomon raises this child to the rank of queen, and becomes beside this queen as a child."[115]

These are the characters; Delitzsch goes on to describe the action by delineating six acts, each of which has two scenes:

1. The mutual affection of the lovers (1:2–2:7), with the conclusion, "I adjure you, ye daughters of Jerusalem."
2. The mutual seeking and finding of the lovers (2:8–3:5), with the conclusion, "I adjure you, ye daughters of Jerusalem."
3. The fetching of the bride and the marriage (3:6–5:1), beginning with "Who is this . . . ?" and ending with "Drink and be drunken, beloved."
4. Love scorned but won again (5:2–6:9).
5. The Shulammite, the attractively fair but humble princess (6:10–8:4), beginning with "Who is this . . . ?" and ending with "I adjure you, ye daughters of Jerusalem."
6. The ratification of the covenant of love in the Shulammite's home (8:5-14), beginning with "Who is this . . . ?"[116]

Three Characters

Another school of thought within the dramatic approach to the Song argued that there were not two but three characters in the narrative. This position goes back at least to Ibn Ezra (twelfth century).[117] This viewpoint, in part at least, was likely motivated by uneasiness concerning Solomon and his love life. Solomon, after all, was seduced into idolatry by his lusts for foreign women (1 Kings 11:1-13). Indeed, as we have already observed, Solomon is pictured at the end of the Song as one who buys and sells love (8:11-12). The three-character view discovered the third character by separating the king from the shepherd in the book, thus producing a love triangle. Generalizing these approaches, the plot surrounds a country girl who has, unfortunately for her, caught the eye of the lustful king Solomon, who wants to carry her away to his harem. She, however, is deeply in love with a shepherd, a country lad, and she does everything that she can to resist the advances of the lascivious king.

114. Delitzsch, *Proverbs, Ecclesiastes, Song of Solomon*, p. 5.
115. Delitzsch, *Proverbs, Ecclesiastes, Song of Solomon*, p. 5.
116. From Delitzsch, *Proverbs, Ecclesiastes, Song of Solomon*, pp. 9-10.
117. At least when he was dealing with the Song on a literal level. He ultimately interpreted the Song in a kind of traditional allegorical manner; cf. S. Horine, "An Integrative Literary Approach to the Song of Songs," Ph.D. dissertation, Westminster Theological Seminary, 1999, pp. 35-36.

Our example of a three-character dramatic approach will be the recent commentary by I. Provan.[118] Provan's view falls into the general pattern of the three-character approach, but with a twist — the woman is already married to Solomon and an unhappy member of his harem. Provan describes his view:

> The woman, already a member of the king's harem, expresses her continuing love for her lover (and, implicitly, her disdain for the king) and he reciprocates (chapters 1–2). The contrast between king and lover is forcibly underlined in chapter 3, where both the woman's determination to overcome threats to her relationship with the man and her negative view of the royal bed and its owner are clear. Both the threats to and depths of the relationship are in evidence in chapters 4–5, where the language and imagery speak of a committed, marital-like relationship between the man and the woman; and chapters 6–7 portray for us in yet further graphic detail the nature of his relationship. Chapter 8 provides us with a strong closing statement of the woman's passion for the man and her resistance to those other males who claim possession of her, whether her brothers or the king. It is a stirring tale of fidelity to first love in the face of power, coercion and all the temptations of the royal court.[119]

Provan's twist then is to see in this three-character love triangle the superiority of true love over legal love.[120]

CRITIQUE OF THE DRAMATIC APPROACH

In my opinion, the dramatic approach has the same fatal shortcoming as the allegorical approach. Nothing in the text supports taking this interpretive strategy. In the first place, the Song is composed of dialogue with absolutely no stage directions. There is no narrative voice that guides readers as they process the speeches of the characters. As a matter of fact, even the rubrics that label the speakers are not in the original Hebrew text and are added by the translator/interpreter.[121] As a matter of fact, as the commentary below

---

118. Provan, *Ecclesiastes and Song of Songs.*
119. Provan, *Ecclesiastes and Song of Songs,* pp. 350-51.
120. See Y. Mazor, "The Song of Songs or the Story of Stories?" *SJOT* 1 (1990): 1-29, and F. Godet, "The Interpretation of the Song of Songs," in *Classical Evangelical Essays in Old Testament Interpretation,* ed. W. C. Kaiser, Jr. (Grand Rapids: Baker, 1972), pp. 151-82, for variations on the attempt to re-create a plot based on a three-character hypothesis.
121. The earliest examples being the Alexandrinus and Sinaiticus, fourth-century manuscripts of the Greek text; cf. E. C. Webster, "Pattern in the Song of Songs," *JSOT* 22 (1982): 73-93.

will make explicit, we cannot be absolutely certain who is speaking in about 10 percent of the cases.

Furthermore, close attention to the writings of advocates of the dramatic approach show that they must overinterpret the text in order to make the plot work. The simplest example of this is the insistence that the shepherd and the king are separate individuals, which is highly unlikely.

I consider these objections insuperable. For that reason, I advocate the view that the Song is a collection of love poems.

LOVE POETRY

Human beings have a strong narrative impulse. We tend to make stories out of the most disparate elements. It is my contention that it is this impulse rather than anything in the Song that leads to the dramatic approach. In the verse-by-verse study that follows in the body of the commentary, we will see that, while there are clear poems in the text, the individual poems are of uncertain and often even of doubtful connection with one another. In the section to follow on Structure, we will admit to literary dynamics that cause us to see an overall coherence to the book, but not a strict narrative unity, that is, a plot. We thus conclude that the Song is an anthology of love poems, a kind of erotic psalter.

However, we must immediately recognize that this psalter is not clearly delineated. In other words, tradition has not passed down to us a canonical division between poems, and as a result we are left with some ambiguity in terms of the number of songs that it contains. Those who argue in favor of an anthological approach to the Song often differ over the precise number of poems that it contains. In a sense, on a practical level, it does not matter whether there are eighty or six poems; the pressing concern of exegesis of the Song is unpacking the metaphors and explaining the effect that it has on us as readers. However, in our study we find ourselves in the midst of the extremes of those who advocate a number of poems in the Song, like F. Landsberger, who does not give us a full study but in his article gives us the impression that virtually every verse is a separate song.[122] We also disagree with M. D. Goulder, however, who argues that there are only fourteen songs.[123] We find ourselves most close to the analysis of M. Falk, who is also to be credited with influencing the most recent flare of popularity of the anthological approach to the Song.[124] Nonetheless, we do not agree with her

---

122. F. Landsberger, "Poetic Units within the Song of Songs," *JBL* 73 (1954): 203-16.

123. Goulder, *The Song of Fourteen Songs*.

124. M. Falk, *Love Lyrics in the Bible* (Sheffield: Almond, 1982).

in detail, since she describes thirty-one songs in the Song, while our analysis below will offer twenty-three. In the introduction to each poem we will give the evidence for our division as well as an indication of how strongly we feel that evidence is.

The conclusion that the Song is an anthology of love poetry as opposed to a drama significantly affects the task of the commentator. It turns attention away from the explanation of a story, or, more pointedly, the construction of a story, to the explication of the meaning of words and metaphors and an attempt to bring out the emotional texture of the poems.

ALTERNATIVE THEORIES

Our previous discussion of the history of interpretation has focused on the two large issues that have shaped readers' approaches to the Song. First, is it an allegory that describes the love between God and his creatures or love poetry that evokes the love of a man for a woman? We have concluded the latter is the intention of the Song. Second, then, is the Song a drama/narrative or a collection/anthology of poems? We have agreed with the latter position. However, we cannot leave the subject of the history of the Song without comment on two other interpretive strategies that have been much discussed in the literature on the Song, namely, the cultic approach and the psychological approach.

Cultic Interpretations

As described above, the nineteenth century A.D. saw the rediscovery of the great civilizations and literature of the ancient Near East and, in particular, the recovery of love poems that bear similarity to the Song. In addition, texts associated with a sacred marriage ritual also were made public.[125] The sacred marriage ceremony in its oldest known form involved the coupling of Dumuz and Inanna, two Sumerian deities, in order to ensure fertility for the coming year. This Sumerian version found a reflex in the Akkadian sacred marriage between Tammuz and Ishtar, and a Canaanite version as well. On a human plane, this divine marriage was acted out by the king and queen or, alternatively, by a priestess of the goddess.

In the early twentieth century, certain scholars, most eminently T. J. Meek, argued that the Song of Songs was a Hebrew reflex to this ancient

---

125. The most recent and full treatment of the texts associated with the Sumerian myth and ritual may be found in Y. Sefati, *Love Songs in Sumerian Literature: Critical Edition of the Dumuz-Inanna Songs* (Ramat-Gan: Bar-Ilan University Press, 1998).

Near Eastern myth and ritual.[126] More recently, Meek's viewpoint has been articulated by the legendary Sumerologist S. N. Kramer: "there is good reason to conclude that at least some of the passionate and rhapsodic love songs of which the book [Song of Songs] is composed are cultic in origin, and were sung in the course of the *hieros gamos,* or 'sacred marriage,' between a king and a votary of Astarte, the Canaanite goddess of love and procreation whom even as wise a Hebrew king as Solomon worshipped and adored. . . ."[127]

Nothing in the Song itself supports the idea that it is part of a Hebrew sacred marriage ritual, and, indeed, there is no hint of a marriage ritual anywhere in the Old Testament. To be sure, we have clear evidence that some Israelites worshipped a female counterpart to Yahweh, but the canon as we have it today certainly distances and indeed rejects any threat to monotheism. There are some who argue that the texts of the Old Testament betray an earlier layer before monotheism came to dominate Israelite theological thinking,[128] but such an opinion is highly speculative and cannot be supported by the texts as we have them. In any case, no one writing on the Song today supports Meek's version of a mythological approach to the Song.[129]

More recently, and often discussed, is Marvin Pope's attempt to situate the Song in the context of the ancient Near Eastern *marzēaḥ* festival. No one has devoted more attention to this festival and its purported echoes down through the ages than Pope.[130] The *marzēaḥ* was a meal — at times Pope describes it as an institution — that asserted the force of life, with which he includes sex, over against death. This meal involved heavy drinking, eating, singing, and sexual acts in the context of a funerary cult. Pope argues that the climax of the Song is found in 8:6c, d:

> For love is strong as Death,
> Passion fierce as Hell.[131]

---

126. T. J. Meek, "Canticles and the Tammuz Cult," *AJSL* 39 (1922-23): 1-14; idem, "Babylonian Parallels to the Song of Songs," *JBL* 43 (1924): 245-52.

127. S. N. Kramer, "The Biblical 'Song of Songs' and the Sumerian Love Songs," *Expedition* 5 (1962): 25.

128. M. S. Smith, *The Early History of God: Yahweh and the Other Deities in Ancient Israel* (New York: Harper & Row, 1990).

129. Gaster ("What 'The Song of Songs' Means," p. 321) had this trenchant criticism of Meek's approach: "while Ishtar and Tammuz were lovers, not all lovers are Ishtar and Tammuz. An erotic cult will naturally use the language of ordinary erotic experience, but that does not mean that any normal employment of it must necessarily be referred to a ritual origin. Are the sonnets of Shakespeare likewise relics of the Ishtar cult?"

130. Pope, *Song of Songs,* pp. 210-29.

131. This translation is Pope's; cf. *Song of Songs,* p. 653.

Pope explains the connection of the *marzēaḥ* with the Song in the following way:

> This fear [of death] may be the covert concern of the Canticle, the response to inexorable human fate with the assertion of Love as the only power that frustrates the complete victory of Death. The sacred marriage was a celebration and affirmation of this vital force. Life and love come into stark confrontation with Death in mortuary observances, not only in the wake and burial but in the ongoing concern to commune with the departed and provide for their needs in the infernal realm with offerings of food and drink.

In response to Pope, we acknowledge that the Old Testament is aware of the *marzēaḥ* festival. However, in the two places where it is mentioned it is castigated as sinful (Amos 6:7; Jer. 16:5). Furthermore, not only is *marzēaḥ* not mentioned positively in the Song, it is never mentioned. Thus, it is more likely that both the *marzēaḥ* and the Song acknowledge the power of love over death independently than that there is some kind of connection between the two.[132]

PSYCHOLOGICAL INTERPRETATION: F. LANDY[133]

Landy's study of the Song starts on the right foot when he states, "My contention, briefly put, is that as Wisdom literature[134] the Song inquires into and expresses the nature of love and therefore of man, with a profundity and compression that has rarely been equalled and in ancient times perhaps only by Sappho."[135] Thus far, he stands in the tradition of interpreting the Song as love poetry. He believes that the Song is composed of love lyrics. Where Landy's approach becomes innovative, and obscuring, is in his psychological readings of the characters and metaphors of the Song. He applies Freudian and Jungian categories and concepts to the text. Not to deny that there are important intuitions and insights into the text such as his insistence that the lovers of the Song are types of lovers and not real individuals, these insights are

---

132. For a trenchant critique of Pope, see the helpful study of J. Sasson, "Unlocking the Poetry of Love in the Song of Songs," *BR* 1 (1985): 11-19.

133. Landy, *Paradoxes of Paradise*. Also, G. Krinetzki (*Kommentar zum Hohelied* [Frankfurt am Main/Bern: Peter Lang, 1981]) adopts a psychological approach to the Song heavily influenced by the perspective of Carl Jung.

134. Below, we will explore the connection between the Song and wisdom literature.

135. Landy, *Paradoxes of Paradise*, p. 33.

clear without the psychological jargon. Typical of the latter is the conclusion that ". . . both lovers derive from and reconstitute the bisexual mother, the ambivalent archetype."[136] As one reads Landy's work, one gets the uncomfortable feeling that we are learning more about the scholar than the object of his study. Moreover, once again we encounter a type of allegory, in this case the allegory of one's psyche, rather than an exposition of the text.[137]

POLITICAL INTERPRETATION: L. STADELMANN[138]

Stadelmann begins by alluding to the medieval idea that the Song needs a key in order to unlock the code that hides the meaning of the book from a plain reading of the text. In his case, though, the book is not a theological allegory but a political one, and the purpose for couching the political message in the form of love poetry was to hide a revolutionary message from the eyes of an oppressive power.

The original setting, according to Stadelmann, is the Persian domination of Judah, and the message concerns the hopes, desires, and intention to restore a Davidic descendant on the throne of Judah. The various characters in the Song represent political entities in postexilic Judah. For instance, Solomon is "representative of the monarchical state of the Davidic dynasty," and the woman represents "the native population of Judah."[139] The love between Solomon and the Shulammite is thus a cipher based on treaty/covenant language, and it refers to the relationship between vassal and king, to the bond between king and people.

Stadelmann thus presents an innovative understanding of the Song — Luther may provide a kind of precursor in that he too saw a political lesson behind the text. Yet Stadlemann's analysis suffers the weakness of all allegorical readings: the lack of any indication within the text that we are to read the text in the manner he describes. It assumes that we need a key to unlock its mysteries. On the contrary, we have argued that there is no reason to avoid the obvious sexual meaning of the text.

---

136. Landy, *Paradoxes of Paradise,* p. 92.

137. Two recent studies from a psychological perspective appeared during the final stages of the preparation of this commentary. They are R. Boer, "The Second Coming: Repetition and Insatiable Desire in the Song of Songs," *Biblical Interpretation* 8 (2000): 276-301, and F. C. Black, "Beauty or the Beast? The Grotesque Body in the Song of Songs," *Biblical Interpretation* 8 (2000): 302-23.

138. L. Stadelmann, *Love and Politics: A New Commentary on the Song of Songs* (New York/Mahwah, N.J.: Paulist, 1990).

139. Stadelmann, *Love and Politics,* p. 2.

VIII. GENRE

The lengthy section above provides the argumentation for the conclusions drawn in this section on the genre of the text. We have surveyed the major options and have anticipated our identification of the Song as an anthology of love poetry. More specifically, the Song is lyric poetry that expresses the thoughts and feelings of the poet(s) via the characters of his artistic creation with the intention of evoking those thoughts and feelings in the heart and mind of the reader. There is really nothing quite like the Song in the Hebrew Bible; its closest connections, we have seen above, are with other ancient Near Eastern love poems. A text like Psalm 45 is similar,[140] but there the love between the king and his queen-to-be is described by a third party, not expressed by the man and the woman themselves.

In terms of the structure of the Song, we will below explicate the relationship between the poems; for now suffice it to say that they are only loosely connected by recurrent refrains, a consistency of persona, and repetition of themes and metaphors.

This conclusion concerning genre shapes how the verse-by-verse commentary will proceed.[141] Our focus will not be on creating a narrative story line as in the dramatic approach or identifying the hidden referents of an allegory — whether historical, political, psychological, or cultic. Our genre identification, rather, triggers a reading strategy that will concentrate on unpacking metaphors, recovering ancient customs and conventions, and describing the thoughts and emotions evoked by the poet.

B. S. Childs,[142] F. Landy,[143] and others[144] have called the Song a work of wisdom literature. This is in addition to, not in place of, its identification as love poetry. Others have rejected this identification. Certainly, there is a

---

140. C. Schroeder, "'A Love Song': Psalm 45 in the Light of Ancient Near Eastern Marriage Texts," *CBQ* 58 (1996): 417-32.

141. For the relationship between genre and reading strategy, consult T. Longman III, "Form Criticism, Recent Developments in Genre Theory, and the Evangelical," *WTJ* 44 (1985): 46-67; idem, *Literary Approaches to Biblical Interpretation* (Grand Rapids: Zondervan, 1987), pp. 76-83, and idem, *Fictional Akkadian Autobiography* (Winona Lake, IN: Eisenbrauns, 1991), pp. 39-48.

142. B. S. Childs (*Introduction to the Old Testament as Scripture* [Philadelphia: Fortress, 1979], pp. 573-75), who also notes the connection to wisdom via the superscription, which associates the Song with Solomon, the wisdom teacher *par excellence*.

143. Landy, *Paradoxes of Paradise*, p. 33.

144. M. Sadgrove ("The Song of Songs as Wisdom Literature," in *Studia Biblica 1978* [Sheffield: JSOT Press, 1978], pp. 245-48), who sees in particular 8:6-7 as the introduction of a wisdom admonition at the climax of the Song. See also N. Tromp, "Wisdom and the Canticle: Ct., 8, 6c-7b: Text, Character, Message and Import," in *La sagesse de l'ancien Testament,* ed. M. Gilbert (Leuven: Leuven University Press, 1990), pp. 88-95.

clear difference between the Song and a blatantly didactic work like the book of Proverbs. However, if wisdom is broadly conceived, as suggested by the just-named scholars, then a case can be made for the appropriateness of wisdom as descriptive of the Song. Wisdom is the application of God's will to the nitty-gritty of life. This, at least, is a partial perspective on the topic. By describing a love that is intense, exclusive, and faithful in spite of obstacles, the Song indirectly but passionately reveals God's will for that special relationship between a man and a woman. Murphy insightfully points out that the Song might be read as an "explication" of Proverbs 30:19: "the way of a man with a maiden."[145] It is certainly not out of keeping with wisdom literature to note that explicit theological language is lacking in the Song, though below we will insist that, when read canonically, the book is rich in insight into the relationship between God and his people. J. M. Munro may be on the right track when she notices a wisdom connection in the relationship between the young woman and the chorus, composed of other young women, whom she is instructing in the ways of love.[146]

We should also pay attention to the form of the individual poems that constitute the Song. The introduction to each poem will comment on its form and, when helpful, give a description. Here we will just list the different forms and give examples in parentheses. First, we see the use of both monologue (2:18-17; 7:12-14) and dialogue (1:15-17; 2:1-7; 4:1–5:1; 8:13-14). Second, in terms of content we have noted admiration songs (1:15-17; 2:1-3; 3:6-11), descriptions of experience (2:4-7; 5:2-7; 6:11-12), songs of yearning (3:1-5; 8:1-4; 8:13-14), invitations (2:10-14; 4:8-9; 7:12-14), the tease (1:7-8), and the *wasf* (4:1-7, 12-14; 5:10-16; 6:4-6; 7:2-8).

IX. ANCIENT NEAR EASTERN BACKGROUND

The Song of Songs did not appear in a literary and cultural vacuum. Above, we alluded to the fact that the broader Near East attests to the presence of literary texts that are similar to what we find in the Song. In anticipation of this evidence, we argued that the Song speaks primarily of human, not divine, love. The most important evidence comes from Egypt, but we will also mention the love poetry from Mesopotamian, Northwest Semitic, early Arabic, and Indian literature. This evidence shows similarities to the Song's genre, theme, motifs, language, and poetic techniques.[147]

---

145. R. E. Murphy, *Wisdom Literature: Job, Proverbs, Ruth, Canticles, Ecclesiastes, and Esther,* FOTL 13 (Grand Rapids: Eerdmans, 1981), p. 104.

146. Munro, *Spikenard and Saffron,* pp. 146-47.

147. For a survey of the various literatures and their connections to the Songs in

EGYPTIAN LOVE POETRY

Egyptian love poetry comes from the Ramesside period (19th and 20th Dynasty: 1305-1150 B.C.) and is found in four places: Chester Beatty Papyrus I, Papyrus Harris 500, the Turin Papyrus, and the Cairo Love Songs.[148] M. V. Fox has argued that the purpose of these songs was entertainment, probably at banquets. In any case, there is no indication that they served a cultic or ritual purpose.

Like the Song, these writings do not tell a story but are a collection of an unspecified number of love poems. Some of the poems are monologues, but others have both speakers present. Nonetheless, contrary to the Song, even when both lovers are present, they appear to speak about each other rather than to each other.[149] However, as in the Song, the man and the woman are not concrete historical personages but rather types of a man and a woman in love.

That Egyptian love poems exude the same mood as the Song is demonstrated by a quotation from number 18 in Papyrus Harris 500:

> In it are *s"m*-trees;
>> before them one is exalted:
>>> I am your favorite girl.
> I am yours like the field
>> planted with flowers
>>> and with all sorts of fragrant plants.
> Pleasant is the canal within it,
>> which your hand scooped out,
>>> while we cooled ourselves in the north wind:
>>>> A lovely place for strolling about,
>>> with your hand upon mine!
> My body is satisfied,
>> and my heart rejoices
>>> in our walking about together.

---

these areas, see W. G. E. Watson, "Some Ancient Near Eastern Parallels to the Song of Songs," in *Words Remembered, Texts Renewed,* ed. J. Davies et al. (Sheffield: Sheffield Academic Press, 1995), pp. 253-71.

148. The most important studies of the Egyptian love poems in relationship to the Song of Songs may be found in J. B. White, *A Study of the Language of Love in the Song of Songs and Ancient Egyptian Love Poetry* (Missoula, MT: Scholars Press, 1975), and Fox, *The Song of Songs.* S. Israelit-Groll ("Ostracon Nash 12 and Chapter 5 of Song of Songs," in *Proceedings of the Tenth World Congress of Jewish Studies* [Jerusalem, 1990], pp. 131-35) argues that we should add the text named in the title to the list of Egyptian love poems.

149. M. V. Fox, "Love, Passion, and Perception in Israelite and Egyptian Love Poetry," *JBL* 102 (1983): 220-21.

To hear your voice is pomegranate wine (to me):
    I draw life from hearing it.
Could I see you with every glance,
    it would be better for me
        than to eat or to drink.[150]

The use of floral imagery, particularly the woman as the field, as well as water imagery (cf. 4:12-15) is immediately reminiscent of the Song. The romantic mood and the joy of being in each other's presence are also similar.

There are a number of other, more detailed similarities. For instance, the man refers to the woman as his "sister," reminiscent of Song of Songs 4:10-12. In Papyrus Harris 500 (number 6), the boy says:

I will lie down inside,
    and then I will feign illness.
Then my neighbors will enter to see,
    and then my sister
        will come with them.
She'll put the doctors to shame
    for she (alone) will understand my illness.

In addition, the physical descriptions of the man and the woman bear some similarities to the *wasfs* of the Song. For an example, we cite number 31 of Papyrus Chester Beatty I:

One alone is my sister, having no peer: more gracious than all other
    women.
Behold her, like Sothis rising
    at the beginning of a good year:
shining, precious, white of skin,
    lovely of eyes when gazing.
Sweet her lips when speaking:
    she has no excess of words.
Long of neck, white of breast,
    her hair true lapis lazuli.
Her arms surpass gold,
    her fingers are like lotuses.
Full (?) her derriere, narrow (?) her waist,
    her thighs carry on her beauties.
Lovely of walk when she strides on the ground,

---

150. This translation as well as the rest of the quotations from the Egyptian love poems are taken from M. V. Fox, in *Scripture in Context*, vol. 1 (Leiden: Brill, 1997), pp. 125-30.

she has captured my heart in her embrace.
She makes the heads of all men
    turn about when seeing her.
Fortunate is whoever embraces her —
    he is like the foremost of lovers.
Her coming forth appears
    like (that of) the one yonder — the Unique One.

MESOPOTAMIAN LOVE POETRY

Under this heading we will treat both Sumerian and Akkadian literature. While the former has a number of relevant texts, there is little that is exactly like the Song of Songs. Akkadian has less love poetry than Sumerian.

As J. G. Westenholz neatly explains, there are three basic types of love poetry in Sumerian. It includes poetry where "(1) deities assume the role of lovers; (2) individual Sumerian kings are praised as they unite with their consorts or with the goddess Inanna; and (3) lovers are not gods or kings."[151] In all three categories, however, there is nothing quite like the Song of Songs even though there are similar metaphors, themes, and epithets. Perhaps the closest parallel may be found in the so-called Message of Ludingirra to His Mother. Of course, as the title of this Old Babylonian (ca. 1800-1600 B.C.) tablet written in Sumerian implies, this is not a letter from one lover to another but from a son to a mother. However, as J. Cooper points out, the son's description of his mother cannot help but bring to mind the descriptive songs of the Song:

My mother is brilliant in the heavens, a doe in the mountains,
A morning star abroad at noon,
Precious carnelian, a topaz from Marhasi
A prize for the king's daughter, full of charm,
A *nír*-stone seal, an ornament like the sun,
A bracelet of tin, a ring of *antasura,*
A shining piece of gold and silver,

. . . .

An alabaster statuette set on a lapis pedestal,
A living rod of ivory, whose limbs are filled with charm.[152]

151. J. G. Westenholz, "Love Lyrics from the Ancient Near East," in *Civilizations of the Ancient Near East,* vol. 4, ed. J. M. Sasson (New York: Charles Scribner's Songs, 1995), p. 2471.

152. From the translation by J. S. Cooper, "New Cuneiform Parallels to the Song of Songs," *JBL* 90 (1971): 160.

In the following commentary, we will occasionally bring to mind the Sumerian and Akkadian texts[153] that have specific connections with particular verses in the Song.

LOVE POETRY IN NORTHWEST SEMITIC LITERATURE

So far no equivalent to the Song has been found outside of Hebrew in Northwest Semitic poetry. Nonetheless, mention must be made of snippets of texts that bear some similarity to individual poems. One example is the description of Hurriya in the Ugaritic text Kirtu. King Kirtu has just been told by 'Ilu that he should get a new wife by besieging the city of Udum and compelling its king Pabil to turn over his daughter Hurriya, who is described to Pabil by Kirtu as:

> The best girl of your firstborn offspring;
> Whose goodness is like that of 'Anatu,
> whose beauty is like that of 'Aṭiratu;
> The pupils (of whose eyes) are of pure lapis-lazuli,
> whose eyes are like alabaster bowls,
> who is girded with ruby. . . .[154]

Nonetheless, in spite of this and similar love poems in the Ugaritic epics, we will find little that is really illuminating of the Song in Northwest Semitic.

OTHER ANCIENT LITERATURE

Scholarly work has pointed to similarities elsewhere, most notably in the so-called pre-Islamic Arabian odes, written in the two centuries before the rise of Islam. M. Jinbachian has argued that these odes have great similarity to the Song and are relevant because they preserve ancient Semitic poetic conventions.[155] A. Mariaselvam has also compared the Song to ancient Tamil

153. W. G. Lambert ("Divine Love Lyrics from Babylon," *JSS* 4 [1959]: 1-15) presented four fragmentary Akkadian texts that he argued were love poems, but further study did not bear this out. Note, however, the presence of an Old Akkadian love poem published by J. M. Sasson, "A Further Cuneiform Parallel to the Song of Songs?" *ZAW* 85 (1973): 359-60. For this same text see J. Westenholz and A. Westenholz, "Help for Rejected Suitors: The Old Akkadian Love Incantation MAD V 8," *Orientalia* 46 (1977): 198-219.

154. Translation is from D. Pardee in *The Context of Scripture*, p. 335.

155. J. M. Jinbachian, "The Genre of Love Poetry in the Song of Songs and the Pre-Islamic Arabian Odes," *The Bible Translator* 48 (1997): 123-37.

love poetry.[156] The similarities are there, but what is at doubt is the genetic relationship between the Song and this Indian poetry. In any case, Egyptian love poetry provides a closer parallel.

SIGNIFICANCE

The ancient parallels to the Song from Egypt, Mesopotamia, Ugarit, and India demonstrate that the language of love crosses national and linguistic boundaries. We are not suggesting any kind of direct borrowing of songs between these cultures, but there was likely an awareness of love songs from other countries, at least among the elite, similar to the awareness of wise sayings from abroad (1 Kings 4:29-34).

We believe that the similarities between the Song and the above-described love poems were obvious from their presentation. However, by way of summary, we would say that the Song shares the same general topic of human love and sexuality, similar forms (notably the "descriptive poem"), and analogous epithets and images.

Differences are also apparent. This includes the lack of true dialogue in the non-Hebrew examples. In the case of the Ugaritic example, it is pure narrative description; for the others, the poems are monologues. Perhaps we could suggest a difference in intention as well. As we observed with the Egyptian love songs, the purpose was entertainment. As we will attempt to show in the commentary, it is possible to discern in the relationship between the young woman and the chorus in the Song an intention to teach the latter, by example and admonition, the nature of love and its appropriate behavior.

X. STRUCTURE

The question of the structure of the Song is a difficult one, as is demonstrated by the plethora of hypotheses found in the secondary literature. No two scholars agree in detail, though there are what might be called schools of thought on the subject. While we feel confident in the general conclusions

---

156. A. Mariaselvam, *The Song of Songs and Ancient Tamil Love Poetry* (Rome: Editrice Pontifico Istituto Biblico, 1988). See the earlier study of Rabin, "The Song of Songs and Tamil Poetry," as well as the effective criticisms of P. C. Craigie, "Biblical and Tamil Poetry: Some Further Reflections," *SR* 8 (1979): 169-75, and Brenner, "Aromatics and Perfumes."

reached regarding the structure of the Song, we have no illusions that the following is the final word.[157]

One's approach to the structure of the Song is heavily affected by genre identification. Those who advocate a dramatic approach to the Song are committed to an overall unity of plot for the book; the structure follows the movement of that plot, which usually flows from the ups and downs in the relationship between the man and the woman. We have already rejected the dramatic approach as overly eisegetical.

Those of us who conclude that the Song is a collection of love poems, however, differ as to the coherence of the collection as a whole. On the one hand, there are scholars who believe that the Song may be divided into six to eight poems that have an "overarching macrostructure."[158] On the other hand, there are scholars who suggest a larger number of poems, "each with its own independent microstructure," with no substantial connection between the poems.[159]

Early on in this introduction, we tipped our hand in favor of a balanced view of the structure of the book, playing on the title Song of Songs. It is a single Song composed of many different Songs. Thus, in the language of D. Grossberg,[160] we find centripetal and centrifugal forces in the book. The literary unity[161] of the Song may be seen in the book's verbal echoes, consis-

---

157. As I finish this commentary, my doctoral student Philip Roberts is completing his extensive and detailed study of the Song's structure based on a minute literary analysis ("'Let Me See His Form': Seeking Poetic Structure in the Song of Songs," Ph.D. dissertation, Westminster Theological Seminary, 2001). I thank him for letting me see his work in process, which shows great promise for progress in delineating the structure of the book.

158. Those who would be in this school of thought include D. A. Dorsey, "Literary Structuring in the Song of Songs," *JSOT* 46 (1990): 81-96; idem, *The Literary Structure of the Old Testament* (Grand Rapids: Baker, 1999), pp. 199-213; D. Buzy, "La Composition Littéraire du Cantique des Cantiques," *RB* 49 (1940): 169-84; J. C. Exum, "A Literary and Structural Analysis of the Song of Songs," *ZAW* 85 (1973): 47-79; J. Angenieux, "Structure du Cantique des Cantiques," *ETL* 41 (1965): 96-142; idem, "Les Trois Portraits du Cantique des Cantiques," *ETL* 42 (1966): 582-86; idem, "Le Cantique des Cantiques en huit chants à Refrains Alternants," *ETL* 44 (1968): 87-140. E. R. Wendland ("Seeking the Path through a Forest of Symbols: A Figurative and Structural Survey of the Song of Songs," *Journal of Translation and Textlinguistics* 7 [1995]: 13-59) uses the language of discourse analysis and the phenomena of recursion and imagery to suggest eight units.

159. Roberts ("Let Me See Your Form") describes these two schools of thought and suggests the language of macrostructure and microstructure.

160. Grossberg, *Centripetal and Centrifugal Structures*, pp. 55-82.

161. It is my opinion that literary unity does not necessarily imply authorial unity. Various authors could write poems that are of the same genre, using similar vocabulary; their collection then would set off some interesting echoes. At most, it is suggestive of the literary sensitivity of the final redactor.

tency of characters, repetition of scenes, and the refrains[162] that run through the book. In the commentary to follow we will point out the most relevant of these in the introductions to the separate units. In addition, we will describe the boundaries between the poems, which lead us to the conclusion that the Song does flow as with a progression. Our overall conclusion agrees with that of P. Cotterell, who says, "the Song is a collection of songs on a common and generally erotic theme, legitimated by the naming of Solomon, skillfully welded together both by allusion and by the repetition of key vocabulary, but offering no narrative time line maintained through the work."[163]

At this point, we will add one further note concerning attempts to find chiastic structures in the Song. As will be pointed out in the commentary, there surely are echoes throughout the Song, some stronger than others. However, the chiastic schemes suggested by scholars like J. C. Exum, W. H. Shea, and E. C. Webster[164] are produced by varying the size of the matched units and drawing out selective content for comparison.[165] The fact that these scholars do not agree in their analyses bears out the subtle manipulation of the evidence necessary to make their patterns work.

XI. CANON

The status and function of canon are much in discussion these days. Is "canonical" an achieved status or does the term describe an inherent authority that is later recognized by the people of God?[166] In other words, does the Church make the canon or does the canon make the Church? Herman Ridderbos provides the best defense of the latter, while disputing the former. He ar-

---

162. Fox (*The Song of Songs,* pp. 209-10) prefers the term repetend to refrain because the latter appear at regular intervals in a text, unlike the situation in the Song.

163. P. Cotterell, "The Greatest Song: Some Linguistic Considerations," *The Bible Translator* 47 (1996): 106.

164. Exum, "A Literary and Structural Analysis"; W. H. Shea, "The Chiastic Structure of the Song of Songs," *ZAW* 92 (1980): 379-96; W. C. Webster, "Pattern in the Song of Songs," *JSOT* 22 (1982): 73-93; G. L. Carr, "Song of Songs," in *A Complete Literary Guide to the Bible,* ed. L. Ryken and T. Longman III (Grand Rapids: Zondervan, 1993), p. 291.

165. See J. A. Emerton, "An Examination of Some Attempts to Defend the Unity of the Flood Narrative in Genesis, Part I," *VT* 37 (1987): 401-20, and "Part II," *VT* 38 (1988): 1-21 (see in particular p. 2 of this article).

166. See H. Ridderbos, *The Authority of the New Testament Scriptures,* trans. H. De Jongste (Grand Rapids: Baker, 1963), for a definition and insightful discussion of self-attestation. Though his book deals specifically with the New Testament canon, the principle applies to the Old Testament as well.

gues that the canonical books are self-attesting and accepted by faith, rather than provable by an external criterion such as authorship.

While I agree with Ridderbos on this issue, I will now address the issue of the external attestation to the canonical status of the Song of Songs. We begin with a restatement of Rabbi Aqiba's famous exclamation: "God forbid! — no man in Israel ever disputed about the Song of Songs [that he should say] that it does not render the hands unclean, for all the ages are not worth the day on which the Song of Songs was given to Israel; for all the Writings are holy, but the Song of Songs is the Holy of Holies."[167] Of course, from the tone, we know that this statement was uttered in the midst of a disagreement about the status of the Song, and apparently it was Rabbi Yose who was on the receiving end.

Nonetheless, it is fair to say that the Song was one of a handful of books about which disagreement festered.[168] There are difficulties reconstructing the nature of the dispute because of the obscurity of the ancient language used to refer to a book's canonicity. Most scholars, however, conclude that the Song was well situated within the canon as early as we have mention of such matters. For instance, it is explicitly included in the canons of Aquila, Melito, and Tertullian in the second century A.D., and it is likely implied in Josephus's mention of twenty-two books and 2 Esdras's (4 Ezra) citation of twenty-four books.[169] The latter probably provides testimony that reflects opinion as early as the second century B.C. However, the rabbis raised questions from time to time. These questions likely arose because of the secular nature of the book. The dispute concerned whether the Song "defiled the hands" or not, a phrase about which there is some controversy. Most understand the phrase to signify what we call canonicity because its holy nature means that touching it required ritual cleansing. Thus, when a passage in the Talmud doubts that the Song defiles the hands, it is questioning the book's authoritative status. However, some scholars, as explained by M. J. Broyde, argue that a denial that the Song defiles the hands is not a rejection of a book's place in the canon but rather an acknowledgment that the book (along with Ecclesiastes and Esther) nowhere uses the Tetragrammaton to refer to God.[170] The nomenclature, again according to Broyde, has to do with protecting scrolls that contain God's name from being nibbled by rodents and other ani-

167. So quoted in Murphy, *The Song of Songs,* p. 6. See further discussion of this quotation under "History of Interpretation."

168. The others were Proverbs, Ecclesiastes, Ezekiel, and Esther. For a recent and extremely thorough study of canonicity, including the status of the Song, see R. Beckwith, *The Old Testament Canon of the New Testament Church* (London: SPCK, 1985), particularly pp. 1-2, 275-76, 279, 282-84, 308-22.

169. Beckwith, *The Old Testament Canon,* pp. 321-22.

170. Please see my later discussion at 8:6 in the commentary.

mals since scholars ate while studying the scrolls or because the scrolls were stored with sacred food. Such nomenclature causes students of the sacred scrolls to wash their hands for fear that they will soil those scrolls with food and the name of Yahweh be defaced by hungry rodents.

In summary, there is no doubt that the Song was well situated in the canon as early as we have evidence (2 Esdras, Josephus, Aquila, Melito, Tertullian), though a significant undercurrent of doubt is expressed, especially if "defile the hands" is equated with what we call canonicity and not with the simple recognition of the absence of the Tetragrammaton. However, we do not know why the Song was first placed in the canon. Christians, of course, simply followed Jewish acceptance of the book, but the process of its inclusion in a Jewish canon is long lost to us. Many think it is either the connection with Solomon[171] or else the allegorical interpretation of the Song[172] that won the day. However, there are putative Solomonic writings that never made it into the mainstream canon (Wisdom of Solomon), and it is much more likely that the allegorization of the Song was a product of the book's inclusion in the canon rather than vice versa.[173]

XII. THE SIGNIFICANCE AND THEOLOGY OF THE SONG OF SONGS

AS LOVE POETRY

The burden of the Introduction has been to demonstrate and describe the Song of Songs as an anthology of love poems. In light of the history of interpretation, with its impulse to bypass the obviously sensual meaning of the book, it is important to insist on the Song's primary significance in relationship to an important aspect of our humanity: love and sexuality. Above, we

171. This is the view of M. Saebo, "On the Canonicity of the Song of Songs," in *Texts, Temples, and Traditions,* ed. M. V. Fox et al. (Winona Lake, IN: Eisenbrauns, 1996), pp. 260-77.

172. The view of Gerleman (*Ruth, Das Hohelied,* p. 51), who said that the allegorization of the Septuagint is what gave the Song its "erforderte religiose Legitimierung" for canonization.

173. So well stated by D. Garrett, *Proverbs, Ecclesiastes, Song of Songs,* NAC (Nashville: Broadman and Holman, 1993), p. 367. We also cannot agree with A. Bentzen, "Remarks on the Canonization of the Song of Solomon," *Studia Orientalia* 1 (1953): 41-47, who argues that the Song became associated with Passover because of an incidental connection with springtime, and that the connection with Passover led to its inclusion in the canon.

have observed how the Song's obvious meaning was hijacked because of the imposition of nonbiblical ideas on the Bible. The burden of proof now lies with those who would deny the Song's application to human love relationships.

Indeed, as human love poetry, the Song plays a crucial role in the Bible as a whole. In answer to the question, "What is a book like the Song of Songs doing in the canon?" we respond by asking the reader to imagine a Bible without the Song. Without the Song, the Church and synagogue would be left with spare and virtually exclusively negative words about an important aspect of our lives. Sexuality is a major aspect of the human experience, and God in his wisdom has spoken through the poet(s) of the Song to encourage us as well as warn us about its power in our lives.

God is interested in us as whole people. We are not souls encased in a husk of flesh. The Song celebrates the joys of physical touch, the exhilaration of exotic scents, the sweet sound of an intimate voice, the taste of another's body. Furthermore, the book explores human emotion — the thrill and power of love as well as its often attendant pain. The Song affirms human love, intimate relationship, sensuality, and sexuality.

The Church has a tendency to make the topic of sexuality a taboo; it is rarely spoken about or discussed in the context of Christian fellowship. The Song, however, affirms the importance of love and sex and provides encouragement and a platform for frank talk about sex among God's people. Unfortunately, it is my observation that Christian leaders rarely teach or preach on the Song. In a word, the Song celebrates human sexuality and love.

This last statement raises the issue of the relationship between the lover and the beloved in the poems of the Song. Are they married?[174] This question is most difficult for those who believe that the Song tells a story. After all, toward the end of the book there are poems where the couple is not married (8:8-10), even though early in the book they are sexually intimate (1:17; 2:1-7; 4:1–5:1). Furthermore, the text only rarely uses the language of marriage,[175] perhaps raising the question in the minds of some readers whether the Song is a celebration of love apart from marriage. A. LaCocque, for instance, has the temerity to say that "the entire Song strums the chord of 'free love,' neither recognized nor institutionalized."[176] B. S. Childs is surely right, in spite of LaCocque's modernist reading of the context, to approach this question in the light of the canon as a whole, when he states: "The Song

---

174. I benefited much in regard to this question from the study of my student S. Horine, "An Integrative Literary Approach."

175. Among the rare associations with marriage is the language of Solomon's wedding in 3:6-11 and the use of the epithet "bride" in 4:8, 9, 10, 11, 12.

176. LaCocque, *Romance She Wrote,* p. 8.

is wisdom's reflection on the joyful and mysterious nature of love between a man and a woman within the institution of marriage. . . . The writer simply assumes the Hebrew order of the family as a part of the given order of his society, and seeks to explore and unravel its mysteries from within."[177] We must read the Song within its broader context, which means the entire canon, and in this context the intimacies described between the man and the woman must be understood within the bounds of marriage.[178] However, we must bear in mind that the book is an anthology of poems. In some poems the man and the woman are probably courting, while in others their intimacies reach an intensity that the biblical worldview only thought appropriate in a context of public commitment.

In much recent writing, the Song has been correctly understood as love poetry but incorrectly used in order to promote specific dating or sexual practices.[179] It is important to remember that the Song is not a dating guide or a sex manual. It is not a "how-to" book, but rather poetry intent on evoking a mood more than making mandates to the reader concerning specific types of behavior. Nonetheless, the Song's passionate and intimate descriptions of sensual touch may serve the purpose of freeing married couples to experiment and experience a physical relationship they wrongly thought proscribed by their Christian commitment.

In spite of the predominant note of celebration, the Song also issues a warning about the danger of love, and not just illicit sex. Love is a potent force, as is most vigorously articulated in Song 8:6-7:

> Set me like a seal on your heart,
>   like a seal on your arm.
> For stronger than death is love,
>   severe like the grave is jealousy.
> Its flame is an intense fire,
>   a god-like flame.
> Many waters are not able to extinguish love,
>   nor rivers flood it.
> Even if a person gave all the wealth of his house for love,
>   he would be completely despised.

177. Childs, *Introduction to the Old Testament*, p. 575. I believe Childs's conclusion here is supported by the study of D. Grossberg, "Two Kinds of Sexual Relationships in the Hebrew Bible," *Hebrew Studies* 35 (1994): 7-25, in which he contrasts the illicit love of Proverbs 7 with the "joyful and ideal sexual relationship" (p. 7) in Song of Songs, and these in a wisdom context.

178. "It would be anachronistic to interpret the Song of Songs as infatuations and sexual experimentation of promiscuous youth"; so rightly Phipps, "The Plight," p. 83.

179. J. C. Dillow, *Solomon on Sex* (Nashville: Thomas Nelson, 1977).

This potent force can lead not only to ecstatic joy but also to heartbreak and a longing that makes one faint or even sick (2:5; 5:8). It is this that leads the woman to warn the "daughters of Jerusalem" not to arouse love before its time (2:7; 3:5; 8:4).[180]

Thus, the Song presents us with both celebration and warning concerning that most intense and fragile of all human emotions, romantic love, and its physical expression, sexuality. Nothing brings more comfort this side of heaven than an intimate relationship with another. Marriage is indeed the most intimate of all human relationships.[181] However, as the most intimate, we can also be reminded of the blessings of other relationships as well. Friendship, for instance, whether with people of our own and the opposite sex, can bring joy into a difficult and hard world.[182] They can also disturb and trouble. Again, the Song can serve as a reminder of the dual nature of love in other than marital human relationships.

The Song not only addresses the predominant attitudes of the Church but also of our society. If the Church tends to understand sex and even human love as taboo, society at large in our time treats it as an idol. An idol is anything besides God where we try to find the ultimate meaning of life. It goes without saying that people live for sex in the twenty-first century, and the advertisers know it. If medieval society was influenced by Platonic and Aristotelian philosophy, our own postmodern age has been influenced by Hugh Heffner and the *Playboy* revolution. To many, a life without sex is a life that is not worth living — and not just sex, but sexuality without constraints. Again, though, the Song reminds us of the danger and the power of sexuality. To make sex the center of one's life is to devote one's life to a capricious and dangerous god. Love and sex have important roles in our lives, but they should always be subordinate to our devotion to God. Just as the Song finds its proper interpretation only in the context of the canon as a whole, so our sexual life finds its place only in the broader context of our devotion toward God. Love and sex are not the final answer to life's troubles or meaning. Indeed, our human relationships are always in the process of becoming or growing. With that in mind, we see how appropriate it is that the Song ends not with a climactic and finally satisfying embrace, but an expression of yearning for union:

---

180. I am indebted to my student G. Schwab, "The Song of Songs' Cautionary Message concerning Human Love," Ph.D. dissertation, Westminster Theological Seminary, 1999), for pointing out to me the importance of this "subsidiary theme" in the book.

181. D. B. Allender and T. Longman III, *Intimate Allies* (Wheaton: Tyndale House, 1995).

182. It is interesting to note that even Qohelet (the Teacher) in the book of Ecclesiastes speaks with reluctant approval of human relationships in the midst of a meaningless world (Eccles. 4:7-12).

The Man
You who dwell in the gardens,
  companions are listening.
Let me hear your voice!

The Woman
Sneak away, my lover, and be like a gazelle,
  or a young stag on the mountains of spices. (Song 8:13-14)

Married couples are usually well aware of the fact that the answers to one's problems are not all found in marriage. There is no such thing as a perfect marriage this side of heaven. We are always left wanting something more in all of our relationships, particularly marriage. The Song's cautionary poems remind us of this. In this way, the Song communicates to singles as well as married couples. Indeed, this is particularly true if we are right to identify the chorus, the daughters of Jerusalem, as a group of unmarried women who are being schooled in love by the main speaker, the young woman. Perhaps more than anyone, single men and women expect more out of marriage than it can deliver. The Song thus provides a healthy balance between celebrating and cautioning about human love.

Thus, we believe that the Song's primary intention is to address the issues of human love and relationships. According to the Song, love is mutual, exclusive, total, and beautiful.[183] To ignore or suppress this is to distort the message of the book. The man and the woman of the Song are not historical personages but rather poetic types, and as such the poet invites the readers to identify with them. In this way, the work encourages intimate, passionate love.

As we conclude this section, however, we want to do so with a warning. David Carr has pointed out that the shift in the nineteenth century from an allegorical to a literal reading was accompanied by what he calls a "functional decanonization" of the Song.[184] That is, while the academy and the Church now recognize the sexual nature of the Song, this has led to less actual use of the text in sermons and even academic writing. Those of us who believe that the whole canon is relevant to modern Church and society would conclude then that the battle is only half won if, when the text's true nature is recognized, it is not then used.

---

183. The terms are D. Hubbard's, from his *Ecclesiastes, Song of Solomon*, Communicator's Commentary (Dallas: Word, 1991), pp. 260-63.

184. D. M. Carr, "The Song of Songs as a Microcosm of the Canonization and Decanonization Process," in *Canonization and Decanonization*, ed. A. van der Kooij and K. van der Toorn (Leiden: Brill, 1998), p. 185.

AS THE STORY OF SEXUALITY REDEEMED

In the immediately preceding section, we reserved our comments to the Song of Songs itself. Once we understand the Song, we can begin to situate it in the context of the Bible as a whole. The next two sections of the Introduction will address the canonical significance of the book. My thinking in the present section has been deeply shaped by the work of Phyllis Trible,[185] who delineates a movement from the creation of the sexual relationship, to its distortion, and then finally to its redemption.

The story begins in the Garden (Genesis 2). God created Adam from the dust of the ground and God's own breath. The raw materials used in the creation of Adam show his fundamental connection to both creation and the Creator. His distinctive relationship with God is further underlined by the fact that he is created in the divine image, something that will also be affirmed of the female, Eve (Gen. 1:27). Adam was not technically alone in the garden. Besides God himself, the other creatures, the animals, were there, and through naming the animals God shows Adam that he is in relationship with them. It is also likely that Adam's naming of the animals shows that he is their superior. Thus, at the beginning Adam is in the Garden with God and the animals, a being far superior to him and creatures that are inferior. The result is that something is missing; he is lonely ("But for Adam no suitable helper was found" [Gen. 2:20b]).

God responded to Adam's needs by creating a partner:

> So the LORD God caused the man to fall into a deep sleep; and while he was sleeping, he took one of the man's ribs and closed up the place with flesh. Then the LORD God made a woman from the rib he had taken out of the man, and he brought her to the man.

The significance of the creation of the woman from the man's rib[186] has been debated over the years. For one thing, some scholars believe that the Hebrew word and its use here is due to the fact that in Sumerian the words for "life" and "rib" sound similar ($ti[l]$).[187] Perhaps so, but the symbolic meaning

---

185. P. Trible, *God and the Rhetoric of Sexuality* (Philadelphia: Fortress, 1978), though it is important to point out that Trible would likely not affirm everything in this section or necessarily the use to which I am putting her material. See also F. Landy, "The Song of Songs and the Garden of Eden," *JSOT* 98 (1979): 513-28.

186. V. P. Hamilton (*The Book of Genesis: Chapters 1–17* [Grand Rapids: Eerdmans, 1990], p. 178) is in the minority when he argues that ṣēlāʾ, here translated "rib," should really be translated in the general sense of "side."

187. For instance, S. N. Kramer, *The Sumerians* (Chicago: The University of Chicago Press, 1963), p. 149.

goes further than this explanation. In the first place, the process of the woman's creation shows that she and the man are intimately connected. She came out of the man, as Adam's poetic response to her creation indicates (see below). Yet it also addresses the equality of the man and the woman. G. J. Wenham cites the great Baptist preacher Charles Haddon Spurgeon to this effect. Eve is "not made out of his head to top him, not out of his feet to be trampled upon by him, but out of his side to be equal with him, under his arm to be protected, and near his heart to be beloved."[188]

The chapter concludes with Adam's hymn of joy at the creation of his equal partner Eve, which emphasizes their equality and intimacy:

> "This is now bone of my bones
>   and flesh of my flesh;
> she shall be called 'woman,'
>   for she was taken out of man." (Gen. 2:23)

Perhaps most relevant for our understanding of this text's relationship with the Song of Songs is the concluding statement of the chapter: "The man and his wife were both naked, and they felt no shame." It is precisely in the area of sexuality ("nakedness") that their intimacy and total vulnerability to one another is expressed most powerfully.

In the Garden, Adam and Eve experienced harmony and complete vulnerability toward one another. However, by the very next chapter they cover themselves with fig leaves, seeking refuge from the gaze of the other (Gen. 3:7). Why such a radical transformation in their relationship?

The story of the Fall accounts for the change. The narrative begins with the sudden appearance of a talking serpent. Due to the abruptness of his appearance, the identity of the serpent is difficult to discuss within the context of the passage.[189] In any case, the serpent is an evil force intending to lead God's human creatures into an act of rebellion. In the previous chapter God had given just one prohibition, and that was that Adam and Eve could not eat the fruit of the tree of the knowledge of good and evil (Gen. 2:16-17). The serpent, though, questioned God's motive for making this prohibition. God said they would die if they ate the fruit; the serpent countered by saying that they would become God-like in their wisdom if they ate it. Eve was persuaded and ate the fruit. Adam, apparently in the presence of the serpent and Eve during their conversation (Gen. 3:6), did not even utter a protest or question his wife's offer of the fruit, and he too ate it.

---

188. G. J. Wenham, *Genesis 1–15* (Waco, TX: Word, 1987), p. 69.

189. The New Testament authors understand the serpent to be Satan (Rom. 16:20; Rev. 12:9), but there is a question over whether it is appropriate to read this New Testament understanding back into the original Old Testament context.

The result was sin, rebellion against God, and the consequence of the sin was a fracture between Adam and Eve and God. It is interesting, though, that the first manifestation that something was wrong in the Garden appears in the area of Adam's and Eve's sexuality: "Then the eyes of both of them were opened, and they realized they were naked; so they sewed fig leaves together and made coverings for themselves" (Gen. 3:7). Soon God himself appeared to Adam, who was hiding from him, and confronted him with his sin. He responded by pointing the finger at Eve ("The woman you put here with me — she gave me some fruit from the tree, and I ate it" [Gen. 3:12]). Eve, in her turn, blamed the serpent ("The serpent deceived me, and I ate" [Gen. 3:13]). God then cursed serpent, man, and woman. The most relevant curse for the purposes of our present study is the second part of the one given to Eve: "Your desire will be for your husband, and he will rule over you" (Gen. 3:16). There is more than one possible interpretation of this curse. On the one hand, it may refer to the fact that the woman desires to have a relationship with a man, but he will dominate her. On the other hand, it is more likely that the desire for domination works both ways. As Susan Foh points out,[190] the word "desire" (*t^ešûqâ*) occurs again in Genesis 4:7, where it refers to sin crouching at the door desiring to overtake Cain. In this context we can clearly see that the word does not signify a tender desire but a desire to control and consume. In other words, Eve desires to dominate Adam, but Adam will counter by trying to control her. The Bible traces destructive power struggles between the genders back to the Fall and the rebellion of humans against God himself.

No longer are Adam and Eve naked and feeling no shame. They immediately cover themselves with fig leaves. From vulnerability and openness they move to self-consciousness, which is seen in their concern with their nakedness. They now have something to hide. God in his grace does not kill them immediately, though this moment is the time when death is introduced at least in the world of humanity. As a token of his continuing involvement with fallen humanity, God creates clothes for them out of animal skins before he ejects them from the Garden.

It is with this background in Genesis 2–3 that we return again to the Song of Songs. In this section, we will simply provide a perspective, an overview of our reading of the Song's contribution to the theme of sexuality or intimacy redeemed. The commentary proper will argue for the specific interpretations presented here. In the Song of Songs we read about the man and the woman in the garden. They are naked, and feel no shame. Specific poems that support this statement include 1:15-17; 2:1-7, 8-17; 4:10–5:1; 6:1-3;[191]

190. S. Foh, "What Is the Woman's Desire?" *WTJ* 37 (1974-75): 376-83.
191. This unit is at the end of a longer poem that includes 5:2–6:3.

6:11-12; 7:7-11 (English 7:6-10);[192] 7:12-14 (English 7:11-13). One cannot help but hear echoes of the Garden of Eden while reading these poems. The implication of a canonical reading of the Song is that the book speaks of the healing of intimacy. Not that that healing is fully accomplished. On the one hand, the Song celebrates their union and proclaims that intimacy happens in this world. On the other hand, the cautionary poems show that lapses occur in even the best relationships. The redemption of our intimate human relationships, indeed like the redemption of our relationships with God, is an already–not yet phenomenon.

Indeed, one of the most remarked-upon features of the Song is the confident voice of the woman as she pursues relationship with the man. The man responds in kind, and it is fair to characterize their relationship as egalitarian. There is no power play between them, no domination of one against the other. This observation is particularly significant in light of our comments above about the curse on the woman. It is striking that the word "desire" *(tešûqâ),* which we discussed above in reference to Genesis 3:16 and 4:7, occurs only one more time — in Song of Songs 7:11 (English 7:10): "I belong to my lover, and his desire is for me." Here the use is clearly positive. It is also in a refrain of mutual love, affection, and possession.

However, as will be pointed out later in reference to individual passages, not all is healed in the area of human relationships. A significant number of passages express the truth that problems of intimacy still exist in the world of the Song. Little foxes are "ruining our vineyard, our vineyard in bloom" (2:15). The city is often the setting of those poems where union is difficult or impossible (3:1-3; 5:2-7[193]). While rejoicing in love, three times (2:7; 3:5; 8:4) the young woman warns the chorus of the dangers of premature love: "I adjure you, daughters of Jerusalem, by the gazelles or the deer of the field, not to awaken or arouse love until it desires."

In a word, relationships, broken by sin, may experience the healing of redemption, but it is an already–not yet phenomenon. The consummation of relationships will not take place until the eschaton, but precisely what that means is beyond precise description. Much that is relevant to this claim will be present in the next section, but here we will deal with one enigmatic passage that speaks of marriage in heaven, Luke 20:27-40. There Jesus is confronted by the Sadducees, who do not believe in resurrection after death. They use a hypothetical situation in an attempt to ridicule Jesus. They speak of a woman who at the end of her life had had seven husbands, each of whom had in turn predeceased her before producing offspring. To whom will she be married in heaven?

192. This unit is found in a larger poem that includes 7:1-11 (English 6:13–7:10).
193. In the context of the longer poem of 5:2–6:3.

Jesus' words are enigmatic in large part because he refused to allow the Sadducees to misdirect the conversation. The part relevant to our discussion is 20:34-36: "The people of this age marry and are given in marriage. But those who are considered worthy of taking part in that age and in the resurrection from the dead will neither marry nor be given in marriage, and they can no longer die; for they are like the angels." This passage has led too quickly to the conclusion that there is nothing like sexuality or intimacy in heaven. However, we must suspend our hasty judgments. We really do not know what the angels are like in this regard.[194] We must remain open as to the nature of relationships in heaven and not impose a cold, sterile, nonsensual understanding on the biblical text. What we do know is that both divine-human and human-human relationships will be healed and completely restored in heaven, and that brings us to our final point about the significance of the teaching of the Song of Songs.

AS ILLUMINATING THE DIVINE-HUMAN RELATIONSHIP

Earlier we criticized an allegorical approach to the Song that read a theological meaning onto the surface of the book, and in its place we argued support for the idea that the Song is a collection of poems that celebrate and caution concerning human love. However, we now come full circle in order to affirm the legitimacy of a theological reading of the book. Read within the context of the canon, the Song has a clear and obvious relevance to the divine-human relationship. After all, throughout the Bible God's relationship to humankind is likened to a marriage.[195] In this metaphor God is the husband and his people are his wife. It is not that God is male or that there are no female images of God in the Bible (see Psalm 131; Proverbs 6–8; Isa. 66:13). In Israelite society the man was the head of the household, and thus, within the marriage metaphor, it is understandable that God is cast within the role of the husband, and humans, both male and female, play the female role.

Indeed, we may start by noting that Malachi speaks of marriage as a covenant (Mal. 2:14), a relationship that is built on mutual love but finds expression in a legal form. Israel's relationship with God in the Old Testament is also covenantal, as witnessed in the books of Exodus (19–24) and Deuter-

---

194. Indeed, Gen. 6:1-4 and Jude 6, when understood in its context, suggests otherwise. The nonsexual nature of angels may be an imposition of Platonic ideas on the biblical picture.

195. The best recent study of this theme is N. Stienstra, *YHWH Is the Husband of His People: Analysis of a Biblical Metaphor with Special Reference to Translation* (Kampen: Pharos, 1993).

onomy. Israel's breaking of its covenant with God is likened to the breaking of the marriage bond. Hosea may be the first to use this marriage metaphor when he describes the alienation between Israel and God as a break in their marriage vows. God commands the prophet to marry "an adulterous wife" (Hos. 1:2), and later Hosea commands his children to admonish her in a way that challenges the spiritual apostasy of the people of God:

> Rebuke your mother, rebuke her,
>> for she is not my wife,
>> and I am not her husband.
> Let her remove the adulterous look from her face
>> and the unfaithfulness from between her breasts. (Hos. 2:2)

The prophet Ezekiel develops the metaphor of marriage as spiritual symbol to its greatest extent. He dedicates two long chapters to recounting the perversity of Israel's relationship to God using sexual terms. We will pass over Ezekiel 16 and illustrate the prophet's argument with Ezekiel 23. Ezekiel describes two sisters, identifying the first, Oholah, with Samaria and the second, Oholibah, with Jerusalem. These sisters became prostitutes in Egypt, where "their breasts were fondled and their virgin bosoms caressed" (Ezek. 23:3).

God then complains that Oholah lusted after Assyrian soldiers even when he was still married to her (Ezek. 23:5-8). As a result, he simply gave her to them, and they humiliated her and then killed her (Ezek. 23:9-10). Oholibah did not learn a lesson from her sister's fate. She found herself attracted to the Babylonians. Her rejection of the marriage bed was intense, since "she lusted after her lovers whose genitals were like those of donkeys and whose emission was like that of horses" (Ezek. 23:20). In the end God will judge Oholibah, his unfaithful wife, as he did Oholah.

Other prophets also exploit the resemblance of Israel's unfaithfulness to a broken marriage covenant. In Jeremiah, God remembers when his relationship with Israel was good, using these terms:

> I remember the devotion of your youth,
>> how as a bride you loved me
> and followed me through the desert,
>> through a land not sown. (Jer. 2:1)

Yet in the present, Israel commits spiritual adultery. Idolatry is adultery, as Jeremiah 3:6 makes clear: "Have you seen what faithless Israel has done? She has gone up on every high hill and under every spreading tree and has committed adultery there."

Isaiah too makes the literary connection between idolatry and adultery. God has divorced his wife Israel because of her adultery (Isa. 50:1). However, Isaiah also speaks of Israel's future salvation as a restoration of the marriage relationship.

> The LORD will call you back
>   as if you were a wife deserted and distressed in spirit —
> a wife who married young,
>   only to be rejected. . . .
> For a brief moment I abandoned you,
>   but with deep compassion I will bring you back. (Isa. 54:6-7; see
> the whole of ch. 54)

The prophets exploit the marriage metaphor most dramatically, but its contours can be discerned elsewhere in the Old Testament as well. In the Pentateuch we hear of Yahweh's jealousy, an emotion that is only proper to an exclusive relationship like marriage (Exod. 19:3-6; 20:2-6; 34:14). Also, Israel's rebellion is described as adultery and prostitution (Exod. 34:15-16; Lev. 17:7).

The use of the marriage relationship as a metaphor of the relationship between God and his people continues in the New Testament. Most notably, Paul in the book of Ephesians instructs Christians that their connection with Christ is like a marriage (Eph. 5:21-33). Accordingly, wives should submit to their husbands as the Church submits to Christ, and husbands should love their wives with the sacrificial love that Christ has for the Church.[196]

The book of Revelation describes the end of history, when God will once and for all destroy all evil. His faithful people will be united with him forever in glory. It is not surprising, considering the development of the marriage metaphor up to this point in the Bible, that this final union between God and his people is described as a marriage:

> Hallelujah!
>   For our Lord God Almighty reigns.
> Let us rejoice and be glad
>   and give him glory!
> For the wedding of the Lamb has come,
>   and his bride has made herself ready.
> Fine linen, bright and clean,
>   was given her to wear. (Rev. 19:6-8)

---

196. This passage should not be read as if only the wife submits to the husband or, for that matter, that only the husband should love the wife. The command for the wife to submit in Eph. 5:20 needs to be read in the context of 5:21, which demands mutual submission.

The allegorical approach was not wrong in insisting that we read the Song as relevant to our relationship to God. The more we understand about marriage, the more we understand about our relationship with God. More than any other human relationship marriage reflects the divine-human relationship. There are only two relationships that are mutually exclusive to humans. We may have only one spouse and only one God. Accordingly, these are the only two relationships where jealousy can be a positive emotion.[197] The allegorical approach erred in two ways, however. First, allegorists suppressed the human love dimension of the Song, and, second, they pressed the details in arbitrary ways in order to elicit specific theological meaning from the text.[198]

CONCLUSION

In summary, then, the Song of Songs has a large, but often neglected, contribution to make to the religious community and to society. In the first place, it affirms love, sex, and, if read properly within the context of the canon, marriage. Second, it warns readers that such an intense emotion has its dangers. Though the Song's surface meaning is clearly concerned with human sexuality, a canonical reading offers at least two other major avenues of understanding the Song. (1) Human sexuality is part of the story of the creation, fall, and redemption of human relationships. God created marriage (Genesis 2), but that relationship was harmed by sin (Genesis 3). Yet the Song holds out the promise of healing, though complete harmony in relationships awaits the eschaton. (2) Throughout the Bible relationship with God is described by the metaphor of marriage. As with any metaphor, the reader must observe a proper reticence in terms of pressing the analogy. Nonetheless, from the Song we learn about the emotional intensity, intimacy, and exclusivity of our relationship with the God of the universe.

XIII. BIBLIOGRAPHY

Abegg, M., Jr., P. Flint, and E. Ulrich. *The Dead Sea Scrolls Bible.* San Francisco: HarperSanFrancisco, 1999.

197. See the discussion of this in Song of Songs 8:6.
198. See examples above, for instance, Hippolytus reading Song 1:13 and understanding the sachet of myrrh to refer to Jesus and the breasts to the Old and New Testaments.

Abrams, M. H. *A Glossary of Literary Terms.* 4th ed. New York: Holt, Rinehart and Winston, 1981.

Albrektson, B. "Singing or Pruning?" *The Bible Translator* 47 (1996): 109-13.

Albright, W. F. "Archaic Survivals in the Text of Canticles." In *Hebrew and Semitic Studies Presented to Godfrey Rolles Driver,* edited by D. Winton Thomas and W. D. McHardy, pp. 1-7. Oxford: Clarendon, 1963.

Alden, R. L. "Song of Songs 8:12a: Who Said It?" *JETS* 31 (1988): 271-78.

Alexander, P. S. "The Song of Songs as Historical Allegory: Notes on the Development of an Exegetical Tradition." In *Targumic and Cognate Studies: Essays in Honour of Martin McNamara,* edited by K. J. Cathcart and M. Maher, pp. 14-29. Sheffield: Sheffield Academic Press, 1996.

Alexeev, A. A. "The Song of Songs in the Slavonic Bible Tradition." *The Bible Translator* 47 (1996): 119-25.

Allender, D. B., and T. Longman III. *Intimate Allies.* Wheaton: Tyndale House, 1995.

Alter, R. *The Art of Biblical Poetry.* New York: Basic Books, 1985.

Angenieux, J. "Structure du Cantique des Cantiques." *ETL* 41 (1965): 96-142.

———. "Les Trois Portraits du Cantique des Cantiques." *ETL* 42 (1966): 582-86.

———. "Le Cantique des Cantiques en huit Chants à Refrains Alternants." *ETL* 44 (1968): 87-140.

Archer, G. L., Jr. *A Survey of Old Testament Introduction.* Chicago: Moody, 1974.

Ayo, N. *Sacred Marriage: The Wisdom of the Song of Songs.* New York: Continuum, 1997.

Baars, W. "The Peshitta Text of Song of Songs in Barhebraeus' Ausar Raze." *VT* 18 (1968): 281-89.

Balchin, J. "Song of Songs." In *The New Bible Commentary,* 4th ed., pp. 619-28. Downers Grove, IL: InterVarsity, 1994.

Barbiero, G. "Die Liebe der Töchter Jerusalems: Hld 3,10b MT im Kontext von 3,6-11." *BZ* 39 (1995): 96-104.

———. "Die 'Wagen meines edlen Volkes' (Hld 6,12): eine strukturelle Analyse." *Bib* 78 (1997): 174-89.

Bartholomew, C. *Reading Ecclesiastes: Old Testament Exegesis and Hermeneutical Theory.* Rome: Editrice Pontificio Istituto Biblico, 1998.

Beckwith, R. *The Old Testament Canon of the New Testament Church.* London: SPCK, 1985.

Bentzen, A. "Remarks on the Canonization of the Song of Solomon." *Studia Orientalia* 1 (1953): 41-47.

Bergant, D. "'My Beloved Is Mine and I Am His' (Song 2:16): The Song of Songs and Honor and Shame." *Semeia* 68 (1996): 23-41.

Berlin, A. *The Dynamics of Biblical Parallelism.* Bloomington: Indiana University Press, 1984.

Black, F. C. "Beauty or the Beast? The Grotesque Body in the Song of Songs." *Biblical Interpretation* 8 (2000): 302-23.

Bloch, A., and C. Bloch. *The Song of Songs: A New Translation.* New York: Random House, 1995.

Blumenthal, D. R. "Where God Is Not: The Book of Esther and Song of Songs." *Judaism* 173 (1995): 80-90.

Boer, R. "The Second Coming: Repetition and Insatiable Desire in the Song of Songs." *Biblical Interpretation* 8 (2000): 276-301.

Borowski, O. "The Sharon — Symbol of God's Abundance." *BR* 4 (1988): 40-43.

Bosshard-Nepustil, E. "Zu Struktur und Sachprofil des Hoheliedes." *BN* 81 (1996): 45-71.

Boyarin, D. "The Song of Songs: Lock or Key? Intertextuality, Allegory and Midrash." In *The Book and the Text: The Bible and Literary Theory,* edited by R. Schwartz, pp. 214-30. Oxford: Blackwell, 1990.

Brenner, A. "Aromatics and Perfumes in the Song of Songs." *JSOT* 25 (1983): 75-81.

———. "A Note on *Bat-Rabbîm* (Song of Songs VII 5)." *VT* 42 (1992): 113-15.

———. "To See Is to Assume: Whose Love Is Celebrated in the Song of Songs?" *Biblical Interpretation* 1 (1993): 265-84.

Brenner, A., ed. *A Feminist Companion to the Song of Songs.* Sheffield: JSOT Press, 1993.

Broyde, M. J. "Defilement of the Hands, Canonization of the Bible, and the Special Status of Esther, Ecclesiastes, and Song of Songs." *Judaism* 173 (1995): 65-79.

Burrows, M. S. "Foundations for an Erotic Christology: Bernard of Clairvaux on Jesus as 'Tender Lover.'" *ATR* 80 (1998): 477-91.

Button, M. D. "The Watchmen and the Shulammite: Toward a Psychoanalytical Interpretation of the 'Watchman' Passages of Song of Songs 3:3, 4 and 5:7." Unpublished paper.

Buzy, D. "La Composition Littéraire du Cantique des Cantiques." *RB* 49 (1940): 169-84.

Cainion, I. J. "An Analogy of the Song of Songs and Genesis Chapters Two and Three." *SJOT* 14 (2000): 219-59.

Calloud, J. "Esquisse: Propositions une interpretation raisonnee du Cantique des Cantiques." *Semiotique & Bible* 65 (1992): 43-60.

Cantwell, L. "The Allegory of the Canticle of Canticles." *Scripture* 16 (1964): 76-93.

Carr, D. M. "The Song of Songs as a Microcosm of the Canonization and Decanonization Process." In *Canonization and Decanonization,* edited by A. van der Kooij and K. van der Toorn, pp. 173-89. Leiden: Brill, 1998.

————. "Gender and the Shaping of Desire in the Song of Songs and Its Interpretations." *JBL* 119 (2000): 233-48.

Carr, G. L. "The Old Testament Love Songs and Their Use in the New Testament." *JETS* 24 (1981): 97-105.

————. *The Song of Solomon.* TOTC. Downers Grove, IL: InterVarsity, 1984.

————. "Song of Songs." In *A Complete Literary Guide to the Bible,* edited by L. Ryken and T. Longman III, pp. 281-96. Grand Rapids: Zondervan, 1993.

Casimir, Brother. "On the Song of Songs: The First Homily by St. Gregory of Nyssa." *Word and Spirit* 3 (1981): 161-77.

Chappuzeua, G. "Die Exegese von Hohelied 1,2a.b und 7 bei den Kirchenvätern von Hippolyt bis Bernhard." *Jahrbuch für Antike und Christentum* 18 (1975): 91-143.

Chave, P. "Towards a Not Too Rosy Picture of the Song of Songs." *Feminist Theology* 18 (1998): 41-53.

Childs, B. S. *Introduction to the Old Testament as Scripture.* Philadelphia: Fortress, 1979.

Clines, D. J. A. "Why Is There a Song of Songs and What Does It Do to You If You Read It?" *Jian Dao* 1 (1994): 1-27.

Collins, A. Y. "The Song of Songs in Comparative Perspective." In *Hebrew Bible or Old Testament?: Studying the Bible in Judaism and Christianity,* pp. 217-19. Notre Dame, IN: University of Notre Dame Press, 1990.

Cooper, A. "Biblical Poetics: A Linguistic Approach." Ph.D. dissertation. Yale University, 1976.

Cooper, J. S. "New Cuneiform Parallels to the Song of Songs." *JBL* 90 (1971): 157-62.

Cornelius, I. "The Garden in the Iconography of the Ancient Near East: A Study of Selected Material from Egypt." *JSS* 1.2 (1989): 204-28.

Corney, R. W. "What Does 'Literal Meaning' Mean? Some Commentaries on the Song of Songs." *ATR* 80 (1998): 494-516.

Cotterell, P. "The Greatest Song: Some Linguistic Considerations." *The Bible Translator* 47 (1996): 101-8.

Dahood, M. J. "Canticle 7,9 and UT 52,61." *Bib* 57 (1976): 109-10.

————. "Love and Death at Ebla and Their Biblical Reflections." In *Love and Death in the Ancient Near East,* edited by J. H. Marks and R. M. Good, pp. 93-99. Guilford, CT: Four Quarters, 1987.

Davidson, R. M. "Theology of Sexuality in the Song of Songs: Return to Eden." *AUSS* 27 (1989): 1-19.

Davis, E. F. "Romance of the Land in the Song of Songs." *ATR* 80 (1998): 533-46.

Delcor, M. "Two Special Meanings of the Word *yd* in Biblical Hebrew." *JSS* 12 (1967): 230-40.

Delitzsch, F. *Proverbs, Ecclesiastes, Song of Solomon.* Translated by M. G. Easton. Grand Rapids: Eerdmans, 1975 (1885).

Dijk-Hemmes, F. "The Imagination of Power and the Power of Imagination: An Intertextual Analysis of Two Biblical Love Songs: The Song of Songs and Hosea 2." *JSOT* 44 (1989): 75-88.

Dillard, R. B., and T. Longman III. *An Introduction to the Old Testament.* Grand Rapids: Zondervan, 1994.

Dillow, J. C. *Solomon on Sex.* Nashville: Thomas Nelson, 1977.

Dirksen, P. B. "Song of Songs III 6-7." *VT* 39 (1989): 219-25.

————. "The Peshitta of the Song of Songs." *Textus* 19 (1998): 171-83.

Dorsey, D. A. "Literary Structuring in the Song of Song." *JSOT* 46 (1990): 81-96.

————. *The Literary Structure of the Old Testament.* Grand Rapids: Baker, 1999.

Dove, M. "Sex, Allegory and Censorship: A Reconsideration of Medieval Commentaries on the Song of Songs." *Literature and Theology* 10 (1996): 316-28.

Driver, G. R. "Supposed Arabisms in the Old Testament." *JBL* 55 (1936): 101-20.

————. "Lice in the Old Testament." *PEQ* 106 (1974): 159-60.

Edmee, Sr. "The Song of Songs and the Cutting of Roots." *ATR* 90 (1998): 547-61.

Elliott, M. T. *The Literary Unity of the Canticle.* EHS. Frankfurt am Main: Peter Lang, 1989.

————. "Ethics and Aesthetics in the Song of Songs." *TynBul* 45 (1994): 137-52.

Emerton, J. A. "An Examination of Some Attempts to Defend the Unity of the Flood Narrative in Genesis, Part I." *VT* 37 (1987): 401-20; "Part II," *VT* 38 (1988): 1-21.

————. "Lice or a Veil in the Song of Songs 1,7?" In *Understanding Poets and Prophets,* edited by A. G. Auld, pp. 127-40. Sheffield: Sheffield Academic Press, 1993.

Emmerson, G. I. "The Song of Songs: Mystification, Ambiguity and Humour." In *Crossing the Boundaries: Essays in Biblical Interpretation in Honour of Michael D. Goulder,* edited by S. E. Porter, P. Joyce, and D. E. Orton, pp. 97-111. Leiden: Brill, 1994.

Exum, J. C. "A Literary and Structural Analysis of the Song of Songs." *ZAW* 85 (1973): 47-79.

————. "Asseverative '*al* in Canticles 1,6?" *Bib* 62 (1981): 416-19.

Falk, M. *Love Lyrics in the Bible.* Sheffield: Almond, 1982.

Feuillet, A. *Le Cantique des Cantiques.* Paris: Les Editions du Cerf, 1953.

————. "La formule d'appartenance mutuelle (II,16) et les interpretations divergentes du Cantique des Cantiques." *RB* 68 (1961): 5-38.

————. "'S'asseoir a l'ombre' de l'époux (Os., xiv,8a et Cant., ii,3)." *RB* 78 (1971): 391-405.

————. "Perspectives nouvelles à propos de l'intérpretation du Cantique des Cantiques." *Civitas Vaticana* 34 (1990): 203-19.

————. "La double insertion du Cantique des Cantiques dans la vie de la communauté chrétienne et dans la tradition religieuse de l'Ancien Testament." *Divinitas* 35 (1991): 5-18.

Foh, S. "What Is the Woman's Desire?" *WTJ* (1974-75): 376-83.

Fox, M. V. "Scholia to Canticles (I 4b, ii 4, I 4ba, iv 3, v 8, vi 12)." *VT* 33 (1983): 199-206.

————. "Love, Passion, and Perception in Israelite and Egyptian Love Poetry." *JBL* 102 (1983): 219-28.

————. *The Song of Songs and the Ancient Egyptian Love Songs.* Madison: University of Wisconsin Press, 1985.

Fredericks, D. *Qohelet's Language: Re-evaluating Its Nature and Date.* Lewiston, NY; Queenstown, Ontario: Edwin Mellon, 1988.

Froehlich, K. "'Aminadab's Chariot': The Predicament of Biblical Interpretation." *Princeton Seminary Bulletin* 18 (1997): 262-78.

Frolov, S. "No Return for the Shulammite: Reflections on Cant. 7,1." *ZAW* 110 (1998): 256-58.

Fulton, R. "Mimetic Devotion, Marian Exegesis, and the Historical Sense of the Song of Songs." *Viator: Medieval and Renaissance Studies* 27 (1996): 85-116.

Garrett, D. *Proverbs, Ecclesiastes, Song of Songs.* NAC. Nashville: Broadman and Holman, 1993.

Gaster, T. H. "What 'The Song of Songs' Means." *Commentary* 13 (1952): 316-22.

————. "Canticles i.4." *ExpT* 72 (1961): 72.

Geller, M. *Parallelism in Early Hebrew Poetry.* Missoula, MT: Scholars Press, 1979.

Gerleman, G. *Ruth, Das Hohelied.* BKAT 18. Neukirchen-Vluyn: Neukirchener, 1965.

Ginsburg, C. D. *The Song of Songs and Coheleth,* edited by H. M. Orlinsky. New York: KTAV, 1970 (1861).

Gledhill, T. *The Message of the Song of Songs.* BST. Downers Grove, IL: InterVarsity, 1994.

Glickman, S. C. *A Song for Lovers.* Downers Grove, IL: InterVarsity, 1978.

Godet, F., "The Interpretation of the Song of Songs." In *Classical Evangelical Essays in Old Testament Interpretation,* edited by W. C. Kaiser, Jr., pp. 151-82. Grand Rapids: Baker, 1972.

Goiten, S. D. "*Ayumma Kannidgalot* (Song of Songs VI.10) 'Splendid Like the Brilliant Stars,'" *JSS* 10 (1965): 220-21.

Gordis, R. "The Root *dgl* in the Song of Songs." *JBL* 88 (1969): 203-4.

———. *The Song of Songs and Lamentations: A Study, Modern Translation, and Commentary.* Rev. and augmented ed. New York: KTAV, 1974.

Gordon, C. H. "New Directions." *Bulletin of the American Society of Papyrologists* 15 (1978): 59-66.

———. "Asymmetric Janus Parallelism." *Eretz-Israel* 16 (1982): 80-81.

Gorg, M. "Eine Salbenbezeichnung in HL 1,3." *BN* 38-39 (1987): 36-38.

———. "'Kanäle' oder 'Zweige' in Hld 4,13?" *BN* 72 (1994): 20-23.

Goulder, M. D. *The Song of Fourteen Songs.* JSOTS 36. Sheffield: JSOT Press, 1986.

Grossberg, D. "Canticles 3:10 in the Light of a Homeric Analogue and Biblical Poetics." *BTB* 11 (1981): 74-76.

———. "Sexual Desire: Abstract and Concrete." *Hebrew Studies* 22 (1981): 59-60.

———. *Centripetal and Centrifugal Structures in Hebrew Poetry.* Atlanta: Scholars Press, 1989.

———. "Two Kinds of Sexual Relationships in the Hebrew Bible." *Hebrew Studies* 35 (1994): 7-25.

Hallo, W. W. "'As the Seal upon Thy Heart': Glyptic Roles in the Biblical World." *BR* 1 (1985): 20-27.

———. "For Love Is Strong as Death." *JANES* 22 (1993): 45-50.

Hallo, W. W., and K. L. Young, eds., *The Context of Scripture,* 1. Leiden: Brill, 1997.

Harman, A. H. "Modern Discussion on the Song of Songs." *RTR* 37 (1978): 65-72.

Heinevetter, H.-J. *Komm nun, mein Liebster, Dein Garten ruft Dich. Das Hohelied als programmatische Komposition.* Bonner Biblische Beiträge 69. Frankfurt am Main: Athenäum, 1988.

Hicks, R. L. "The Door of Love." In *Love and Death in the Ancient Near East: Essays in Honor of Marvin H. Pope,* edited by J. H. Marks and R. M. Good, pp. 153-58. Guilford, CT: Four Quarters, 1987.

Holmyard, III, H. R. "Solomon's Perfect One." *BibSac* 155 (1998): 164-71.

Horine, S. "An Integrative Literary Approach to the Song of Songs." Unpublished Ph.D. dissertation, Westminster Theological Seminary, 1999.

Hostetter, E. C. "Mistranslation in Cant 1:5." *AUSS* 34 (1996): 35-36.

Hubbard, D. *Ecclesiastes, Song of Solomon.* Communicator's Commentary. Dallas: Word, 1991.

Hubbard, R. *The Book of Ruth.* NICOT. Grand Rapids: Eerdmans, 1988.

Hunt, P. N. "Subtle Paronomasia in the Canticum Canticorum: Hidden Treasures of the Superlative Poet." In *Gelden Apfel in silbern Schalen . . .,* edited by K.-D. Shunck and M. Augustine, pp. 147-54. Beiträge zur Erforschung des Alten Testaments und des antiken Judentums 20. Frankfurt am Main and New York: Peter Lang, 1992.

Hunter, J. H. "The Song of Protest: Reassessing the Song of Songs," *JSOT* 90 (2000): 109-24.

Israelit-Groll, S. "Ostracon Nash 12 and Chapter 5 of Song of Songs." In *Proceedings of the Tenth World Congress of Jewish Studies,* pp. 131-35. Jerusalem, 1990.

Jacobsen, T. "The Battle between Marduk and Tiamat." *JAOS* 88 (1968): 104-5.

Jakobson, R. "Grammatical Parallelism and Its Russian Facet." *Language* 42 (1966): 399-529.

Jinbachian, J. M. "The Genre of Love Poetry in the Song of Songs and the Pre-Islamic Arabian Odes." *The Bible Translator* 48 (1997): 123-37.

Kallas, E. "Martin Luther as Expositor of the Song of Songs." *Lutheran Quarterly* 2 (1988): 323-41.

Kannengiesser, C. "Divine Love Poetry: The Song of Songs." In *Hebrew Bible or Old Testament? Studying the Bible in Judaism and Christianity,* edited by R. Brooks and J. J. Collins, pp. 211-15. Notre Dame, IN: University of Notre Dame Press, 1990.

Keel, O. *The Song of Songs.* A Continental Commentary. Minneapolis: Fortress, 1994.

Kellner, M. *Commentary on Song of Songs: Levi ben Gershom (Gersonides).* New Haven: Yale University Press, 1998.

Kinlaw, D. F. "Song of Songs." In *The Expositor's Bible Commentary,* vol. 5. Grand Rapids: Zondervan, 1991, 1199-1244.

Kimelman, R. "Rabbi Yohanan and Origen on the Song of Songs: A Third-Century Jewish-Christian Disputation." *HTR* 73 (1980): 567-95.

Kramer, S. N. "The Biblical 'Song of Songs' and the Sumerian Love Songs." *Expedition* 5 (1962): 25-31.

Krauss, S. "The Archaeological Background of Some Passages in the Song of Songs." *JQR* 32 (1941-42): 115-37.

Krinetzki, G. *Kommentar zum Hohelied.* Frankfurt am Main and Bern: Peter Lang, 1981.

Kugel, J. *The Idea of Biblical Poetry.* New Haven: Yale University Press, 1981.

LaCocque, A. *Romance She Wrote: A Hermeutical Essay on Song of Songs.* Harrisburg, PA: Trinity Press International, 1998.

Lambert, W. G. "Divine Love Lyrics from Babylon." *JSS* 4 (1959): 1-15.

———. "A New Look at the Babylonian Background of Genesis." *JTS* 16 (1965): 287-300.

Landsberger, F. "Poetic Units within the Song of Songs." *JBL* 73 (1954): 203-16.

Landy, F. "The Song of Songs and the Garden of Eden." *JSOT* 98 (1979): 513-28.

———. "Beauty and the Enigma: An Inquiry into Some Interrelated Episodes of the Song of Songs." *JSOT* 17 (1980): 55-106.

———. *Paradoxes of Paradise: Identity and Difference in the Song of Songs.* Sheffield: Almond, 1983.

————. "The Song of Songs." In *The Literary Guide to the Bible,* edited by R. Alter and F. Kermode, pp. 305-19. Grand Rapids: Zondervan, 1987.

Lavoie, J.-J. "Festin érotique et tendresse cannibalique dans le Cantique des Cantiques." *SR* 24 (1995): 131-46.

Lemaire, A. "*Zāmīr* dans la tablette de Gezer et le Cantique des Cantiques." *VT* 35 (1975): 15-26.

Lenzi, A. "The Translation of Song of Songs 5:8." *The Bible Translator* 49 (1998): 116-23.

Lewis, C. S. *Reflections on the Psalms.* New York: Harcourt Brace, 1961.

Loewe, R. "Apologetic Motifs in the Targum to the Song of Songs." In *Biblical Motifs: Origins and Transformations,* edited by A. Altmann, pp. 159-96. Cambridge, MA: Harvard University Press, 1966.

Lombard, D. "Le Cantique des Cantiques (3,6–5,1)." *Semiotique & Bible* 66 (1992): 45-52.

Long, G. A. "A Lover, Cities, and Heavenly Bodies: Co-Text and the Translation of Two Similes in Canticles (6:4c; 6:10d)." *JBL* 115 (1996): 703-9.

Longman, III, T. "A Critique of Two Recent Metrical Systems." *Bib* 63 (1982): 230-54.

————. "Form Criticism, Recent Developments in Genre Theory, and the Evangelical." *WTJ* 44 (1985): 46-67.

————. *Literary Approaches to Biblical Interpretation.* Grand Rapids: Zondervan, 1987.

————. *Fictional Akkadian Autobiography.* Winona Lake, IN: Eisenbrauns, 1991.

————. *The Book of Ecclesiastes.* NICOT. Grand Rapids: Eerdmans, 1998.

Loretz, O. "Zum Problem des Eros im Hohelied." *BZ* 8 (1964): 191-216.

————. "Cant 4,8 auf dem Hintergrund ugaritischer und assyrischer Beschreibungen des Libanons und Antilibanons." In *Ernten, was man sat: Festschrift für Klaus Koch zu seinem 65. Geburtstag,* edited by E. R. Daniels, U. Glessmer, and M. Rosel, pp. 131-41. Neukirchen-Vluyn: Neukirchener, 1991.

Lundbom, J. R. "Song of Songs 3:1-4." *Interp* 49 (1995): 172-75.

Luthi, K. "Das Hohe Lied der Bibel und seine Impulse für eine geutige Ethik der Geschlechter." *TZ* 49 (1993): 97-118.

Lys, D. *Le Plus Beau Chant de la Creation.* Paris: Les Editions du Cerf, 1968.

Madl, H. "Hld 2,8-14: Die Begenung der Geliebten im Bild des Fruhlings. Versuch einer Exegese." In *Der Orientalische Mensch und seine Beziehungen zum Umwelt,* edited by B. Scholz, pp. 123-35. Graz: R. M. Druck, 1987.

Malul, M. "Janus Parallelism in Biblical Hebrew: Two More Cases (Canticles 4,9.10)." *BZ* 41 (1997): 247-48.

Mariaselvam, A. *The Song of Songs and Ancient Tamil Love Poetry.* Rome: Editrice Pontifico Istituto Biblico, 1988.

Matter, E. A. *The Voice of My Beloved: The Song of Songs in Western Christianity*. Philadelphia: University of Pennsylvania Press, 1990.

Mazor, Y. "The Song of Songs or the Story of Stories?" *SJOT* 1 (1990): 1-29.

McGinn, B. "With 'the Kisses of the Mouth': Recent Works on the Song of Songs." *Journal of Religion* 72 (1992): 269-75.

Meek, T. J. "Canticles and the Tammuz Cult." *AJSL* 39 (1922-23): 1-14.

———. "Babylonian Parallels to the Song of Songs." *JBL* 43 (1924): 245-52.

Meleka, F. "A Review of Origen's Commentary on the Song of Songs." *Coptic Church Review* 1 (1980): 73-77, 125-29.

Meyers, C. "Gender Imagery in the Song of Songs." *HAR* 10 (1986): 209-23.

Miller, P. C. "'Pleasure of the Text, Text of Pleasure': Eros and Language in Origen's Commentary on the Song of Songs." *JAAR* 54 (1986): 241-53.

Moye, J. "Song of Songs — Back to Allegory? Some Hermeneutical Considerations." *AJT* 4 (1990): 120-25.

Mulder, M. J. "Does Canticles 6,12 Make Sense?" In *The Scriptures and the Scrolls: Studies in Honour of A. S. van der Woude on the Occasion of His 65th Birthday,* edited by F. Garcia Martinez et al., pp. 104-13. Leiden: Brill, 1992.

Munro, J. M. *Spikenard and Saffron: A Study in the Poetic Language of the Song of Songs*. Sheffield: Sheffield Academic Press, 1995.

Murphy, R. E. "Towards a Commentary on the Song of Songs." *CBQ* 39 (1977): 482-96.

———. *Wisdom Literature: Job, Proverbs, Ruth, Canticles, Ecclesiastes, and Esther.* FOTL 13. Grand Rapids: Eerdmans, 1981.

———. "Cant 2:8-17 — A Unified Poem?" In *Melange bibliques et orientaux en l'honneur de M. Mathias Delcor,* edited by A. Caquot, S. Legasse, and M. Tardieu, pp. 305-10. Kevelaer: Butzon und Bercker, 1985.

———. "History of Exegesis as a Hermeneutical Tool: The Song of Songs." *BTB* 16 (1986): 87-91.

———. "Dance and Death in the Song of Songs." In *Love and Death in the Ancient Near East: Essays in Honor of Marvin H. Pope,* edited by J. H. Marks and R. M. Good, pp. 117-19. Guilford, CT: Four Quarters, 1987.

———. *The Song of Songs*. Hermeneia. Minneapolis: Fortress, 1990.

Norris, R. A. "The Soul Takes Flight: Gregory of Nyssa and the Song of Songs." *ATR* 80 (1990): 517-32.

O'Connor, M. *Hebrew Verse Structure*. Winona Lake, IN: Eisenbrauns, 1980.

Ogden, G. S. "Some Translational Issues in the Song of Songs." *The Bible Translator* 41 (1990) 222-27.

Pardee, D. "'As Strong as Death.'" In *Love and Death in the Ancient Near East: Essays in Honor of Marvin H. Pope,* edited by J. H. Marks and R. M. Good, pp. 65-69. Guilford, CT: Four Quarters, 1987.

Parsons, G. W. "Guidelines for Understanding and Utilizing the Song of Songs." *BibSac* 156 (1999): 399-422.

Paul, S. M. "An Unrecognized Medical Idiom in Canticles 6,12 and Job 9,21." *Bib* 59 (1979): 545-47.

———. "The 'Plural of Ecstasy' in Mesopotamian and Biblical Love Poetry." In *Solving Riddles and Untying Knots,* edited by Z. Zevit, S. Gitin, and M. Sokoloff, pp. 585-97. Winona Lake, IN: Eisenbrauns, 1995.

Payne, R. "The Song of Songs: Song of Woman, Song of Man, Song of God." *ExpT* 107 (1995-96): 329-33.

Phipps, W. E. "The Plight of the Song of Songs." *JAAR* 42 (1974): 82-100.

Piras, A. "At ille declinaverat atque transierat (Cant 5,2-8)." *ZAW* 106 (1994): 487-90.

Pleuel, A. "Author and Translator: The Stylist's Work with the Song of Songs." *The Bible Translator* 47 (1996): 114-18.

Polaski, D. C. "What Will Ye See in the Shulammite? Women, Power and Panopticism in the Song of Songs." *Biblical Interpretation* 5 (1997): 64-81.

Pope, M. H. "A Mare in Pharaoh's Chariotry." *BASOR* 200 (1970): 56-61.

———. *Song of Songs.* AB 7C. Garden City, NY: Doubleday, 1977.

Preminger, A., ed. *The Princeton Encyclopedia of Poetry and Poetics.* Princeton: Princeton University Press, 1965.

Provan, I. *Ecclesiastes and Song of Songs.* NIVAC. Grand Rapids: Zondervan, 2001.

———. "The Terrors of the Night: Love, Sex, and Power in Song of Songs 3." In *The Way of Wisdom: Essays in Honor of Bruce K. Waltke.* Ed. J. I. Packer and S. K. Soderlund. Grand Rapids: Zondervan, 2000.

Rabin, C. "The Song of Songs and Tamil Poetry." *SR* 3 (1973): 205-19.

Ridderbos, H. *The Authority of the New Testament Scriptures.* Translated by H. De Jongste. Grand Rapids, MI: Baker, 1963.

Robert, A., R. Tournay, and A. Feuillet. *Le Cantiques des Cantiques: Traduction et commentaire.* Paris: Gabalda, 1963.

Roberts, P. "'Let Me See Your Form': Seeking Poetic Structure in the Song of Songs." Ph.D. dissertation, Westminster Theological Seminary, 2001.

Robertson, D. "The Experience of Reading: Bernard of Clairvaux *Sermons on the Song of Songs,* 1." *Religion and Literature* 19 (1987): 1-20.

Roca-Puig, R. "Song of Songs V.12, 14, 13, VI.4-5: P. Barc. Inv. No. 84." *JTS* 26 (1975): 89-91.

Rogerson, J. W. "The Use of the Song of Songs in J. S. Bach's Church Cantatas." In *Biblical Studies/Cultural Studies,* edited by J. C. Exum and S. D. Moore, pp. 343-51. Sheffield: Sheffield Academic Press, 1998.

Rowley, H. H. "The Interpretation of the Song of Songs," In his *The Servant of the Lord and Other Essays on the Old Testament,* 2nd rev. ed., pp. 187-234. Oxford: Blackwell, 1965.

Rozelaar, M. "An Unrecognized Part of the Human Anatomy." *Judaism* 37 (1988): 97-101.

Rundgren, F. "*'arywn:* Tragsessel, Sänfte." *ZAW* 74 (1962): 70-72.

Ryken, L., and T. Longman III, eds. *A Complete Literary Guide to the Bible.* Grand Rapids: Zondervan, 1993.

Sabar, Y. *An Old Neo-Aramaic Version of the Targum on Song of Songs.* Wiesbaden: Otto Harrassowitz, 1991.

Sadgrove, M. "The Song of Songs as Wisdom Literature." In *Studia Biblica 1978,* pp. 245-48. Sheffield: JSOT Press, 1978.

Saebo, M. "On the Canonicity of the Song of Songs." In *Texts, Temples, and Traditions,* edited by M. V. Fox et al., pp. 260-77. Winona Lake, IN: Eisenbrauns, 1996.

Sasson, J. M. "A Further Cuneiform Parallel to the Song of Songs?" *ZAW* 85 (1973): 359-60.

———. "Unlocking the Poetry of Love in the Song of Songs." *BR* 1 (1985): 11-19.

Sasson, V. "King Solomon and the Dark Lady in the Song of Songs." *VT* 39 (1989): 407-14.

Schroeder, C. "'A Love Song': Psalm 45 in the Light of Ancient Near Eastern Marriage Texts." *CBQ* 58 (1996): 417-32.

Schwab, G. "The Song of Songs' Cautionary Message concerning Human Love." Unpublished Ph.D. dissertation, Westminster Theological Seminary, 1999.

———. "Song of Songs." In *The Expositor's Bible Commentary.* Rev. ed. Grand Rapids: Zondervan, forthcoming.

Schwienhorst-Schonberger, L. "Das Hohelied." In *Einleitung in das Alte Testament,* edited by E. Zenger et al. Stuttgart: Kohlhammer, 1995.

Sefati, Y. *Love Songs in Sumerian Literature: Critical Edition of the Dumuz-Inanna Songs.* Ramat-Gan: Bar-Ilan University Press, 1998.

Segal, M. H. "The Song of Songs." *VT* 12 (1962): 470-90.

Shea, W. H. "The Chiastic Structure of the Song of Songs." *ZAW* 92 (1980): 378-96.

Sibinga, J. S. "Une Citation du Cantique dans la Secunda Petri." *RB* 73 (1966): 107-18.

Silva, M. *Has the Church Misread the Bible?* Grand Rapids: Zondervan, 1987.

Simka, H. "Cant. 1,7f. in altchristlicher Auslegung." *TZ* 18 (1962): 256-67.

Smith, M. S. *The Early History of God: Yahweh and the Other Deities in Ancient Israel.* New York: Harper & Row, 1990.

Snaith, J. G. *Song of Songs.* The New Century Bible Commentary. Grand Rapids: Eerdmans, 1993.

Soulen, R. N. "The *Wasfs* of the Song of Songs and Hermeneutic." *JBL* 86 (1967): 183-90.

Stadelmann, L. *Love and Politics: A New Commentary on the Song of Songs.* New York and Mahwah, NJ: Paulist, 1990.

Steinstra, N. *YHWH Is the Husband of His People: Analysis of a Biblical Metaphor with Special Reference to Translation.* Kampen: Pharos, 1993.

Tanner, J. P. "The History of Interpretation of the Song of Songs." *BibSac* 154 (1997): 23-46.

Tinney, S. "Notes on Sumerian Sexual Lyric." *JNES* 59 (2000): 23-30.

Tournay, R. *Le Cantique des Cantiques.* Paris: Les Editions du Cerf, 1967.

―――. "Abraham et le Cantique des Cantiques." *VT* 25 (1975): 544-52.

―――. "The Song of Songs and Its Concluding Section." *Immanuel* 10 (1980): 5-14.

―――. *Word of God, Song of Love.* New York and Mahwah, NJ: Paulist, 1988.

Trible, P. *God and the Rhetoric of Sexuality.* Philadelphia: Fortress, 1978.

Tromp, N. J. "Wisdom and the Canticle: Ct., 8,6c-7b: Text, Character, Message and Import." In *La sagesse de l'ancien testament,* edited by M. Gilbert, pp. 88-95. Leuven: Leuven University Press, 1990.

Tuell, S. S. "A Riddle Resolved by an Enigma: Hebrew *glš* and Ugaritic *glṯ.*" *JBL* 112 (1993): 99-104.

Turner, D. *Eros and Allegory: Medieval Exegesis and the Song of Songs.* Kalamazoo, MI and Spencer, MA: Cistercian Publications, 1995.

Villiers, D. W., de, and J. J. Burden. "Function and Translation: A Twosome in the Song of Songs." *OTE* 2 (1989): 1-11.

Waldman, N. M. "A Note on Canticles 4 9." *JBL* 89 (1970): 215-17.

Walsh, C. E. "A Startling Voice: Woman's Desire in the Song of Songs." *BTB* 28 (1998): 129-34.

Waltke, B. K., and M. O'Connor. *An Introduction to Biblical Hebrew Syntax.* Winona Lake, IN: Eisenbrauns, 1990.

Walton, J. H., V. H. Matthews, and M. W. Chavalas. *The Bible Background Commentary: Old Testament.* Downers Grove: InterVarsity, 2000.

Waterman, L. *The Song of Songs.* Ann Arbor, MI: University of Michigan Press, 1948.

Watson, W. G. E. "Some Ancient Near Eastern Parallels to the Song of Songs." In *Words Remembered, Texts Renewed,* edited by J. Davies et al., pp. 253-71. Sheffield: Sheffield Academic Press, 1995.

―――. *Classical Hebrew Poetry.* JSOTS 26. Sheffield: JSOT Press, 1984.

―――. "Love and Death Once More (Song of Songs VIII 6)." *VT* 47 (1997): 385-86.

Webb, B. "The Song of Songs: A Love Poem and as Holy Scripture." *RTR* 49 (1990): 91-99.

Webster, E. C. "Pattern in the Song of Songs." *JSOT* 22 (1982): 73-93.

Wendland, E. R. "Seeking the Path through a Forest of Symbols: A Figurative and Structural Survey of the Song of Songs." *Journal of Translation and Textlinguistics* 7 (1995): 13-59.

Westenholz, J. G. "Love Lyrics from the Ancient Near East." In *Civilizations of the Ancient Near East,* vol. 4, edited by J. M. Sasson, pp. 2471-84. New York: Charles Scribner's Sons, 1995.

Westenholz, J. G., and A. Westenholz. "Help for Rejected Suitors: The Old Akkadian Love Incantation MAD V 8." *Orientalia* 46 (1977): 198-219.

Wetzstein, J. G. "Die Syrische Dreschtafel." *Zeitschrift für Ethnologie* 5 (1873): 270-302.

White, J. B. *A Study of the Language of Love in the Song of Songs and Ancient Egyptian Love Poetry.* Missoula, MT: Scholars Press, 1975.

Whitesell, C. J. "Behold, Thou Art Fair, My Beloved." *Parabola* 20 (1995): 92-99.

Wirt, S. E. "Some New Thoughts about the Song of Solomon." *JETS* 33 (1990): 433-36.

Zevit, Z. "Roman Jakobson, Psycholinguistics, and Biblical Poetry." *JBL* 109 (1990): 385-401.

SONG OF SONGS

CHAPTER ONE

SUPERSCRIPTION (1:1)

1. *The song of songs, which[1] concerns[2] Solomon.*

The Song of Songs opens with a superscription.[3] The first verse is a detached description of the contents of the book; what follows in the rest of the book is passionate love poetry. Superscriptions appear at the beginning of many other biblical books, most consistently with works of prophecy. The superscription is like the title page of a modern book in that it provides information about the genre, author, and occasionally the subject matter and date of a book (e.g., Isa. 1:1; Jer. 1:1-3; Nah. 1:1). Superscriptions are found in other wisdom contexts as well (Prov. 1:1; Eccles. 1:1), where, interestingly, Solomon is either mentioned or implied.

In the case of the Song, two items appear in the superscription. The first is *song of songs,* a construct phrase built from the singular and then the plural of the same noun "song" *(šîr).* This grammatical structure often indicates the superlative. Analogies include "completely meaningless" (*habēl hᵃbālîm;* Eccles. 1:2) and "Holy of Holies," in reference to the most holy spot on earth (Exod. 29:37) — see other analogies in Deuteronomy 10:14 ("heaven of heavens") and Genesis 9:25 ("servant of servants"). Indeed, M. H. Pope cites Jewish commentary on the book that highlights the Song as the best biblical song; and Origen, a third-century Christian theologian, re-

---

1. The relative pronoun *ᵃšer* occurs only here in the Song of Songs; elsewhere the relative is *še.* This datum supports the idea that the superscription was a later addition to the book.

2. The preposition *l-* does not necessarily indicate authorship (see Introduction: Authorship), though the Targum understood it as such (cf. M. H. Pope, *Song of Songs,* AB 7C (Garden City, NY: Doubleday, 1977), pp. 295-96.

3. Note that the Vulgate omits this superscription altogether.

fers to seven songs in the Bible of which the Song of Songs was the apex.[4] In this context, however, the expression may also point to the composite nature of the book. As described in the Introduction, the Song of Songs is a single poem composed of many poems, literally, then, a song of songs.[5]

Song (šîr) is a genre designation, but a broad one. It indicates a literary text with a musical accompaniment. While it can designate a host of different types of songs,[6] Pope says it more often than not indicates a "glad song."[7] "Song" leaves the composition ambiguously related to the cult and religious expression.[8]

More difficult to discern is the function of the phrase *which concerns Solomon (ʾᵃšer lišᵉlōmōh)*. The problem has to do with the force of the preposition *lᵉ*. The semantic range of the preposition is wide, and it theoretically could be translated "of," "to," "by," or *concerning*. The choice of translation usually derives from the context of the preposition within a sentence, but the superscription does not provide such a sentence context to guide us. The ancient audience presumably would have been well aware of the force of the preposition in a superscription, but we are distanced and ignorant of that information. The ambiguity is the same as that in the title of the Psalms, but the same answer is not necessary in both cases.

Some scholars[9] argue that the superscription was added late as tour de force to provide the book with authority or to link it with the wisdom tradition. Perhaps this is the case. However, it is also conceivable, on analogy with Proverbs,[10] that Solomon, though not the author of the book as a whole, was the originator of some of the poems within the collection. Solomon himself is mentioned only twice in the book (3:6-11; 8:10-12), once rather favorably and the second time rather unfavorably. (For more detailed discussion, see the Introduction: Authorship.)

4. Pope, *Song of Songs,* pp. 296-97.

5. In agreement with M. Falk, *Love Lyrics in the Bible* (Sheffield: Almond, 1982), pp. 107-8, contra F. Delitzsch, *Proverbs, Ecclesiastes, The Song of Songs,* trans. M. G. Easton (Grand Rapids; Eerdmans, 1975 [1885]), p. 17, who asserts that the title "denotes that it is a connected whole, and is the work of one author."

6. For instance, a religious song (Amos 8:3), a thanksgiving song (2 Sam. 22:1), a victory hymn (Exod. 15:1), and an eschatological hymn (Isa. 26:1); see *NIDOTTE,* vol. 4, p. 99.

7. Pope, *Song of Songs,* p. 293.

8. O. Keel, *The Song of Songs,* A Continental Commentary (Minneapolis: Fortress, 1994), p. 38.

9. R. E. Murphy, *Wisdom Literature: Job, Proverbs, Ruth, Canticles, Ecclesiastes, and Esther,* FOTL 13 (Grand Rapids: Eerdmans, 1981), p. 105.

10. R. B. Dillard and T. Longman III, *An Introduction to the Old Testament* (Grand Rapids: Zondervan, 1994), pp. 263-64.

POEM ONE:
THE WOMAN'S PURSUIT (1:2-4)

The Song proper begins with an explosion of words. Bernard of Clairvaux noted that the woman's speech presupposes a conversation and relationship that has already begun, and he calls this line a "beginning without a beginning."[11] It sets a dynamic tone that never ends throughout the book. Indeed, the last poem, as we will see, does not impart a distinct sense of closure.

The first of the songs begins with an expression of the woman's desire for the man. As is frequently the case throughout the Song, the woman takes the initiative. Indeed, A. LaCocque and S. D. Goitein[12] point out that the woman speaks 53 percent of the time in the Song, while the man speaks 39 percent of the time. Perhaps the text was subversive in its ancient context;[13] it certainly is in the present in Christian contexts where females are expected to keep their proper place in life and romance. The characters of the Song may not be identified with historical figures or any actually existing human beings; neither do the poems carry a narrative. They express universal emotions. As is the case in the Psalms, the voice of the poet is intended to be our voice at the proper time and in the proper place.

This poem was not always taken as a reference to physical lovemaking (cf. Introduction). Perhaps the most notable allegorical interpretation of this poem is that which takes it as a reference to the Exodus. The woman, Israel, beckons her man, God, to take her into his bedroom, Palestine.

The form of these three verses is a poem of yearning (see Introduction: Genre for other examples). The name, of course, derives from the woman's expressed desire for union with the man.

The Woman
2. *Let him kiss me with the kisses of his mouth,*
    for your[14] love[15] is better than wine.

---

11. From his first sermon, see D. Robertson, "The Experience of Reading: Bernard of Clairvaux's *Sermons on the Song of Songs, 1,*" *Religion and Literature* 19 (1987): 19.

12. See the reference in A. LaCocque, *Romance She Wrote: A Hermeneutical Essay on Song of Songs* (Harrisburg, PA: Trinity Press International, 1998), p. 41. A. Brenner ("Women Poets and Authors," in *The Feminine Companion to the Song of Songs,* ed. A. Brenner [Sheffield: JSOT Press, 1993], p. 88) breaks it down by verse: 61½ are by the woman, 40 by the man, 11 by various choruses, and 9 she considers to be ambiguous.

13. D. Bergant, looking at the Song from a social anthropological perspective, comes to this conclusion in "'My Beloved Is Mine and I Am His' (Song 2:16): The Song of Songs and Honor and Shame," *Semeia* 68 (1996): 23-41.

14. Here the woman shifts from third person to second person in reference to the man. It strikes us as odd, but it has analogies in Egyptian love poetry. Pope (*Song of*

3. *How wonderful[16] is the scent of your oils;*
   your name is poured out[17] oil.[18]
   Therefore, the young women love you.
4. *Draw me after you; let's run!*
   The king has brought me into his bedroom.[19]

The Women of Jerusalem
We will rejoice and feel happy for you!
We will praise[20] your love more than wine!

The Woman
They rightly[21] love you![22]

Songs, p. 297), indeed, points out that the device, called enallage, is not uncommon in poetry in general.

15. Note that the Septuagint has *mastoi sou* "your breasts," reflecting Hebrew *daddêkā*, which does not make a lot of sense in the context of the woman speaking about the man. D. Garrett (*Proverbs, Ecclesiastes, Song of Songs,* New American Commentary [Nashville: Broadman and Holman, 1993], p. 385) represents a view that *dwd* means the act of lovemaking rather than the abstract quality. The passages he quotes (particularly Ezek. 16:8; 23:17) demonstrate that it can have the more concrete meaning, but not in every context.

16. The preposition *le* could be marking a *casus pendens* ("as for your scent") or an emphatic (as taken in our translation). See J. G. Snaith, *Song of Songs,* The New Century Bible Commentary (Grand Rapids: Eerdmans, 1993), p. 3.

17. Taking *tûraq* as a hophal of the verb *ryq* "to empty." It is true that the feminine form of the verb appears to conflict with the masculine "oil" *(šemen),* but it is not all that unusual to lack gender concord in Hebrew. M. V. Fox (*The Song of Songs and the Ancient Egyptian Love Songs* [Madison: University of Wisconsin Press, 1985], p. 97) takes it as a reference to a geographical area attested in an Ugaritic text, "oil of Turaq." M. Gorg ("Eine Salbenbezeichnung in HL 1,3," *BN* 38/39 [1987]: 36-38) understands *tûraq* to be an Egyptian loanword and translates "strong scented oil" ("stark duftendes Salbol").

18. Note the wordplay on "name" *(šēm)* and oil *(šemen).*

19. According to LaCocque, *Romance She Wrote,* p. 70, *ḥeder* "designates an inner room, especially a bedroom. It can allude to royal chambers or to private apartments."

20. The verbal root *zkr* is "to remember," and so the hiphil, as here, means "cause to remember," therefore, to celebrate or to praise.

21. T. H. Gaster ("Canticles i.4," *ExpT* 72 [1961]: 195) suggests unnecessarily to take this as *mimeyras ahabeka* "your caresses more than new wine" (where Ugaritic *meyraš* would be equivalent to Hebrew *tîrôš;* cf. Song 7:10 [English 7:9]). With R. E. Murphy (*The Song of Songs,* Hermeneia [Minneapolis: Fortress, 1990], p. 126), we take the word as a "abstract adverbial accusative."

22. The Qumran text of the Song (6QCant) has "rightly are they loved" *('āḥûbîm).* The Septuagint translates *euthytēs ēgapēsen se,* which R. Beckwith (*The Old Testament Canon of the New Testament Church* [London: SPCK, 1985], p. 314) argues should be taken as "righteousness loved you" and understood as a hint of an allegorical approach, but the Greek word could be taken as "they honestly [or sincerely] loved you."

2   The first poem is a passionate exclamation on the part of the woman, who desires union with the man. The woman takes the initiative here and in many of the poems of the Song. The aggressiveness of the woman in the Song undermines our stereotypes of ancient gender roles and instructs those today who look to the Bible for guidance in matters of relationships. This book will not support a dominance of the male over the female. Nonetheless, her initiative does not go so far as to say "I will kiss him," but rather her exclamation wants to prod him to action *(let him kiss me)*.

The characters of the Song are not specific. That is, the woman is not a particular woman but stands for all women. The same may be said for the man. These characters are developed intentionally in a nonspecific way since they are not reporting about a particular couple. These poems invite later readers to place themselves in the position of the woman and the man. In this way, the Song is similar to the book of Psalms, where the reader is implicitly encouraged to put him- or herself in the place of the first person speaker.[23]

The motif is the invitation for intimacy expressed in the form of a wish.[24] The Song expresses the couple's yearning for complete union and thus appeals to every sense. The woman begins with the erotic touch of a *kiss.* The expression *let him kiss me with the kisses of his mouth,* though it sounds awkward and even ponderous to us, expresses her exuberance. F. Delitzsch certainly stretches the phrase when he makes the preposterous comment that the expression means that she only got a few of Solomon's rather promiscuous kisses.[25] The specification of kisses on the mouth may suggest that there were other intimate gestures, perhaps, for instance, nose kisses,[26] but then the specification may also be a function of poetic rhythm.

In what a prosaic person would call a "motive clause," she likens his *love* to the taste of *wine,* a rich and sensuous liquid. The bouquet of the wine as well as its taste creates an enticing metaphor for the physical aspects of love, especially the kiss. Drinking wine intoxicates, and kissing the woman arouses the man, making him lightheaded. Indeed, she insists not only that the man's love is like wine, but that it is *better than wine.*[27]

3   After praising his taste, the woman celebrates his scent. Men appar-

---

23. T. Longman III, *How to Read the Psalms* (Downers Grove, IL: InterVarsity, 1988).

24. Expressed by the jussive. Keel (*The Song of Songs,* pp. 41-42) documents the antiquity of kissing in the ancient Near East and reproduces artistic representations.

25. Delitzsch, *Proverbs, Ecclesiastes, Song of Songs,* p. 19.

26. So M. V. Fox, *The Song of Songs and the Ancient Egyptian Love Songs* (Madison: University of Wisconsin Press, 1985), p. 97.

27. For a history of early Christian interpretation of this book, see G. Chappuzeau, "Die Exegesie von Hohelied 1,2a.b und 7 bei den Kirchenvätern von Hippolyt bis Bernhard," *Jahrbuch für Antike und Christentum* 18 (1975): 91-113.

ently wore aromatic *oils,* what we today would call cologne. All of her senses are aroused by his presence. The man's physical smell leads to a comment on his reputation as well, signified by his *name.* His reputation goes before him positively like his scent. He is loved not only by the woman, but also by all the *young women.* These women are unspecified, but their function here is to confirm the good taste of the female speaker. She is not deluded by love; others love her man as well, thus confirming her choice. Pope points out that this particular word for *young woman (ᶜªlāmôt)* indicates "sexual ripeness without presumption one way or the other as to virginity or sexual experience."[28]

We should note that verses 2b and 3a form a chiasm, beginning and ending with the Hebrew *ṭôbîm,* taken as a comparative *better* in 2b and as *wonderful* in 3a. To preserve the chiasm we would render the line:

> For good is your love more than wine;
> as for the scent, your oils are good.

4 The allegorical approach understands the reference to *the king* as indicating God or, in Christian tradition, Jesus. For those taking the poem as historical, the reference to the king has been taken to refer to Solomon, but since the work of J. G. Wetzstein and his comparison with nineteenth-century wedding celebrations in Syria, some have taken the title as pointing to a wedding ritual.[29] The weddings he observed included a ritual where the bride and groom crowned each other queen and king. Yet even this interpretation is unnecessary. It is best to take the reference neither historically nor ritually, but rather as a poetic device. It is love language. She refers to him as king, but this must not be taken literally. In her eyes, he is a king, the best and most powerful male in her life, worthy of the highest honor. Elsewhere, she calls him a shepherd (1:7), but that is not literal either. These are terms of endearment. The Song is best understood as creating a poetic world, not as describing actual events.

The woman invites the man to get away with her *(draw me after you).* She is the initiator of the relationship in this poem, a theme that we will encounter many times in the Song. She expresses her urgency with the verb *run* (from *rûṣ*). She is in haste to be intimate with her lover.

She wants him to take her into his *bedroom (ḥeder).*[30] The bedroom is

---

28. Pope, *Song of Songs,* p. 300.

29. See the Introduction (pp. 37-38) for an overview of J. G. Wetzstein's impact on the interpretation of the Song of Songs.

30. It is not always clear that *ḥeder* is a *bedroom* (and in Prov. 24:4 it seems to be a storeroom), although it is clearly an interior room, a private enclosure. For instance, the *ḥeder* is the room where Joseph goes to weep (Gen. 43:30) — even there, though, bedroom may be intended. Certainly in many instances a bedroom is explicitly meant (e.g., 2 Sam. 4:7), and in an erotic context like Song 1:4, *bedroom* is surely intended.

obviously a private place where the couple can be alone. We will see the theme of flight to privacy take on many permutations in the Song, but this verse is the first occurrence. We have not been told where they are — that is unimportant, but what is important is that she urges him to bring her into his bedroom. Thus, she desires (and I believe we are to assume that she gets) intimate sexual union with the man. It is verses like these that render attempts to build a narrative out of the Song, climaxing (poetically and sexually) at the end of the fourth chapter, so wrong-minded.

Elsewhere in the Old Testament where a man and a woman are alone in a bedroom (ḥeder) — for example, Samson and Delilah (Judg. 15:1) and David and Abishag (1 Kings 15:1) — it is a place of an intimate, often sexual, relationship. Its connection with marriage may be most strongly seen in Joel 2:16, where it occurs in parallel with "bridal chamber" (ḥuppâ):

> Gather the people,
>   consecrate the assembly;
> bring together the elders,
>   gather the children,
>   those nursing at the breast.
> Let the bridegroom leave his room (ḥeder)
>   and the bride her chamber (ḥuppâ).

Stephen Horine has made a strong case that this reference in verse 4b, along with that in 8:13-14, with which it forms an inclusio, indicates that the Song as a whole finds its setting within a marriage relationship.[31]

Celebration breaks out upon their entry into the bedchamber (*We will rejoice . . .*). The shift here to the first person plural has caused some discussion. Pope describes how this shift from second person (*draw me after you*) to third person (*the king has brought me*) to first person plural (*we will rejoice . . .*) led some, such as C. D. Ginsburg,[32] to adopt the three-character dramatic approach to the Song (see Introduction).[33] The king has taken her to his bedroom, but she is in love with another whom she addresses in the second person. A simpler explanation for the shift in grammatical reference is enallage, noted above in verse 2. M. V. Fox cites Egyptian parallels and offers the following explanation: "The girl moves back and forth between the first person plural, where she includes the other girls in her appreciation of her lover's beauties, and the third person plural, where she dances verbally

---

31. S. Horine, "An Integrative Literary Approach to the Song of Songs," Ph.D. dissertation, Westminster Theological Seminary, 1998.

32. C. D. Ginsburg, *The Song of Songs and Coheleth*, ed. H. M. Orlinsky (New York: KTAV, 1970 [1861]).

33. Pope, *Song of Songs*, p. 303.

out of the group in order to add a certain objectivity to her statement about the public estimation of his loveworthiness."[34] Upon their entry into the bed-chamber, the chorus of women chimes in with their happy approval of this union. In essence, they provide their blessing for the relationship. They confirm their love and also echo the woman's sentiment that their love is better than wine. The other two places where a benediction accompanies the relationship between a man and a woman are marriage contexts (Psalm 45; Prov. 5:18), and Horine argues on this basis that the opening poem of the Song also implies a marriage relationship.[35]

There is some debate over the identity of the chorus. Even over R. E. Murphy's objections,[36] it seems most natural to take the speakers as the "young women" or maidens (*ʿᵃlāmôt*) of 1:3. There is further debate over whether the young woman includes herself with the maidens, but this seems stretched and unnecessary.[37] A third issue is whether we should associate the "young woman" here with the "daughters of Jerusalem" mentioned later in the poem (2:7; 3:5, 10, 11; 5:8, 16; 8:4). O. Keel differentiates the two. The "young women" are the speaker's intimates, while the "daughters of Jerusalem" are the "stereotypical public," a group of "spoiled, idle, and curious women of the capital city" who were "especially versed in matters of beauty and love." However, Keel's description of the latter comes more from prophetic diatribes against the "daughters of Jerusalem" than from the Song, and we should be cautious in making this transference.[38] The simplest theory is that the "young women" (*ʿᵃlāmôt*), the "daughters of Jerusalem" (*bᵉnôt yᵉrûšālayim*), and the "daughters of Zion" (*bᵉnôt ṣîyyôn*) are variant references to the same chorus.[39] The poem ends with the woman again affirming that other women are right to love the man. She is not the only one; she is not deluded. He is indeed a worthy recipient of her adoration. The chorus often serves as a mirror of the woman's emotions, a sounding board as it were, throughout the book. As she addresses the chorus (see below), we learn more about the woman's values and feelings.[40]

34. M. V. Fox, "Scholia to Canticles (I 4b, ii 4, I 4ba, iv 3, v 8, vi 12)," *VT* 33 (1983): 200.

35. Horine, "An Integrative Literary Approach," pp. 99-101. He refers also to prophetic uses of the exclamation of joy over a wedding scene in Isa. 62:5; Jer. 7:34; 16:9; 25:10; 33:11.

36. Murphy, *The Song of Songs*, pp. 127-28.

37. Keel, *The Song of Songs*, p. 45 for the argument that the woman did include herself in the chorus.

38. Following Horine, "An Integrative Literary Approach," p. 107.

39. See the parallelism in 6:8-9.

40. For connections with the classical Greek chorus (sixth-fifth centuries B.C.) consult the Introduction.

V. Sasson[41] argues that the phrase *the king has brought me* and particularly the verb *hᵉbî'anî* is an echo of 1 Kings 3:1, where Solomon "brought [his Egyptian bride] to the City of David." He argues on the basis of this and other echoes that the Song is about Solomon's marriage to the Egyptian princess, but this is an extremely weak argument.

POEM TWO:
DARK, BUT BEAUTIFUL (1:5-6)

The unit is set off from the preceding and the following poems by its content and the fact that the woman addresses the daughters of Jerusalem. The mood is also different from what comes before and after, being defensive rather than outgoing. This short poem is a self-description, an apology of sorts for her appearance. Her brothers are introduced as a subject for the first time. They do not speak until 8:8-9.

The Woman
5. *I am dark, but beautiful, daughters of Jerusalem,*
    like the tents of Qedar,
    like the curtains of Solomon.
6. *Don't look at me, because I am swarthy,*
    because the sun scorched[42] me.
My mother's sons were angry with me;
    they made me guard vineyards,
    but my vineyard I did not guard.

5 The woman asserts her beauty in spite of the fact that she has been exposed to the darkening rays of the sun. In verse 6, she claims that the sun has made her "swarthy" (*šᵉharhōret*), which is often taken as a diminutive of "black" (*šāhôr*).[43] In verse 5a there has been much discussion over the relationship between the darkness of her complexion and her beauty. In a nutshell, should we translate the *waw* as a conjunctive "and" or a disjunctive "but"? The context is actually quite clear. She is not happy with her darker

---

41. V. Sasson, "King Solomon and the Dark Lady in the Song of Songs," *VT* 39 (1989): 407-14.
42. The verb often denotes "to gaze, to catch sight of" (Job 20:9; 28:7). Here the sun gazing on the woman produces her scorched skin. According to *NIDOTTE* (p. 74), in postbiblical Hebrew the verb means "to blacken."
43. Pope, *Song of Songs,* p. 322.

than normal skin, so the disjunctive makes sense.[44] In the next verse, she will complain that her brothers forced her to work their vineyard, where she was exposed to the scorching heat of the sun. Her discomfort is accentuated by her command that the other women not look at her. Yet scholars often translate the *waw* as "and."[45] Why? For fear of the appearance of racism. Yet the text, on the surface of it, has nothing to do with race. The Song neither explicitly nor implicitly suggests that white is inherently better or more attractive than black skin. Furthermore, the woman was Semitic and likely had a dark complexion to start with. The darkness about which she complains is not her natural skin color but a tan or burn. Different cultures at different times either esteem or denigrate a tan. Her reaction invites us to suggest that the text assumes a culture where a deep, dark tan or burn is not attractive. Perhaps in the culture at the time the effects of the sun indicated that she was a laborer or lower-class woman.[46] In spite of some ambiguities, the text is clear about two matters: (1) the woman considers her dark skin unattractive, and (2) her dark skin is not her natural skin color but rather the result of a tan.[47] Besides being an indicator of class, the woman's darkness may well be part of the opposition that we frequently see in the Song between the city and the country. Here the contrast would be between the pale city girls (the daughters of Jerusalem) and the dark girl, who is burned while laboring in the country.[48]

The similes that follow her exclamation are historically ambiguous, but from the context they appear to accentuate the depth of her tan. *Tents* in colon b is the common word (*'ohēl*); colon c has the less frequent *curtains* (*y^erî'ôt*), but it is a word that often occurs in parallel with *'ohēl* (cf. Isa. 54:2). Kedar (*qēdār*) is a tribe of nomads from the Syro-Arabian desert, often mentioned in the Bible (Gen. 25:13; Jer. 49:28-29, the latter even refers to the

44. Note the Vulgate "but" (*sed*). See the helpful study of E. C. Hostetter, "Mistranslation in Cant 1:5," *AUSS* 34 (1996): 35-36, in which he argues that those who argue for the conjunction "'and' get off on the wrong foot by their understanding of *s^eharhōret* as "black" rather than "dark" or, as we would render it, *swarthy.*

45. Note Pope, *Song of Songs,* p. 291: "Black am I and beautiful."

46. According to M. Jinbachian ("The Genre of Love Poetry in the Song of Songs and the Pre-Islamic Arabian Odes," *The Bible Translator* 48 [1997]: 126), the situation is the same in the pre-Islamic Arabian Odes, where "whiteness is the preferred complexion of a woman, because darkness of skin caused by exposure to the harshness of the sun was regarded as a sign of membership of the lower social class. A poor girl was obliged to work in the sun while the wealthy sat in the shade of the tent."

47. Pope, *Song of Songs,* pp. 307-18, has a long section devoted to the black goddess, which is interesting but irrelevant to this verse (see Introduction on Pope's idiosyncratic interpretation of the Song). See also Keel, *The Song of Songs,* pp. 47-49.

48. F. Landy, "Beauty and the Enigma: An Inquiry into Some Interrelated Episodes of the Song of Songs," *JSOT* 17 (1980): 64-55.

tents of Kedar in a context of judgment). "The Kidar were among the most powerful of the northern Arabian bedouin tribal groups in the period between the 8th and 4th centuries B.C. They are mentioned in the Assyrian and Neo-Babylonian annals and are tied to the genealogy of Ishmael in Gen 25:13."[49] While we have no indication of the color of the tents of the Kedarites, it is interesting to note that the associated verbal root means "to be dark."[50] In colon c, the *curtains of Solomon* may well refer to Solomon's well-known tent, but again we have no knowledge of this tent apart from this text. It is safe to say with Keel that the association with Solomon makes us "understand them as artistic and precious palace furnishings."[51] The context again directs us to the opinion that the tents and the curtains are especially dark. An alternative understanding that has the support of an argument based on parallelism would be to repoint the word to *salmâ*, taking it as a reference to a south Arabian tribe mentioned in extrabiblical sources.[52]

The woman speaks to the *daughters of Jerusalem*. For their identity and relationship to the "young women" and the "daughters of Zion," see the Introduction and comments at 1:4. Here, the "daughters of Jerusalem" serve as a sounding board for the feelings of the woman. Being the residents of a "big city," they may also elicit the embarrassment of a girl burned by labor in the sun.

6 Verse 6 makes it clear that the woman finds her scorched complexion unattractive.[53] Again, her reaction has nothing to do with race or some transcultural statement on the aesthetics of skin pigmentation. The *sun* has burned her. She has been out in the fields working hard, with the result that her skin is deeply tanned or sun-burnt. We might speculate that her culture prized skin that did not show signs of the physical labors of the lower classes.[54]

Indeed, her burn came as a result of labor that was forced on her by her brothers. She had to work vineyards at the insistence of her *mother's*

---

49. J. Walton, V. H. Matthews, and M. V. Chavalas, *The IVP Bible Background Commentary* (Downers Grove: InterVarsity, 2000), p. 57.

50. See *NIDOTTE*, vol. 3, pp. 875-76.

51. Keel, *The Song of Songs*, p. 46.

52. T. H. Gaster, "What 'The Song of Songs' Means," *Commentary* 13 (1952): 322; Murphy, *The Song of Songs*, p. 126.

53. J. C. Exum ("Asseverative *'al* in Canticles 1,6?" *Bib* 62 [1981]: 416-19) argues that the *'al* is not the negative but rather the strong affirmative particle, thus rendering "Look at me that I am black." Though a noble attempt, *'al* is rare as an asseverative in Hebrew if it occurs at all, and the context still leads one to argue against a positive reading of the woman's artificial darkness.

54. In a personal communication, Robert Hubbard tells me of an analogy in rural Armenia. Farmers are tanned; office workers are more lightly complexioned. A tan thus is a sign of being "just a farmer."

sons. We should probably attach more than poetic significance to the latter phrase. It is more than simply another way of saying "my brothers."[55] By using this more awkward phrase, the woman distances herself from her brothers — after all, the woman clearly is not positively inclined toward them. Here and elsewhere (cf. 8:8-9) they serve the function of keeping her from acting on her sexuality. In the ancient Near East and in Israel itself, the brothers do play a role in the marriage of their sister.[56] Presumably, they also protect her chastity before marriage.

As we will see throughout the book, the image of *vineyard* and other related agricultural language have sexual overtones in the Song. "Fertile vines produced luscious grapes, pleasing to the taste and, when fermented, intoxicating. It is not surprising, considering the general use of agricultural images for sexuality, that the vine is frequently employed in that most sensual of all biblical poems, the Song of Songs. What is perhaps somewhat unexpected is the variety of ways the poet uses the image."[57] In the case of "vineyard," it often connotes the woman's sexuality. The plowing of a vineyard or other type of field, for example, is an apt image of sexual intercourse. It is not that vineyard is a cipher for sexuality or intercourse.[58] The vineyard in the Song of Songs is multivalent. As a matter of fact, it may have two nuances in the present verse. When the verse states that her brothers have made her work in the vineyard and, as a result, the sun scorches her, we think of real physical labor with a real physical consequence. Yet this may suggest the more poetic reference to vineyard, the woman's sexuality, perhaps in this case her sex appeal. The verse seems to state that her work in the vineyard has meant that she could not attend to her own attractiveness. The effect of this poem is that we feel sorry for the woman, but also respect her assertiveness in the face of her domineering brothers.

The verse states that they required her labor because they were *angry* with her. However, the text does not give us an explicit motivation for their anger. Perhaps, given what we stated above about the brothers' role in pro-

55. Snaith (*Song of Songs*, p. 18) cites D. Lys approvingly that this is a way of distinguishing half-brothers from real brothers, but this shows insensitivity to the poetic quality of the verse.

56. In Genesis 32 the brothers of Jacob play a role in the marriage negotiations of their sister Dinah with the Shechemite Hamor and his father. The brothers are irate because he has deflowered their sister, and two of them work revenge against the whole town of Shechem.

57. "Vine, Vineyard," in *The Dictionary of Biblical Imagery,* ed L. Ryken, J. Wilhoit, and T. Longman III (Downers Grove, IL: InterVarsity, 1998), p. 916.

58. Pope (*Song of Songs*, pp. 326-27) is wrong to say that the neglect of the vineyard denotes promiscuity (which he then defends by means of his cultic interpretation [see Introduction]).

tecting their sister's sexuality, they were suspicious of her in this area (again see 8:8-9). T. Gledhill[59] suggests that they are mad because her appearance has deteriorated, but that seems an odd perspective on the verse since it is their anger that leads to her long exposure to the sun.

POEM THREE:
AN INVITATION TO A TRYST (1:7-8)

The woman no longer addresses the daughters of Jerusalem but the man, asking him a question with the intention of meeting him. She addresses him as a shepherd, which evokes a country setting. She will meet him outside the city. The question and the answer are both playful; indeed, the unit might be called a "tease." The question exposes the woman's yearning for the man's company; the language expresses a concern that their meeting remain hidden from others. She needs to know where he will be so that she does not have to ask directions. She indicates that if he does not give her directions, then she will have to pursue him while wearing a veil, to hide her identity from others. He does not answer her directly but says that if she does not know, then she should use the ruse of being a shepherd herself as she comes out to the fields. Thus no one will know her true intent.

It is not totally clear who is speaking in verse 8. We have followed the majority of commentators and versions (NLT, KJV) in ascribing the verse to the man, who is playfully ambiguous in his response to the woman. The NIV[60] ascribes these words to the daughters of Jerusalem, but this seems an unnatural understanding of the interchange since the woman's question is clearly directed to the man himself (cf. the use of the vocative in v. 7).

The end of this poem could be debated,[61] but there is no clear link between verses 7-8 and the following section. Thus, we treat them as separate poems.[62]

---

59. T. Gledhill, *The Message of the Song of Songs,* BST (Downers Grove, IL: InterVarsity, 1994), p. 104.

60. Followed by Garrett, *Proverbs, Ecclesiastes, Song of Songs,* pp. 387-88.

61. Snaith (*Song of Songs,* pp. 17-20) concurs on the ending of the poem at this place, as does Keel (*The Song of Songs,* pp. 51-53).

62. For early Christian allegorical interpretations of this poem (Hippolytus, Origen, Ambrose, Jerome), consult H. Simka, "Cant. 1,7f. in altchristlicher Auslegung," *TZ* 18 (1962): 256-67. For a description of early Christian allegorical approaches to the Song, see the Introduction under History of Interpretation.

The Woman

7. Tell me, one whom I love,[63] where will you graze?
   Where will you make your flocks lie down at noon?
   Why should I be like a veiled woman[64]
   around the flocks of your companions?

The Man

8. If you do not know, most beautiful of women,
   follow the tracks of the sheep,
   and feed your young goats
   by the dwellings of the shepherds.

7 The woman opens the next poem with a tease. She wants a rendezvous with her lover to meet him at midday for a tryst. She addresses him as the one she loves, making clear her feelings for him. The expression *one whom I love* denotes deep affection but not necessarily sexual attraction, as the use of the phrase in the relationship between David and Jonathan makes clear (1 Sam. 20:17). However, in the present context, there is no room for doubt but that she loves him in a sexual way.

She asks him where he is taking his flocks for a rest at noon, presumably so they can dally together while the animals feed. It evokes a pastoral scene for lovemaking. They will be alone in the fields. She prods him for the information by implying that otherwise she will have to go from shepherd tent to shepherd tent looking for him, and she assumes that he does not want her poking around the tents of his male friends and possible rivals.

She asks for directions so that she does not have to steal out as a *veiled woman* (*'ōṭᵉyâ*). This reference to the veil has caused all sorts of speculation as to its significance. It is important to note that it was apparently not common for women to wear a veil in ancient Israel.[65] Veils were for special occasions or certain situations. Weddings are one such occasion, but this seems unlikely in chapter one. Some interpreters[66] argue, on the basis of Genesis 38:14-15,[67] that the veiled woman is a prostitute, and thus the woman reminds her lover that if she is reduced to searching for him, she will look like

---

63. Literally, "one whom my soul loves" (*šeʾāhᵃbâ napšî;* see also 3:1-4).

64. Literally, as Murphy (*The Song of Songs*, p. 131) points out, "one who covers one's self."

65. See the comments and evidence provided by J. M. Munro, *Spikenard and Saffron: A Study in the Poetic Language of the Song of Songs* (Sheffield: Sheffield Academic Press, 1995), pp. 53-54.

66. Munro, *Spikenard and Saffron*, pp. 53-54.

67. Of course, it may be that the veiling of Tamar here is a function of the fact that she wants to deceive Judah concerning her identity.

a whore. However, the veil is not restricted to prostitutes. After all, in the *wasf* in chapter four, the man describes his beloved as having a beautiful temple behind her veil; there is no suggestion of impropriety. The veil in the present verse just adds to the furtiveness of the scene. She is stealing out to be with her beloved. The woman's veiling also adds to her mystique, a quality that will be exploited later in the Song (e.g., 4:3).

Alternative explanations of the phrase include asserting a textual corruption of a form of the root *t'h* "to wander" (a metathesis of *'th*).[68] A rather novel interpretation is to take it from an Arabic root that means "to pick lice,"[69] translating the phrase as "that I not be left picking lice" (see NEB) in the sense of our phrase "not be left twiddling my thumbs." Basing a rather strange meaning on an Arabic cognate seems risky, though, considering the linguistic distance between Hebrew and Arabic.

Gledhill offers a provocative explanation of the lack of objects in cola b and c. We understand the objects to be the shepherd's animals, but perhaps, as he suggests, there is a double entendre here. He points out that *graze (r'h)* has erotic overtones in 6:3. He also notes that the woman may imply that it is she herself whom she wants to "make lie down" in the pasture.[70] M. Falk suggests that "because the garden and its flowers are associated with female sexuality, pasturing is usually symbolic of male sexual activity."[71]

It is important to keep in mind that we are dealing with poetry and not with an actual couple. The latter supposition has gotten interpreters into trouble as they try to figure out how the king in 1:4 relates to the shepherd in this verse. Some speak of a shepherd-king, and others of two figures, a king — often Solomon himself — and a shepherd who is his rival. The shepherd, like the king, is a poetic creation to evoke a romantic scene.[72]

8 Verse 8 is the first time that the man speaks. He answers the woman's question. She initiates, and he responds. The poem reads like a playful, sensual game of hide-and-seek. The invitation for intimate encounter is there, but it is under the surface, not too obvious. This coy response probably intends to arouse deeper desire. He does not tell her the location, only a

---

68. This lies behind the translation of the verse by the Peshitta, the Vulgate, and Symmachus.

69. See A. F. von Gall, "Jeremiah 43,12 und das Zeitwort *'th*," *ZAW* 24 (1904): 105-21, and G. R. Driver, "Lice in the Old Testament," *PEQ* 106 (1974): 159-60. Recently, this translation has been preferred by J. A. Emerton, "Lice or a Veil in the Song of Songs 1.7?" in *Understanding Poets and Prophets*, ed. A. G. Auld (Sheffield: Sheffield Academic Press, 1993), pp. 127-40, and LaCocque, *Romance She Wrote*, p. 75.

70. Gledhill, *The Message of the Song of Songs*, p. 108.

71. Falk, *Love Lyrics in the Bible*, p. 104.

72. For a description of early Christian allegorical approaches to this verse, see Chappuzeau, "Die Exegese von Hohelied," pp. 113-29.

strategy for pursuit, to follow the trail left by his sheep as they wander out to the wilderness. She is to take her goats with her. She is to cover her tracks, so to speak, so that any onlooker will think that she is taking care of her flock. Yet they know it is a cover; she is stealing her way out to be alone with her lover.

He expresses his feelings toward the woman by calling her the most beautiful woman of all. He will exegete her beauty in the verses that immediately follow. Though Proverbs says that beauty is fleeting (31:30), the man defines her beauty in this poem primarily physically.

Again, the pastoral imagery of sheep, goats, and shepherds is part of the romance. It evokes a pleasant scene away from the public eye of the city.

POEM FOUR: A BEAUTIFUL MARE (1:9-11)

The fourth unit of the collection is a poem of admiration. It is spoken by the man concerning the physical beauty of the woman. It begins with a comparison between the woman and a mare and then concentrates more on the woman's ornaments than on the woman's physical features. Jewelry heightens the royal motif (also bolstered by the mention of Pharaoh) as it also enhances the natural beauty of the woman.

The Man
9. *To a mare*[73] *among Pharaoh's chariots*[74]
   I liken you, my darling.
10. *Your cheeks are lovely between earrings;*[75]
    your neck, with a necklace.[76]

---

73. Taking the -*i* ending on "mare" *(l^esusātî)* as a survival of an old genitive ending *(hireq compaginis)*, rather than a possessive (cf. Pope, *Song of Songs,* p. 338).

74. It has long been noted that *rēkbê* is the plural of *rēkeb,* raising a problem in the minds of some interpreters that a singular mare is associated with a plurality of chariots. The interpretation adopted in the commentary solves the problem since the mare is not attached to the chariots but sent out among the chariots in a defensive strategy. However, those scholars who opt for a different interpretation will often invoke the collective plural; see, e.g., Munro, *Spikenard and Saffron,* p. 22.

75. The word is *tôr,* but in the plural. It appears only here in the Hebrew Bible as a piece of jewelry; its other occurrence as a noun is in the singular (Esther 2:12, 15) with a different meaning, but one based on the meaning of the verbal root, which is "to turn about, to go about."

76. "*ḥ^arûzîm,*" *NIDOTTE,* vol. 2, p. 268, points out that this *hapax legomenon*

11. *Earrings of gold we[77] will make for you*
     along with studs of silver.

9 The man now describes the beauty of the woman, beginning with a simile drawing comparison between his beloved and a *mare*. To our modern tastes this analogy does not immediately impress us as complimentary. We might imagine, though, the mare's sleekness, and certainly the evocation of Pharaoh calls to mind opulence. Delitzsch shows his impulse toward historical explanation of the poetic imagery by pointing out that the imagery was appropriate to Solomon, a "keen hippologue."[78] Pope, however, puts forward an attractive hypothesis for the meaning of this verse. He first reminds us that chariot horses were usually stallions, not mares.[79] He then describes an attested defensive strategy against chariot attack. As the stallions rush toward their intended target, a mare in heat is let lose among them, driving them to distraction so that they cannot proceed with the attack. He appeals specifically to the report of an Egyptian attack against Qadesh where this technique was used. It failed, though, when the mare was killed by an Egyptian soldier. To paraphrase the thought of the man, he is saying that she drives all the men crazy with her attractiveness, with the implication that she drives him to distraction as well. He will voice a similar sentiment in 4:9. I find Pope's proposal not only interesting but persuasive.[80]

The man refers to the woman as his *darling (ra'yâ)*. This term occurs only in the Song (see also 1:15; 2:2, 10, 13; 4:1, 7; 5:2; 6:4). It is a term of endearment and familiarity.

10 At first, it is ambiguous whether the description that follows verse 9 refers to the mare or to the woman. As J. M. Munro suggests, repeating a suggestion of R. Alter, "mare and woman shadow each other, tenor and vehicle have become one."[81] The mention of jewels could be in reference to a

gains its meaning by comparison with Aramaic *ḥrz* "to string together" and Arabic *ḥāraz* "necklace of shells or pearls."

77. Perhaps this should be taken as a male version of the "plural of ecstasy" described by S. Paul ("The 'Plural of Ecstasy' in Mesopotamian and Biblical Love Poetry," in *Solving Riddles and Untying Knots,* ed. Z. Zevit, S. Gitin, and M. Sokoloff [Winona Lake, IN: Eisenbrauns, 1995], pp. 585-97). He does not mention this example, which is actually better than the others he does supply from the Song (1:4; 2:15), but perhaps he was blinded by his prejudice that this is only a female phenomenon.

78. Delitzsch, *Proverbs, Ecclesiastes, Song of Songs,* p. 33.

79. See Pope, *Song of Songs,* pp. 336-41, as well as his earlier article "A Mare in Pharaoh's Chariotry," *BASOR* 200 (1970): 56-61.

80. Even in the light of Fox's *(The Song of Songs and the Ancient Egyptian Love Songs)* criticisms and his assertion that it is simply a metaphor of "ornamented beauty."

81. Munro, *Spikenard and Saffron,* p. 56, citing R. Alter, *The Art of Biblical Poetry* (New York: Basic Books, 1985), p. 197.

festooned animal,[82] but in our opinion the mare image fades away to a description of the attractive style of the woman. Her natural beauty is heightened by her jewelry (earrings and necklace). Elsewhere in the Song (4:9; 7:2 [English 7:1]), jewelry is seen as enhancing the woman's beauty. This positive view of jewelry is in keeping with most of the Old Testament. Occasionally the prophets will denigrate jewelry, but, when they do, jewelry is a symbol of political and economic oppression that emanates from an errant view of God (Isa. 3:16-22). Jewelry was also associated with pagan worship (Hos. 2:15 [English 2:13]), which also reaps the denunciation of the prophets. This negative attitude of the prophets likely stands behind the New Testament's cautious attitude toward human use of jewelry (1 Tim. 2:9-10). The Song of Songs indicates that there is not an absolute prohibition against jewelry for people of faith.

11   The earrings are further poetically described. Much remains ambiguous in the verse, since the word *stud (n^equddôt)* occurs only here in the Hebrew Bible.[83] In a recent discussion of the word, A. H. Konkel concludes, "the exact nature of the silver can only be conjectured, but it would seem to be some small type of bead."[84] In spite of the ambiguities, we can clearly see that the verse describes some kind of precious jewelry that enhances the beauty of his beloved.

The verb *we will make (na^aśeh)* indicates that the man includes himself among those who ornament the woman. Again, it is wrong-minded to press this literally as if the man was a jeweler. He expresses the idea that she is beautiful, and he will work to enhance that beauty.

POEM FIVE:
INTIMATE FRAGRANCES (1:12-14)

The fifth song is an admiration poem directed to the man. Her speech, composed in three verses, seems to be centered on the theme of sweet smells. All the senses are involved in the attraction of the couple to each other.

82. This opinion is expressed by Delitzsch, *Proverbs, Ecclesiastes, Song of Songs,* p. 34. Pope (*Song of Songs,* p. 344) attempts to bolster this approach by referring to some Ugaritic texts that mention *tr* in association with chariots, but the contexts are not that clear. Pope ultimately concludes that the description of vv. 10 and 11 could refer to a horse, a woman, or a goddess (the last suggesting his own distinctive interpretation of the book; see Introduction).

83. Though perhaps *nāqôd* "speckled" (Gen. 30:32) and *n^equddîm* "small cake" (Josh. 9:5) are related.

84. A. H. Konkel, *"n^equddôt," NIDOTTE,* vol. 3, pp. 151-52.

Admittedly, the connection between this speech and the ones before and after it is unclear. It is conceivable that the woman is here responding to the immediately preceding admiration speech by the man (1:9-11), but there are no direct connections between the two. Similarly, the poem that immediately follows this poem (found in 1:15-17) may be the man's response to the woman's speech here, but there are no explicit connections between the two.

The Woman
12. *While the king is on his couch*
      my nard gives off its scent.
13. *My lover is to me a sachet of myrrh*
      lodging between my breasts.
14. *A cluster of henna blossoms is my lover to me*
      in the vineyards of En-gedi.

12   The woman is in the man's intimate presence. That is the meaning of the *while* (*'ad-še*), which has such a force with the perfect aspect of the verb.[85] The man is again referred to as *king,* continuing the alternation of pastoral and courtly imagery. He is on his *mēsab,* here translated *couch,* though the word occurs only here in the singular.[86] It derives from the verbal root *sbb* "to go around" and denotes something like a circular couch or table (if the latter, then "at his table"; so NIV). A postbiblical Hebrew cognate may indicate the furniture on which banqueters would lie down as they ate. However, the scene certainly does not imply a crowd. *Couch* suggests a more erotic scene, and she is close enough for him to smell her perfume, specifically *nard* (*nērd;* see also Song of Songs 4:13), a term of Sanskrit derivation, pointing to its origin in India.[87] Lovemaking involves all the senses; here the emphasis is on smell. The sweet smell of perfume arouses other senses and emotions. The woman intends to arouse the king. The anticipation in this verse is palpable. It is the prelude to an embrace. Munro helpfully points out how the motif of fragrance, in this case nard, mediates the courtly realm and the realm of nature. It comes from nature but is affordable and worn by the upper classes.[88]

13   The previous verse expresses a physical closeness and anticipated intimacy that is here articulated in a powerfully suggestive image. If

85. So Pope, *Song of Songs,* p. 347.
86. See 2 Kings 23:5 for the plural in the sense of the "surroundings" of Jerusalem. Indeed, Murphy's translation of Song of Songs 1:12 ("in his enclosure," in *The Song of Songs,* p. 130) suggests a meaning more closely related to the plural.
87. Where, according to Keel, *The Song of Songs,* p. 62, it was used as an aphrodisiac.
88. Munro, *Spikenard and Saffron,* p. 49.

we read a narrative impulse between verses 12 and 13, perhaps the woman has lain down next to her reclined "king" and cradles his head between her breasts. He too is sweet smelling, being likened to a sachet of myrrh, and she imagines him close to one of her most intimate places, her breasts. The word *sachet (ṣᵉrôr)* is a purse-like object that could hold money (Gen. 42:35; Hag. 1:6). This *sachet* holds *myrrh (môr)*, which "is an aromatic gum which exudes from cracks in the bark of the *Bulsamodendron myrrha* which grows in Arabia, Abyssinia, and India."[89] The *sachet* "lodges" *(lyn)* between her breasts, the verb denoting a lengthy, languorous stay. For the first of thirty-one times, the woman refers to the man as her *lover (dwd)*. This noun outside the Song refers most often to an uncle or a close cousin. Keel speculates that it became a term to refer to the lover since the marriage of cousins was common.[90] From the context alone, we determine that this is a term of great intimacy and affection.

This verse stretched the imagination of allegorical interpreters with its explicit sensuality. Cyril of Alexandria is at his creative best when he suggests that the verse describes what we today would call biblical theology. The breasts are the Old and New Testaments, presumably only linked by their two-ness. Jesus Christ is the sachet of myrrh. The New Testament is in the Old concealed; the Old in the New revealed. Jesus spans the testaments as the sachet spans the woman's two breasts.

14 The woman draws another comparison to describe her lover. It actually does more than simply describe him, it reveals her desire for him. She describes him as a *cluster of henna blossoms*. The word *cluster ('eškōl)* is most often found in reference to grapes (cf. Song 7:8, 9 [English 7:7, 8] in connection with the woman's breasts). Here it is connected to the *henna (kōper)*, a shrub, well known in Egypt and Palestine, whose flowers are used for dyeing hair red. The metaphor probably emphasizes his pleasant smell. Yet these are not ordinary henna; they are from the region around *En-gedi,* one of the most delightful locations in all of Israel. En-gedi is on the western bank of the Dead Sea, just north of Masada (which of course did not exist as a fortress until many centuries later). The surrounding landscape is desolate, but En-gedi is a delightful oasis with waterfall and stream. Hidden and private, it is a romantic place, to be sure, contributing to the contrast developed through the Song between the countryside as a place of love and the city as a place of alienation.

89. Pope, *Song of Songs,* p. 350.
90. Keel, *The Song of Songs,* p. 65.

POEM SIX:
OUTDOOR LOVE (1:15-17)

It may be that this poem continues the dialogue of the previous poem, but since the connections are slight, if existent at all, we treat it as a separate dialogue, following a monologue. This dialogue between the man and the woman begins with an exchange of general compliments on their respective attractiveness. Thus, we do well to consider this poem an admiration song. The woman, though, climaxes the poem with a reference to their "bed" and their "house." As explained below, the language indicates that these are not literal. The scene is clearly out in the country. They intimately embrace in the open air. The description evokes a pleasant scene and appeals to the sense of smell as well.

The Man
15. *You are beautiful, my darling.*
    You are beautiful;
    your eyes are doves.

The Woman
16. *You are beautiful, my lover, so lovely;*
    our bed is verdant!
17. *The boards of our house are cedars;*
    its rafters[91] *are junipers.*[92]

15   The man now responds to his lover's song of admiration and desire with the same. He wants his *darling* (cf. commentary at 1:9), and he compliments her beauty. We do not translate the *hinnēh* that opens the first two cola. This word provides emphasis; it is often translated "behold." In this context, that rendition feels awkward. If we were to translate it, perhaps "ah" would be a close approximation. After a general statement calling her *beautiful*, her *eyes* capture his attention. The image is not immediately clear. What is it about *doves* that make them a good metaphor for eyes? While keeping in mind the danger we run in reading our own cultural or individual preferences into the ancient world, we find it hard to think that it might be the color of the dove, which is not particularly striking. It could be the attribute of softness, but

---

91. The Ketib is *raḥîṭ;* the Qere is *raḥîṭ.* The word is cognate with Syriac *rā/aḥṭā* (cf. *NIDOTTE,* vol. 3, p. 1067).

92. A quick look at the commentaries and the translations indicates a great deal of variety in the translation of *bᵉrôt,* reminding us of the difficulty of translating ancient botanical terms into modern ones.

again that is not clear. The article on doves in the *Dictionary of Biblical Imagery* lists a number of qualities that may be at play here when it states, "Because of the dove's softness, beauty of feathers and eyes, and affection for and faithfulness to its mate."[93] However, it is hard to tell what exactly the ancient perception of this bird was like. Indeed, perhaps we are missing a cultural background to this image, but from the context we can be certain that the metaphor is a compliment. In this section, the man praises the woman's physical beauty as a prelude to an intimate rendezvous.

16 The woman responds in kind to her *lover* (*dôdî;* cf. commentary at 1:13). She begins with a general praise of his physical beauty, using the same words as he did in describing her beauty.[94] He follows the first general comment with a second. She is *lovely* (*nāʿîm,* which is an adjective formed from the relatively frequent verb *nʿm* "to be pleasant"). Samuel Meier indicates that the word *nāʿîm* refers to "the intrinsic attractiveness of an object or action."[95] Here, the woman's intrinsic attractiveness is the object of the man's comment, and the context emphasizes that it is primarily her physical beauty that is at issue.

The woman then shifts this conversation from description of the man to description of the place where they are intimate. They have made their *bed* out in the country. The adjective that qualifies the bed is an interesting one. We translate *raʿʿanan* as verdant, meaning flourishing, green, luxurious. This Hebrew adjective is more appropriate to a tree, but that is the point, as we will see in the next verse. We are dealing with figurative language here. We are not to interpret this as an actual event. The Song is not telling the story of a specific couple. The country, as opposed to the city, is a place of private intimacy in the Song.

17 The figurative language of verse 16 continues in this verse. The woman describes the "house" where she will share a moment of intimacy with her lover. The picture is of a well-forested area where there is a grassy opening. As they lie in the grass and look around and above, they are surrounded — that is, protected — by the trees. The trees provide privacy, and more: the *cedar* and the *juniper* are trees that produce a pleasant scent, making this spot a pleasant place for an intimate encounter.

---

93. *Dictionary of Biblical Imagery,* p. 217.

94. *You are beautiful (hinnᵉkā yapeh);* the difference is that the pronominal suffix is understandably masculine, not feminine.

95. Samuel A. Meier, *"nʿm,"* in *NIDOTTE,* vol. 3, p. 121.

CHAPTER TWO

POEM SEVEN:
FLOWERS AND TREES (2:1-7)

The unity of this poem is uncertain. Certainly, 2:1-3 should be treated together. The interchange between the man and the woman in these verses plays on floral imagery.[1] It begins with the woman providing a somewhat self-deprecating description of herself as a common flower. The man picks up the image and turns it into an expression of admiration for his beloved. She may be a simple lily, but everyone else around her is a rough thorn. Then the woman repays the compliment by likening her lover to a fertile, luxuriant, scented apple tree in a forest of ordinary trees. To one another they stand out dramatically from the crowd.

The next four verses (2:4-7) have a subtle connection with the first three through the mention of apples, though it is conceivable that this is a different poem placed in this position because of that catchword. In any case, the woman now tells of an experience she has. She states that her lover has brought her into the wine house, and then she calls for sustenance, implying physical assertions. The poem ends with two verses, both of which serve as refrains in the book (see commentary below).

The Woman
1. *I am a flower of Sharon,*
   a lily of the valleys.

The Man
2. *Like a lily between thorns*
   is my darling among the girls.[2]

---

1. Perhaps suggested by the tree imagery of the preceding poem.
2. Literally, "daughters."

The Woman

3. *Like an apple tree among the trees of the forest*
   is my lover among boys.[3]
   I desire his shade and I dwell there;
   his fruit is sweet to my palate.
4. *He has brought me to the wine house,*
   and his banner over me was "Love."
5. *Sustain me with raisin cakes;*[4]
   refresh[5] *me with apples,*
   for I am faint with love.
6. *His left hand is under my head,*
   and his right embraces me.
7. *I adjure you,*[6] *daughters of Jerusalem,*
   by the gazelles or the deer of the field,
   not to awaken or arouse love until it desires.

1 The woman asserts her own beauty by association with flowers. This verse is a self-description, which initiates an admiration song.[7] The self-description fits in with a pattern of nature imagery used throughout the Song. The question that determines the direction of the interpretation is the symbolic value of the specific flowers that are mentioned in the verse: the *flower (ḥᵃbaṣṣelet)* and the *lily (šôšannâ)*. The former is only found elsewhere in Isaiah 35:1, where the desert will burst into bloom with these flowers. The metaphor indicates the joy of those who are redeemed by God. Our translation understands that the woman refers to herself by a common flower[8] that occurs by the myriad.[9] She further indicates that she is just one flower (the force of the indefinite article) rather than a unique flower (which would have been signaled by the definite article). A traditional translation of the Hebrew word is "rose" (KJV,

---

3. Literally, "sons."

4. Virtually all modern commentators and translations understand the word to refer to a specialty cake made of raisins, but older commentators (and the AV) understood the reference to be to a "flagon of wine."

5. The verb means "to spread, underlay, support" and appears in the qal one time (Job 41:22 [English 41:30]) and two times, including this verse, in the piel (also Job 17:13). The noun *rᵉpîdâ* occurs only in Song of Songs 3:10.

6. The suffix is masculine, though clearly here it refers to the "daughters of Jerusalem." As Murphy points out (*The Song of Songs*, p. 133), this use of the masculine for a feminine reference is not unusual in the book.

7. Murphy, *Wisdom Literature*, p. 114.

8. Significantly, the Septuagint and Vulgate translate *ḥᵃbaṣṣelet* with common terms for flowers.

9. Delitzsch, *Proverbs, Ecclesiastes, Song of Solomon*, p. 40.

NKJV), but this is impossible since this particular flower did not come to Israel until after the Old Testament period. *Sharon* is a plain just between the coast and the foothills of western Israel, north of Jaffa up to Athlit. The reference concretizes the imagery. Perhaps the reference to Sharon enriches the image of the flower since Sharon "is a fertile, lush plain where browsing flocks eat their fill and become fat"[10] (cf. the other four references to Sharon in the Old Testament: Isa. 33:9; 35:2; 65:10; 1 Chron. 27:29).

She is also *a lily of the valleys,* a perhaps even more common reference. The exact referent to *šôšannâ* is disputed, though. While most take it as some form of the lily,[11] M. H. Pope argues for the specific meaning of "lotus," which is a type of lily, with all the supposed erotic overtones of that flower.[12]

The main significance of these flower references is best understood to be a modest expression of her beauty. It does not deny her flower-like attractiveness. T. Gledhill points out that a later reference in Matthew 6:29 negatively compares Solomon's splendor to the splendor of the lilies of the field.[13] Nonetheless, it is nothing outstanding, nothing out of the ordinary — at least in her eyes. In other words, she implies her unworthiness of the man's admiration. If this is a subtle attempt at flirtation, it succeeds. In the next verse, the man will dispute her self-deprecating interpretation.

2   That the man is speaking in this verse is signaled by his reference to *my darling (ra'yātî).* That is the man's term for the woman (cf. 1:15 and references cited there). He picks up on the reference to *lily,* a common flower but a beautiful one (see the discussion on the previous verse), but then places it in a context that magnifies the woman's beauty in his eyes. She is not an ordinary lily but one found among *thorns.* The latter are plain in color and rough looking and contrast vividly with the flower. Indeed, thorns invite anything but intimacy. The analogy is clear. She is the best looking of all the women; the only one worth looking at. Later he will refer to her as the "most beautiful of women."

In this verse, the woman is literally placed in the class of "daughters" *(benôt),* which is a term that may indicate her youth. With this in mind, we have translated the term "girls," not "women."

3   The woman responds with a botanical analogy of her own. Her *lover,* a favorite appellation of the woman toward the man (see already 1:13, 14, 16), is like an *apple tree* in the forest.[14] An apple tree, of course, stands

10. E. Borowski, "The Sharon — Symbol of God's Abundance," *BR* 4 (1988): 40.

11. Perhaps the "water lily." The Septuagint translates *krinon* "lily" and the Vulgate *lilium.*

12. Pope, *Song of Songs,* p. 368.

13. Gledhill, *The Message of the Song of Songs,* p. 122.

14. Though most commentators acknowledge difficulty in making an exact identification with the apple. Falk (*Love Lyrics in the Bible,* p. 174) adopts a suggestion by

out among the common trees of a *forest* by its fruit, which also sends forth an appealing scent.[15] The rest of the trees in the forest are common and stand for the other men, who seem so ordinary in the presence of her partner. The sexual connotations of the apple will be picked up below in verse 5 (see also commentary at 7:9 [English 7:8]; 8:5). Here, the man's youth is emphasized by placing him in the class of "sons" *(bānîm),* here translated *boys.* This reference compares with the girls of the previous verse.

She continues to use the imagery to comment on their intimacy. She not only looks at the apple tree from afar, but she places herself, figuratively, under his protecting and comforting branches *(I desire his shade and I dwell there).* Their physical union is represented by the fact that she tastes his fruit. Pope cites the title of two relatively recent songs to suggest that the sensual nature of the apple tree as a place of romance continues down to the present: "In the Shade of the Old Apple Tree" and "Don't Sit Under the Apple Tree."[16]

A. Feuillet notes that both Song of Songs 2:3c and Hosea 14:8a (English 14:7a) have the phrase *yšb bᵉṣîl* (to sit in the shade).[17] He points out that the image is used of the relationship between God and his people in Hosea. While he argues that this promotes a theological reading of the Song, it is better to simply see it as an obvious image of intimate relationship that can be applied to more than one type of relationship.

4 The love banter between the man and the woman gives way to the woman's narrative about where her lover took her. It is possible that there is a new poem here and a break with 2:1-3.[18] However, this verse through verse 7 are just as naturally taken as a continuation of the preceding verses. The woman exclaims that the man has brought her to the *wine house.* This is the only use of this phrase *(bēt hayyâyin)* in the Bible, but there are near synonyms, including "house for the drinking of wine" *(bēt mištēh hayyâyin)* in Esther 7:8 and the "drinking house" *(bēt mištēh)* in Jeremiah 16:8 and Ecclesiastes 7:2. While there have been a number of attempts to discover some es-

Nogah Hareuveni that the word means quince. She translates "sweet fruit tree," which gets at the point regardless of the specific identification of the fruit.

15. J. G. Westenholz ("Love Lyrics from the Ancient Near East," in *Civilizations of the Ancient Near East,* vol. 4, ed. J. M. Sasson [New York: Charles Scribner's Sons, 1995], p. 2482) gives examples of the apple and apple tree used in a similar symbolic fashion to the Song of Songs in Sumerian, Akkadian, and Egyptian love poems.

16. The second song continues "with anyone else but me." See Pope, *Song of Songs,* p. 372.

17. A. Feuillet, "'S'asseoir a l'ombre' de l'époux (Os., xiv, 8a et Cant., ii, 3)," *RB* 78 (1971): 391-405.

18. As Keel *(The Song of Songs,* p. 84) seems to suggest. He believes that the placement of this poem after 2:1-3 is consequence of the catchword "apple," which can also be taken as an indication that it is indeed a part of the unit begun in 2:1.

oteric connections of the wine house,[19] its significance in the near and far context of the Song of Songs seems clear. The house of wine was a place where wine was drunk. Whether this is to be pictured as a banquet hall, a room in the palace, a private residence, or a tavern is relatively unimportant compared to the sensual associations it evokes. Already in the Song, wine has been associated with love (1:2; see also 4:10; 7:9). The warm, thick liquid that has the potential to send the mind spinning is an appropriate symbol of love and its physical manifestations. He is "intoxicated" with her and has brought her to a place to make love.

The second colon has also been discussed at some length. The predominant use of *degel* in the Hebrew Bible is as a *banner* or "emblem." Its use outside of the Song is restricted to the book of Numbers (1:52; 2:2, 3, 10, 17, 18, 25, 31, 34; 10:14, 18, 22, 25). E. Carpenter and M. Grisanti describe the semantic development of the noun in this way: "Although *degel* originally signified the standard for each tribe's military force, it clearly served to represent the entire tribe as well in their camping and decamping. Eventually, *degel* became extended by association to specify exclusively an army unit."[20] From this definition, the term seems to have military connotations and refers to the emblems that an army unit would fly over their encampment and carry with them in battle. In the ancient Near East these emblems or battle standards would carry the name or symbol of the deity with which the army was associated. The use in Numbers is one of the indications that the wilderness wanderings are perceived as a march into battle and that the wilderness camp is a battle camp. Some scholars hesitate to ascribe military connotations to the term here, but for insubstantial reasons. After all, the effect is to picture the man as a young virile soldier, perhaps paralleled by the martial imagery of the other love song in the Bible, Psalm 45 (see particularly vv. 3-5). It is quite an interesting use of the martial (and royal) image to put it at the service of love. The man has marked her out as his own and has stamped her with a public display of his love. The metaphor implies belonging, inclusion, and commitment.

Among those who balk at the meaning *banner* is Pope, who translates "his intention toward me was love," based on an Akkadian cognate *(diglu)*.[21] G. Gerleman argues on the basis of an Arabic cognate that the connection is with a sign posted outside a drinking party,[22] and R. Gordis, in turn, connects

19. Most interesting and idiosyncratic is that of Pope (*Song of Songs,* p. 375), who wants to connect it to the *bet marzēaḥ* and the use of "wine, especially in association with women and song in worship of the powers of fertility, which cult persisted for millennia in Syria-Palestine."

20. See their article on *degel* in *NIDOTTE,* vol. 1, pp. 919-20.

21. Pope, *Song of Songs,* pp. 375-77.

22. G. Gerleman, *Ruth, Das Hohelied,* BKAT 18 (Neukirchen-Vluyn: Neukirchener, 1965).

the root with a second Akkadian cognate *(dāgalu)* and translates "his glance upon me was loving."[23] Again, we see no reason to depart from the understanding of the root derived from its use in the book of Numbers.

5 Presumably, the woman continues speaking and exclaims that the intensity of her love makes her physically weak. She is exhausted. The broader context indicates that she is appealing to the "daughters of Jerusalem." She needs sustenance and calls for *raisin cakes* and *apples.* The emotion of love can overwhelm a person psychologically, and the physical rigors of lovemaking can wear a person out. The context does not make it clear whether one or the other, or perhaps more likely both, is meant. Raisin cakes and apples may provide more than physical sustenance and may have been understood to be aphrodisiacs.[24] The connection of the former with Canaanite fertility rituals may suggest that it had this power (Hos. 3:1),[25] and O. Keel mentions a cooking press with an image of a goddess on it and speculates that these cakes had such a form put on them.[26] However, like apples, raisin cakes are not always associated with a pagan cult or with fertility (2 Sam. 6:19). R. E. Murphy suggests that the context does not support the idea of an aphrodisiac,[27] but the idea seems to be that she is both worn out and wants more of the same. She is physically tired but wants to continue the intimacy. Pope claims that this cake was made out of crushed dried raisins.[28] The motive clause that occurs as the third colon of the verse gives the reason for the sustenance. Love has made her *faint.* The noun *ḥôlat* from the verb *ḥlh* denotes a loss of physical strength. Often it denotes illness, not just weakness. This phrase could conceivably be translated "I am sick with love," but the meaning is roughly the same. She is overwhelmed emotionally and physically by her love for the man. It is a strong statement of the power of love and may also contain a cautionary note to the effect that love is wonderful but not something to play around with. As G. Schwab points out, "the girl's malady in Cant. 2:5 was not caused by the absence of her lover, but by his amatory presence. It is the activity of love itself that is creating her physical infirmity."[29] He argues that this is why the poem ends in 2:7 with a note of caution to the daughters of Jerusalem.

23. R. Gordis, "The Root *dgl* in the Song of Songs," *JBL* 88 (1969): 203-4.

24. J.-J. Lavoie, "Festin érotique et tendresse cannibalique dans le Cantique des Cantiques," *SR* 24 (1995): 132.

25. F. I. Andersen and D. N. Freedman, *Hosea,* AB 24 (Garden City, NY: Doubleday, 1980), p. 298.

26. Keel, *The Song of Songs,* p. 85, see his figure 43 on p. 90.

27. Murphy, *The Song of Songs,* p. 137.

28. Pope, *Song of Songs,* pp. 378-80.

29. G. Schwab, "The Song of Songs' Cautionary Message concerning Human Love," Ph.D. dissertation, Westminster Theological Seminary, 1999, p. 74.

6   The woman describes her embrace with the man.[30] The best understanding of the verse is that they are lying down and the man has slipped his left arm under her head, and, as he cradles her head on his arm, he has reached over and pulled her toward him. This is not a response to her fatigue but rather an expression of a desire for more lovemaking. This verse recurs in 8:3 and serves as one of the refrains of the Song that bind the whole together (see Introduction: Structure). The context certainly indicates that this is an intimate embrace, but the verb *ḥbq* does not explicitly indicate sexual intercourse. As Pope points out, the verb is used both for "affectionate greeting (Gen 29:13) and of sexual embrace (Prov 5:20)."[31] No doubt the present context is closer to the latter than the former.

7   The section culminates with the woman calling on her listeners, the witnesses to the love relationship (the *daughters of Jerusalem*), to swear an oath.[32] The opening verb *(I adjure you,* the hiphil of *šbʿ)* indicates that she is urging them to make a promise, but what is the nature of the promise? The promise itself is given in the third colon of the verse. She warns them *not to awaken or arouse love until it desires.* The first two verbs, both in the main clause, are variations of the same root *ʿwr.* The first is hiphil and the second is polel. The meaning of *ʿwr* II has to do with arousal or excitation to some activity. The repetition of the root has an emphatic force, similar to "whatever you do, don't arouse. . . ." It is a strong note of caution then. Still, what is she warning against exactly?[33] One suggestion is that the phrase has the force of a "do not disturb sign." Don't disturb us until our love (the love of the man and the woman) has had its fill. Yet this seems an odd way to express the idea. More naturally, the verse is a warning of the woman to other women who may look on the relationship and want to experience something similar; she is, in essence, telling them not to force it. Wait for love to blossom; don't hurry it. In a sense, then, the *daughters of Jerusalem* are surrogates for the reader. We too are to learn the same lesson: Wait for love to blossom; don't try to stimulate it artificially. After all, in the preceding

---

30. Some commentators (see Murphy, *The Song of Songs,* p. 137) understand the verse to indicate a wish rather than describing a present reality. This seems unlikely.

31. Pope, *Song of Songs,* p. 384.

32. Keel (*The Song of Songs,* p. 89) questions the relationship of 2:6, 7 with the preceding unit due to the fact that the woman now addresses the daughters of Jerusalem rather than the man. However, we have seen this kind of change in dialogue partner from the very beginning of the book.

33. D. W. de Villiers and J. J. Burden ("Function and Translation: A Twosome in the Song of Songs," *OTE* 2 [1989]: 1-11) provide a helpful discussion of the issues involved in the proper translation and interpretation of the text. Their study supports the viewpoint adopted in the commentary. See also D. Grossberg, "Sexual Desire: Abstract and Concrete," *Hebrew Studies* 22 (1981): 59-60.

verses we have seen that love takes its toll on the woman. She warns the others not to arouse love until they are ready to meet its rigors, both physical and emotional. Love is not a passing fling but rather a demanding and exhausting relationship.[34]

The woman in love calls on the other women to take the oath by *the gazelles and the deer of the field*. This formulation of an oath strikes us as very odd, but there are good explanations for it. The first is revealed only by comparing the Hebrew of the colon *(biṣbā'ôt 'ô be'aylôt haśśādeh)* to the phrase "by the (LORD) of Hosts or by God Almighty" *(be[YHWH] ṣebā'ôt 'ô be'el šāddai)*. We must remember that the divine name does not occur in the book (see 8:6 for a possible exception); there seems to be a studied avoidance of the use of divine names. Thus, this oath would be a playful allusion to the divine name, while at the same time evoking a pastoral image, in keeping with the tenor of the book.[35]

This verse is repeated with some variation in 3:5 and 8:4 and creates an impression of unity for the work as a whole (see Introduction: Structure).

POEM EIGHT:
A POEM OF SPRING (2:8-17)

Roland Murphy has argued in favor of the unity of this section.[36] While some of the transitions in the poem, particularly surrounding verse 15, are not absolutely clear, I am generally persuaded by his position and follow him in what follows. The poem begins with the woman's excited announcement of her lover's arrival. She likens him to a gazelle or a young stag bounding over the hills and finally arriving at her house, trying to catch sight of her from the other side of the wall as he peers through the window (vv. 8-9).[37] From this vantage point, he calls to her and invites her to a tryst. Even though it is he who is doing the inviting, the speech still belongs to the woman since she is

34. My thanks to Robert Hubbard for his insights into this verse.

35. It has also been pointed out correctly that the gazelle and the deer are animals associated with the goddess of love in ancient Canaanite religion; cf. Keel, *The Song of Songs*, p. 92.

36. R. E. Murphy, "Cant 2:8-17 — A Unified Poem?" in *Melange bibliques et orientaux en l'honneur de M. Mathias Delcor,* ed. A. Caquot, S. Legasse, and M. Tardieu (Kevelaer: Butzon und Bercker, 1985), pp. 305-10.

37. H. Madl ("Hld 2,8-14: Die Begenung der Geliebten im Bild des Fruhlings. Versuch einer Exegese," in *Der Orientalische Mensch und seine Beziehungen zum Umwelt,* ed. B. Scholz [Graz: R. M. Druck, 1989], pp. 123-35) points out that these two verses are bound together by the use of seven participles.

quoting the invitation. Verses 10 and 13, part of the quoted invitation, provide a unit within the broader poem, separated by an inclusio formed by the request expressed by "Rise up, my darling, my beautiful one, and come. . . ." We have named this poem after the imagery embedded in this section of the poem since it is filled with allusions to the springtime. However, the quoted request continues in verse 14 as he asks to hear her voice as well as to see her.

The most difficult verse of the unit to understand is verse 15, which is the cry to catch the foxes, but we follow Murphy and see this as the response of the woman to the man's request to see and hear her. It is an odd response, to be sure, but it may indicate the awareness of obstacles to their intimacy. Finally, in verses 16 and 17, the woman makes it clear that she desires union with the man. The unity of this poem is most convincing by virtue of the inclusio formed by a chiasm, which was noticed by R. Tournay[38] and quoted by Murphy.[39] As the latter points out, when one compares verse 8 and verse 17, one concludes that "the unit begins with mountains, gazelle, stag, and it ends in chiastic fashion with gazelle, stag, mountains."

The Woman

8. *The sound of my lover!*
   See, he is coming,
      leaping over mountains,
      bounding over hills!
9. *My lover is like a gazelle*
      or a young stag.
   He[40] is now[41] standing behind our[42] wall,[43]
      staring through the window,
      peeking through the lattice.[44]
10. *My lover responded and said to me,*
    "Rise up, my darling,
       my beautiful one, and come, . . .

---

38. R. Tournay, "Abraham et le Cantique des Cantiques," *VT* 25 (1975): 544-52.
39. Murphy, "Cant 2:8-17," p. 307, n. 11.
40. For the demonstrative pronoun *zeh*.
41. Rendering the *hinnēh*.
42. Apparently, the woman is in her family's home.
43. This word for wall *(kōtel)* is a *hapax* in biblical Hebrew but is found in biblical Aramaic (Dan. 5:5; Ezra 5:8), though it also has an Akkadian cognate.
44. Window *(ḥallôn)* is the more common word in Hebrew and thus not surprisingly precedes *lattice (ḥārāk),* which is a *hapax legomenon* in biblical Hebrew although it occurs also in postbiblical Hebrew. According to *NIDOTTE,* vol. 2, p. 144, "later Jewish literature, Pesik. Hahod, distinguishes between light coming through a *ḥallôn,* and a *ḥārāk,* lattice window."

11. *For now the winter*[45] *has passed,*
    the rains have come, gone.[46]
12. *Blossoms*[47] *appear in the land.*
    A time of singing has arrived,
    and the sound of turtledoves is heard in our land.
13. *The fig tree ripens its fruit,*
    and the vines, in blossom, spread their fragrance.
    Rise up, my darling,
    my beautiful one, and come. . . .
14. *My dove, in the crevices of the rock,*
    in the hiding place in the cliff,
    let me see your form!
    Let me hear your voice!
    For your voice is agreeable,
    and your form is pleasant."
15. *"Grab*[48] *the foxes,*[49]
    the little foxes!
    They are ruining the vineyards,
    our vineyards in bloom."[50]
16. *My lover is mine and I am his;*
    he grazes[51] *among the lilies.*[52]

---

45. For *s^etāw* (Qere form is *s^etāyw*) — a *hapax legomenon*. The word may refer specifically to the "winter rains"; cf. Murphy, *The Song of Songs*, p. 139, who also mentions that it is an Aramaism.

46. The two verbs here *(ḥālap, ḥālak)* are asyndetic.

47. The Hebrew word here *(niṣṣānîm)* is unique but is closely related to the more common *nēṣ* and *niṣṣâh* (cf. Gen. 40:10; Isa. 18:5; Job 15:33). Pope suggests that the word in the Song is formed with an afformative *-an* (*Song of Songs*, p. 395).

48. Literally, "Grab for us the foxes." The preposition has the force of "for our benefit" but sounds very awkward in English translation. The best understanding of the first person plural "us" is as a reference to the man and the woman. Paul ("The 'Plural of Ecstasy' in Mesopotamian and Biblical Love Poetry," pp. 586-97) seems to create a problem that does not exist in order to solve it with his assertion of a plural of ecstasy. The plural of ecstasy, which he supports with examples from Sumerian and Akkadian literature, may exist elsewhere, but it is an unnecessary hypothesis in this context.

49. Some believe that the Hebrew word *šû'āl* refers to a jackal instead of or alongside of a wolf. This seems an insignificant issue in regard to the verse's meaning.

50. On *in bloom (s^emādar)*, see 2:13.

51. With Murphy (*The Song of Songs*, p. 139) taking the verb intransitively rather than transitively, unlike the Septuagint, which understood the reference to be simply that the lover was pasturing his flock among the lilies.

52. For lilies *(šôšannîm)*, see 3:1.

17. *Until*[53] *the day breaks*[54] *and the shadows flee* —
    turn, my lover, be like a gazelle
    or a young stag on the mountains of Bether.

8 The verse drips with the woman's excited anticipation of the arrival of
her lover. The short, staccato Hebrew clauses communicate her passion. She
describes the movement of her lover, and it is that movement that indicates
his excitement. The first clause has caused some discussion as to its referent;
what is the *sound (qôl)* of her lover? Some say it is an interjection, translated
"Hark!"[55] which expresses that it is hard to know what sound the lover could
be making. However, it is more naturally taken as a noun in construct with
the following noun. While we cannot be precise as to whether the lover is
shouting as he is coming forward or that his rapid movement simply makes a
lot of noise, nonetheless the commotion registers excitement as well. He is
not simply walking or even running; he is *leaping* (from *dlg*) and *bounding*
(from *qpṣ*). The verbs anticipate the metaphor made explicit in the next
verse; the lover is a gazelle. He is moving with agile grace and speed toward
his beloved. The scene evokes a sense of excitement and eagerness. *Leaping*
is the more common of the paired verbs, and so it is not surprising that it
comes first since Hebrew poetry often reserves the rarer word for the second
colon. It is used elsewhere of the joyous leaping of the lame who find healing
in the time of restoration; indeed, the metaphor here also connects the leaping with the deer (Isa. 35:6; cf. Song 2:9). However, it is not always explicitly
connected with animal imagery, as Zephaniah 1:9 demonstrates,[56] where
"leaping over the threshold" appears to be a pagan ritual that the prophet con-
demns. In what seems to be a military context, the psalmist exclaims that
God gives him the ability to leap over a wall (Ps. 18:30 [English 18:29] =
2 Sam. 22:30). The other verb is a *hapax* of what most lexicographers call
qpṣ II.[57] Not only the context, however, but also Arabic and Aramaic cognates make it clear that the verb is in the semantic domain of leaping and
jumping. J. G. Snaith tries to connect *qpṣ* I and *qpṣ* II by saying that the
meaning of I "to draw together" may be a reference to the muscles in the act
of leaping. Perhaps so, but it would be hard to verify.

The excitement of the lover is communicated by the fact that he is

---

53. Or perhaps "while" or "when." The issue is how to translate *'ad-še*. In 1:12,
we chose the translation "while," arguing with Pope that that was the proper force of the
word with the perfect; here, of course, the verb is imperfect (from *pwḥ*).

54. Literally, it means to "blow."

55. Murphy, *The Song of Songs,* p. 138.

56. This is the only use of the verb in the qal. Elsewhere, including Song of
Songs, it is in the piel.

57. For instance, *NIDOTTE,* vol. 3, p. 954.

leaping and bounding over *mountains* and *hills*. These two words are found together frequently in Hebrew poetry, and they are roughly to be taken as synonyms. They communicate that the lover overcomes obstacles in his desire to reach his beloved. This is an indication of his loving commitment, his determination to make a rendezvous.

9 The animal imagery hinted at in the verbs of verse 8 becomes explicit in verse 9. The woman draws a simile between her lover and a *gazelle*. The verb used to construct the simile *(is like,* a qal of the verb *dmh)* is used elsewhere in the Song both in the qal and the piel (2:17; 8:14 [also referring to a gazelle], as well as 1:9; 7:8 [English 7:7]). *Gazelle* here is in parallelism with *young stag ('ōper hā'āyyalîm).* The latter is used five times in the Song of Songs, often in parallel with *gazelle.* The simile raises the issue of how the lover is like these animals. As we noted in verse 8, swiftness is one characteristic of both. The lover approaches her rapidly because of his passionate desire. Gazelles are also beautiful. In the Song the short form of the noun is used *(ṣᵉbî),* which has a similar form to a word for "beautiful." This, of course, is an obvious compliment. It may also be the case that the animal radiates a masculine sexuality that is imputed to the lover. Pope draws our attention to the fact that the gazelle is evoked in Mesopotamian love incantations to dispel impotence.[58]

The lover in the form of a gazelle has rushed over the mountain obstacles to arrive at the woman's home, implied by the windows. The lover comes from the countryside to the urban area to fetch his beloved. He does not cross the threshold of her domicile, however, but stands beyond the wall, still in the romantic countryside, and stares (from the root *šgḥ*) and peeks (from the root *ṣwṣ*) through her window. He is no voyeur, as Pope suggests by calling him a Peeping Tom,[59] but rather beckons his beloved to join him. The fact that he stands quietly and looks intently after such agitated movement also evokes a mood of romantic tension. Will she go with him? How quickly?

10 The next poem begins with a prose phrase in which the woman, who is speaking, reports the speech of her *lover* (for which, see 1:9). There then follows a bicolon in this verse in which the man invites the woman to join him. This bicolon is just the beginning of the invitation, which actually continues down through verse 14 (see introduction to this unit). I believe, under the influence of Murphy cited above in the introduction to this poem, that we are to connect this poem with the previous poem and suggest that the man is speaking from behind the wall (2:9) and calling his beloved out of the house to join him in a more private place.

58. M. H. Pope, *Job,* AB 15 (Garden City, NY: Doubleday, 1973), p. 470.
59. Pope, *Song of Songs,* p. 392.

In any case, the main part of his invitation in verses 10 through 13 has the form of a chiasm (a-b/b'-a'). The two outside members (a/a') are the verbs asking her to move toward him. The middle members of the chiasm are his names for *her (my darling, my beautiful one),* both indicating his affection and passion for her.

This bicolon also serves, along with its almost exact repetition in 2:13c, as an inclusio that gives this speech (2:10-13) a sense of closure.

11   The man's invitation in the previous verse now receives a motive clause. *Winter* is gone and spring has arrived. Springtime is the universal time for love: warmer weather, the fragrance of flowers — a time to go outside, a time for the removal of clothes and intimacy. The couple can leave the urban setting and go out to the countryside, the place of lovemaking and union. While the word for *winter (sᵉtāw)* is rare, the word for *rains (gešem)* is one of the more common words out of the many for rain in Israel. Since winter (October-April) is the only real time for rain in Palestine, the two words are variants on the same theme. Since the rains end in April, it is likely that the scene evokes a temporal setting in May.

12   It's springtime, the right time for love. Springtime is signaled by three events associated with its beginning. First, flowers appear. After the rainy season, the countryside of Israel is filled with wild flowers. Second, there is *singing* in the land. The root of *zāmîr* is debated. Is it from *zmr* "to sing" or *zmr* "to prune"?[60] While the floral context might suggest the latter, many point out that the timing is wrong for pruning, which takes place in July through August. Both renditions have an old pedigree, and Gordon suggests that there may be a double reference here.[61] Third, there is the cooing of the turtledove, a bird known to return to Palestine in early April.

13   This verse provides more clues of early spring. The *fig tree ripens its fruit.* The *blossoms* of the vine give off their scent. The warmth and pleasant fragrance of the early spring draw people outside. *Fig tree (tᵉʾēnâ)* and *vine (gepen)* occur about a dozen times together as a pair and often denote security and prosperity.[62] In the Song, agrarian settings are often the

60. A. Lemaire ("*Zāmîr* dans la tablette de Gezer et le Cantique des Cantiques," *VT* 35 [1975]: 15-26) argues on the basis of the Gezer Calendar that *zmr* means the time of grape gathering (*"vendange"*). However, I remain unclear as to how this helps us decide on the correct choice of the possible cognates.

61. So C. Gordon, "New Directions," *Bulletin of the American Society of Papyrologists* 15 (1978): 59-66, and idem, "Asymmetric Janus Parallelism," *Eretz-Israel* 16 (1982): 80-81. In the latter article, he defines "asymmetric Janus parallelism" as "when a polyseme parallels what precedes it with one meaning, and what follows it with a different meaning." I am skeptical of this supposed poetic device because I doubt that even the most literate reader could be counted on to detect such a subtle use of language.

62. *NIDOTTE,* vol. 4, p. 268.

place of intimacy and lovemaking between the couple. The verb in the first colon *(ripens, from ḥnt)* is unusual; its two other occurrences refer to the act of embalming a corpse (Gen. 50:2, 26). Snaith, citing M. V. Fox, suggests that the concepts of embalming a body and the ripening of a fruit may not be as far apart as first impressions might indicate. The Egyptian practice of embalming a body required that certain liquid spices be introduced into body, while the ripening of a fruit might be understood to be the infusion of sap through the branches into the hard fruit, thus making it soft.[63] The word for the fruit *(pag)* in the first line does refer to the hard green fig before it matures. The word is a *hapax legomenon* in biblical Hebrew but is attested in Arabic and postbiblical Hebrew. That the ripening of the fig is a sign of spring is a figure also exploited in the New Testament (Mark 13:28: "Now, learn a lesson from the fig tree. When its buds become tender and its leaves begin to sprout, you know without being told that summer is near"). Yet it is not only the ripening of the fig but the smell of the vine that is a telltale sign of spring, the auspicious time for lovemaking. The vineyard is mentioned often in the Song (1:6; 2:15; 6:11; 7:9, 13 [English 7:8, 12]; 8:11-12). The word for *blossom (sᵉmādar)* also occurs at 7:10-13 (English 7:9-12). There is debate over exactly what stage of the blossom the word refers to, and some even have suggested that it is a geographical reference (and thus "Semadar vines") based on a reference in the Ebla tablets.[64] However, to suggest a proper or geographical name is a last-ditch effort at understanding the word, and the material from Ebla has not been made accessible enough yet for us to confirm that such a meaning would be appropriate in this context.

Verses 11-13 list a number of phenomena associated with spring. Poetically, it thus evokes a scene of newness, vigor, freshness, joy, expectation — a context for joyous lovemaking.[65]

As mentioned in the commentary at 2:10, this central part of the man's invitation to the woman ends the way it begins, with his invitation for the woman to come away with him, presumably to the country where the smells are sweet.

14 This long verse is in doubtful relationship with the previous verses as the inclusio of 10b and 13c gives those verses a sense of closure. Yet verse 14 continues the theme of the man's invitation to the woman. He wants her to come with him. She is presently separated from him, indeed hidden from him. He wants her to join him. Further, she is in a barren and perhaps threatening environment, and he desires to be with her. The barren rocks

---

63. Snaith, *Song of Songs*, p. 39.
64. *NIDOTTE*, vol. 3, p. 685.
65. My thanks to Robert Hubbard for unpacking the imagery of springtime in this illuminating way (personal communication).

and cliffs where she presently lives may be contrasted with the fruitful, sweet-smelling garden and vineyard locations where lovemaking takes place. We must remember that we are reading a poem and not a historical narrative. There is not a real woman playing hide-and-seek in a real rocky wilderness. The poet rather evokes a mood and sends a message of desire and invitation.

He addresses her as *dove (yônâ)*. He has already compared her eyes to doves in 1:15, but here it is a nickname, an epithet. As Pope informs us, "the gentleness and amativeness of the dove make it a fitting universal symbol of love and peace."[66] As he recognizes, and Keel expands upon,[67] the dove may also have reference to the goddess of love of the ancient Near East. In both Mesopotamia and Canaan, dove figurines have been associated with the love goddess cult. Keel puts it well when he claims that the man's name for the woman "confesses that in the beloved the speaker encounters love — if not the love-goddess — in person." *The Dictionary of Biblical Imagery* suggests that in this context another quality of the dove is highlighted, that is, its "ability to hide and nest in hidden, out-of-the-way places." Similar uses may be found in Jeremiah 48:28 and Ezekiel 7:16.[68]

The poem locates the woman in the *rock (selaʿ)* or the *cliff (madrēgâ)*. The first word is a general term for rocks, usually indicating rocks of substantial size. It is relatively common. The second word is rare, occurring in Jeremiah 49:16 and Obadiah 3 in reference to the cliffs in which the Edomites lived. A place like Petra with its narrow passes and its caves may give us a good picture of the scene. After all, she hides in the *crevices (ḥagwê)* or the *hiding place (sēter)*. The man's invitation calls her out of hiding. Her inaccessibility heightens his desire. His excitement rises as he waits for his first glimpse of her.

He wants her to come out so that he might see her. That is the effect of the motive clause (beginning with *kî*) that concludes the verse. In the process of the invitation, he also compliments her. She is a pleasure of sight and sound. Her form and her voice are attractive. The first, her *form (marēh)*, is a difficult word to render especially in its first occurrence in the verse. It is a noun form of the common verbal root "to see" *(rʾh)*, and its most natural translation is "appearance," but that English word does not work well in the line with the verb "see." *Form* seems a good rendition, though somewhat vague. Some scholars[69] assert that the word should be translated "face." The adjectives that he uses to compliment her *voice (agreeable: ʿarēb)* and her *form (pleasant: nāʾweh)* are strongly, but not overpoweringly, positive. We

---

66. Pope, *Song of Songs*, p. 399.
67. Keel, *The Song of Songs*, p. 106.
68. *The Dictionary of Biblical Imagery*, p. 217.
69. Murphy, *The Song of Songs*, p. 139.

have chosen to render them agreeable and pleasant, respectively. Notice that there is a chiastic relationship in the last four cola:

let me see your *form!* Let me hear your *voice!*
For your *voice* is agreeable, and your *form* is pleasant.

15   This little ditty is easy to understand in isolation but difficult in context — not that the former has no ambiguities, as, e.g., who is speaking and who is addressed. Murphy suggests that the woman speaks, in answer to the man's request to hear her voice. He even goes so far as to suggest that her brief song has no real meaning to the context; she is just answering his desire to hear her voice. This approach seems a strategy of last resort. It may well be, as Keel proposes, a separate poem, placed in its present position by the catchword *in bloom (m^esādar),* for which see 2:13. On the surface, however, the picture that the verse evokes is easy enough to understand. There are *foxes (šû'ālîm)* loose in the vineyard, destroying the fruit. That foxes were pests in a vineyard is attested by a poem of Theocritus of Comatas from approximately 275 B.C.: "I hate the brushtail foxes, that soon as day declines/ Come creeping to their vintaging mid goodman Micon's vines."[70] As F. Landy points out, "foxes are guileful, riddling creatures in fable and proverb; and thus comparable to the cunning serpent."[71] Elsewhere in the Song, the vineyard represents the woman (1:6) or the place of lovemaking (6:11). In either case, the presence of the foxes implies a threat to the relationship.[72] Identifying that threat more closely, say as rival, unwanted suitors, stretches the text beyond what we can honestly defend.[73] We should just adopt a gen-

70. Quoted in Keel, *The Song of Songs,* pp. 109-10, citing Theocritus, "The Goatherd and the Shepherd," in *The Greek Bucolic Poets,* trans. J. M. Edmonds (London: William Heinemann; New York: G. P. Putnam's Sons, 1912), p. 77.

71. F. Landy, *Paradoxes of Paradise: Identity and Difference in the Song of Songs* (Sheffield: Almond, 1983), p. 240. He also suggests that the fact that the foxes are little indicates the problems are small as well. This may be pressing the metaphor a bit too far, though such judgments are a matter of intuition.

72. That foxes have a negative connotation may be supported by the study of Robin Way, who concluded that in the Bible the fox and jackal, along with other carnivorous animals, "are related to death"; cf. *NIDOTTE,* vol. 4, p. 311. For a brief listing of some minor interpretive options on this verse and the identification of the foxes with concrete referents, see A. Pleuel, "Author and Translator: The Stylist's Work with the Song of Songs," *The Bible Translator* 47 (1996): 116.

73. Though Walton, Matthews, and Chavalas (*The Bible Background Commentary: Old Testament,* p. 578) suggest a connection with Egyptian love poems where "the foxes represent sexually aggressive men, rather like the term 'wolf' in American idiom." It is certainly illegitimate to understand the use of fox here in the light of Jesus calling Herod "that fox" (so P. Cotterell, "The Greatest Song: Some Linguistic Considerations,"

eral interpretation, associating the foxes with obstacles to the blossoming relationship. This approach is taken by George Schwab in his excellent study of passages within the Song that raise caution about the dangers of love.[74] Keel alerts us to the fact that the fox represents a mischievous lover in ancient Egyptian love poetry, citing Papyrus Harris 500, group A, no. 4:

> My heart is not yet done with your lovemaking,
>> my (little) [fox]!
>>> Your liquor is (your) lovemaking.[75]

16   While the speaker of the previous verse is ambiguous, we have no doubt about the fact that it is the woman who speaks here.[76] In a phrase that recurs at 6:3 (with slight variation of word order; see also 7:12 [English 7:11]), she affirms their mutual affection. She uses the language of ownership: she belongs to him and he belongs to her. This idea may offend some modern notions of relationship between the sexes, but it should not since it is a voluntary relationship of concern and love; it is not abuse. It has a rough parallel in the covenant formula "I will be their God, and they will be my people" (Jer. 7:23; 11:4; Ezek. 34:30).[77] That he *grazes among the lilies* seems to indicate some act of intimacy. She is elsewhere likened to a vineyard or garden, and he is there partaking of it. In 4:5 we see the same idiom, but it there refers to her two breasts, which are like fawns that graze among the lilies (see commentary there for the significance of the metaphor in reference to the breasts). We might also point to 5:13, where the man's lips are said to be like perfumed lilies, and suggest that there the reference is to the woman's lips on which he feeds. Some scholars do not take the lilies as

---

The Bible Translator 47 [1996]: 104, who concludes that "the vineyards (of this verse) represent the virginity of the northern girls and the foxes, the little foxes, are the young men who despoil them").

74. Schwab, "The Song of Songs' Cautionary Message," pp. 95-97.

75. Fox takes the interesting approach that it is the woman speaking in this verse and that she is teasing the man with a kind of "come on." The man is the fox and she, a young woman, is the vineyard.

76. She says that she is "his" *(lô)*.

77. Contra Snaith, *Song of Songs,* p. 42, who for some unknown reason argues that the relationship between the covenant formula and this phrase cannot be relevant because of the sexual overtones in the Song. The parallel certainly cannot be used to argue for an allegorical approach to the text, as suggested in A. Feuillet, "La forumule d'appartenance mutuelle (II, 16) et les interpretations divergentes du Cantique des Cantiques," *RB* 68 (1961): 5-38. The primary meaning is sexual. Yet in the light of the extensive use of the marriage metaphor to describe the relationship between God and humanity in the rest of Scripture (see Introduction: Theology), it seems odd to suggest that the two are mutually exclusive.

symbolic of the woman herself but as simply evoking a pastoral scene and feeling.[78]

17 The chapter ends with a verse that evokes romantic and sensual feelings, but when it comes down to a precise description of what the woman is saying, we are left with our heads shaking. First of all, what is the time reference of the verse? The temporal prepositional phrase that begins the verse (*'ad-še*) could be translated "until," "when," or perhaps "while," and that is just the beginning of the problems. When is it that the *day breaks* (literally the "day breathes"). Is it in the morning as the sun rises or in the evening when the cool winds come to blow away the morning's heat?[79] In short, is she asking him to stay all day or to stay all night? In the final analysis, we cannot decide with absolute certainty. One might expect the nighttime to be the more appropriate moment for a tryst, but there is the possibility of afternoon delights as well. At least we can see (and feel) her desire for intimacy in the verse.

Second, what is the force of the main verb of the verse, the imperative *turn*. Does this mean that he is turning to her or from her? Has he been absent? Here, the context suggests that she desires him to turn toward her, to be with her.

Third, what does it mean for him *to be like a gazelle or a young stag?* She earlier described her lover as a gazelle and stag in 2:9, highlighting the speed of the animals and also their sensuality. Here she commands him to be like these animals, showing her desire for his sensuality. Yet where is he to direct his energies? On *the mountains of Bether* raises the final major issue of this enigmatic verse. What or perhaps where are these mountains? Even though we simply transliterate the name Bether, it is unlikely that it is simply a place name. If so, we know of no such place from other sources. The root *btr* means "to cut into pieces" or, perhaps more relevantly to this context, "to cut in half." Many scholars suggest that the root connotes cleavage and that she is inviting him to play with her breasts. Pope goes one further and notes another mound-like erogenous zone of the female (the so-called *mons veneris*).[80] Perhaps Murphy is on safest grounds when he simply suggests that these mountains "seem to be a symbol of the woman herself."[81]

---

78. Gerleman, *Ruth, Das Hohelied,* pp. 127-28.

79. As Murphy (*The Song of Songs,* p. 139) puts it, "In one case the words are understood to mean the afternoon breeze (Gen 3:8), and the lengthening of the shadows, as night approaches. In the other, the reference would be to the morning wind, and the disappearance of darkness, as day dawns."

80. Pope, *Song of Songs,* p. 410. While I certainly do not insist on Pope's understanding of this phrase, I do not find Snaith's (*Song of Songs,* p. 44) objection that the woman's vagina would only be a single mountain convincing. After all, as with breasts, there is a cleavage, or slit if you will, in the woman's vagina as well.

81. Murphy, *The Song of Songs,* p. 139.

CHAPTER THREE

POEM NINE:
SEEKING AND (NOT) FINDING (3:1-5)

As we move from poem eight to poem nine, we have, in the words of T. Gledhill,[1] "a sudden change in mood. It progresses from yearning for his presence, through fear of loss and abandonment, to panicky action, leading to a rushing torrent of relief when she finds him, clutches him, and will not let him go until they have consummated their relationship." Besides the mood change, we also have a theme change with an emphasis on the woman seeking and, at first, not finding, but then eventually finding.[2] The theme of seeking her absent lover is repeated in the poem of 5:2–6:2, but there her search takes on a much darker tone.

The setting of the present poem begins in the woman's bed (v. 1), moves to the public areas of the city (vv. 2-4b), and then to the privacy of the mother's bedroom (vv. 4c-5). The whole scene is somewhat surreal, and indeed it has been debated on the basis of the opening words of the poem (*on my bed at night*) whether or not this was a dream fantasy rather than reality. Our own view of the song undercuts this discussion, as explained in the commentary on the first verse, since we believe the poet is creating a world rather than describing an actual event.

This poem is a poem of yearning that finds fulfillment at the end. However, it expresses her yearning through the description of an experience. It is not entirely clear to whom the woman is speaking at first. Nonetheless, in the very last verse of the poem (v. 5), the woman turns to the chorus and, for a second time (see 2:7), cautions them concerning love. In the light of this

1. Gledhill, *The Message of the Song of Songs*, p. 144.
2. See comment on this theme in G. S. Ogden, "Some Translational Issues in the Song of Songs," *The Bible Translator* 41 (1990): 225.

final verse, it is possible that the entire poem should be understood as an address to them.

In an interesting study, Jack Lundbom suggests that Song of Songs 3:1-4 shapes the episode reported in John 20:11-18. In the latter text, Mary Magdalene comes to the tomb looking for Jesus. She cannot find his body, and so she questions two angels about his location. She turns and, though she does not recognize him at first, encounters the risen Jesus. She holds onto him, but he says he must go. Lundbom's study is provocative and persuasive as he maps not only the similarities but also the differences between the two texts. The most poignant of the latter is "that although he will not come to her mother's house, Mary — along with others — will go to his, to a heavenly paradise where God is Father and Jesus is Son." Like the beloved in the Song of Songs (see Introduction: Theological Message), Mary has a sense of "paradise regained."[3]

The Woman

1. *On my bed[4] at night[5] I searched for the one my soul loves.*
    I searched for him, but I did not find him.[6]
2. *"I will get up and go around in the city,*
        in the streets[7] and the public areas.[8]
    I will search for the one my soul loves."
    I searched, but I did not find him.
3. *The guards found me, those who patrol the city.*
        "Have you seen the one my soul loves?"
4. *It was a little while after I left them that I found the one my soul*
        loves.

3. J. R. Lundbom, "Song of Songs 3:1-4," *Interp* 49 (1995): 172-75. Both quotes are from p. 175.

4. As in today's language, the word *bed (miškāb)* can indicate "a place for sexual intimacies" (*NIDOTTE,* vol. 3, p. 1129).

5. Literally, "at nights," the plural of night *(lēlôt)* is used here. Some (NEB; Fox [*The Song of Songs and the Ancient Egyptian Love Songs,* p. 60]; Garrett [*Proverbs, Ecclesiastes, Song of Songs,* p. 397]) think that this means it is a desire that happens on many nights; others, such as Snaith (*Song of Songs,* p. 46), argue, more persuasively, that "the plural form here is a so-called plural of composition denoting not a succession of nights but rather night-time in general" (also Pope, *Song of Songs,* p. 415).

6. The LXX adds a sentence here: "I called him, but he did not answer me" *(ekalesa auton kai ouch hypēkousen mou).* The NEB and the RSV (check the NRSV) also add it, but it may well be a harmonizing gloss based on 5:6.

7. The word *šûq* only occurs four times in the Hebrew Bible (Prov. 7:8; Eccles. 12:4, 5; and here). Its Arabic cognate means market, a meaning that is also found in postbiblical Hebrew.

8. The *rᵉhôb* is a large open space in a city, a public square or a plaza of some sort (*NIDOTTE,* vol. 3, pp. 1092-93).

I grabbed him and would not let him go
until I brought him to my mother's house,
to the room where she conceived me.[9]
5. *I adjure you, daughters of Jerusalem,*
by the gazelles or the deer of the field,
not to awaken or arouse love until it desires.

1 The opening phrase of this five-verse poem is enigmatic. Does *on my bed at night* (*'al-miškābî balêlôt*) indicate that this is a night fantasy? Did she really get up and go around the city searching for her lover or did she just imagine the scene? Does it mean that she first looked for him in bed, where she expected to find him, but when he was nowhere to be found, she got up and set off searching for him in the city? Once we remember that this is poetry and not the account of an actual event, then the issue becomes less pressing. In any case, the central motive of the poem is quite clear: she is pining for her absent lover and she pursues him until she finds him and brings him back to a place of intimacy where they can experience union. Thus, again, we get a pattern that we have seen and will see repeated numerous times in the Song: absence and longing lead to search and discovery, which results in intimacy and joy.

Throughout this poem the lover is called *the one my soul loves*. He is named by her desire. We should not misunderstand the role of the word *soul* here, as if it indicates some kind of disembodied love. She is interested not only in his internal self but also in his body, as so much of the Song makes clear. Soul (*nepeš*) in the Old Testament does not refer to the intangible parts of a human being but often means the whole person (e.g., Ps. 7:3 [English 7:2]; Lev. 26:11).

Her initial search results in failure *(I did not find him)*, and thus she sets off on a broader quest that is described in the following verses.

2 In the opening verse of the poem, the woman initiated a search

---

9. Note should be taken of Ogden's ("Some Translational Issues in the Song of Songs," pp. 225-27) interpretation of the phrase *ḥeder hōrātî* as a participle that looks to the near future with a suffixed personal pronoun that is possessive, with the result that the colon does not relate to her mother's past conception but to her hope that she will conceive in the near future. However, the parallel with mother here in the preceding colon and the use of the phrase in Hos. 2:7 (English 2:5) militates against this understanding. Also, perhaps we can find some support for the traditional rendering of this phrase from the fact that the Sumerian love songs talk about the "entry into the bride's house as the first formal act of marriage, after which came the union of the couple"; so Y. Sefati, *Love Songs in Sumerian Literature* (Ramat-Gan: Bar-Ilan University Press, 1999), pp. 3-5. He further comments that there are many examples where the groom goes to the house of the bride's parents, but only one where the reverse happens.

for her lover that began when she discovered him missing from her bed. Now she determines to get up and pursue him in the city.[10] The city is a place hostile to intimate relationship (see the similar theme in 5:2-7), particularly when compared with the safety and privacy of the bedroom. After all, the city, especially the *street (šûq)* and the *public square (rᵉḥôb)*, is a place teeming with people, hardly conducive to romance. Even at night, when the crowds are not as large, the city is a hostile location, as we will observe in the next verse. In spite of the dangers, her mission is to find him and bring him back to the solitude of the bedroom, but, again, at least initially, her mission failed.

3 Her pursuit in bed and through the city has been futile thus far, and so she keeps looking, drawing the attention of the city guards. They are watchmen, the ones who patrol the city to keep things in order, and a desperate woman has caught their attention *(the guards found*[11] *me)*. She takes the opportunity to ask them whether they have seen her lover. Perhaps, she may have thought, they had noticed him while on their rounds. In the next encounter (5:7) with the city *guards (haššōmmᵉrîm)*, they will treat her roughly, but here they do not respond, at least explicitly, at all. In this context the encounter allows her to express her desire one more time with the question, *Have you seen the one my soul loves?* (for the lover's epithet, see 3:1).

D. Garrett[12] adopts a bizarre, quasi-allegorical view when he argues, on the basis of the metaphor of 6:4, that the woman is as beautiful as Jerusalem, that the city is the woman herself. If the city is the woman, then the guards must be her self-discipline to keep her virginity. Besides the fact that this approach does not respect the loose association of poems in the Song or the flexibility of metaphor, the woman hasn't been a virgin for quite some time in the Song, or in this particular poem (remember she expected to find him in her bed).

4 The passage does not say whether or not the city patrol led her to him, but it was soon thereafter that she finally found him. When she did, she grabbed him ardently and pulled him back to the privacy of her mother's bedroom. These actions certainly dispel a typical stereotype of the woman's "role" in a relationship. She is no passive wallflower waiting for the advances of the more active male. She grabs him and hauls him off to the privacy of the bedroom. Now, at least to us, the mother's bedroom is not necessarily the most romantic of places, but in the world of the Song it is a place associated

---

10. Notice that the first three verbs of this verse are cohortatives, which according to Murphy (*The Song of Songs,* p. 145) express "a simple resolution of will."

11. With Murphy (*The Song of Songs,* p. 145) note the irony that she was searching to find, but in turn she herself is found, not by the lover but by the guards.

12. Garrett, *Proverbs, Ecclesiastes, Song of Songs,* p. 398.

with intimacies.[13] It is the place of the previous generation's romantic liaison and thus an indirect way to indicate that the woman's intention is to make love. We will see a similar movement from a public place to the privacy of the mother's bedroom in 8:2. As J. M. Munro states, "her mother's house (3:4; 8:2) is also the place of security *par excellence.*"[14] Perhaps further the mother's room is noted because mothers played an integral role in arranging marriages for their daughters. That is the persuasive conclusion reached by D. Hubbard in his comments on Naomi's charge to her two bereaved daughters-in-law to return to their "mother's house" (Ruth 1:8-9). He notes further that Isaac and Rebekah consummate their marriage in their mother's tent, according to Genesis 24:67. In addition, it is interesting to note that it is Solomon's mother who crowns him on the day of his marriage (Song 3:11).[15]

Another possibility for understanding "the house of the mother" and the "place where she conceived me" is the womb.[16] If so, the reference is to the act of sex.

5   That this poem culminates in the act of love is underlined by the warning that the woman brings to the circle of young women around here. Her passion led her in an energetic pursuit of her man. Once she found him, she brought him to a place of intimacy. What woman would not want to feel her passion and find its satisfaction? Yet the woman wisely tells the others not to rush into love, but rather to wait for the right moment (see comments at 2:7), the moment indeed she has apparently found.

This warning is a leitmotif that runs through the Song. It appeared for the first time in 2:7, and the commentary there may be consulted for the details of the verse (see also 8:4).

POEM TEN:
A ROYAL WEDDING PROCESSION (3:6-11)

Song of Songs 3:6-11 clearly stands out as a separate poetic unit. It begins with a question that draws the reader's attention out to the wilderness where what is soon to be identified as a palanquin (and later a litter) is kicking up

13. It is interesting to note that in the Sumerian love poems "the groom is the one who goes or is brought to the house of the bride's parents. By contrast, we find only one example in which the lover brings his beloved bride to his home, and it does not belong to the marriage ceremony"; so Sefati, *Love Songs in Sumerian Literature,* p. 104.

14. Munro, *Spikenard and Saffron,* p. 70.

15. R. Hubbard, *The Book of Ruth,* NICOT (Grand Rapids: Eerdmans, 1988), pp. 101-2.

16. Gledhill, *The Message of the Song of Songs,* p. 145.

dust that looks like a pillar of smoke (3:6). The remainder of the poem describes this luxurious vehicle as well as the guards that accompany it. The poem concludes with a focus on the wedding crown of Solomon (3:11).

Indeed, King Solomon plays a major, though enigmatic, role in this poem. Solomon's name occurs a mere seven times in the book, including once in the superscription (1:1), a second time in a description of tent curtains (1:5), and two times at the end of the book (8:11, 12). Here, his name occurs three times (3:7, 9, 11), but his role is still not certain, as will become clear when we discuss interpretive options.

We may describe three main schools of thought concerning the role of Solomon and the meaning of the poem, though even these schools have variations. Each school reflects the interpreter's overall understanding of the Song of Songs (see the Introduction for extensive description and analysis).

First, perhaps the least likely (see criticism in the Introduction) interpretation is a mythological approach to the text. T. J. Meek argued that in the original form of the poem it was not Solomon but rather a god whose name was Shulman (or Shelem) who was being brought to the temple for the sacred marriage rite. More recently, G. Gerleman connects the poem to "a description of a procession to and from the Theban necropolis in Egypt during the annual Opet festival, when the god Amun was transported at night from Karnak to Luxor."[17] Such interpretations arise from those commentators who have a cultic/mythological approach to the Song, which was criticized in the Introduction (see pp. 44-46). The only textual evidence used to support this approach is the reference to the pillar or column of smoke. In the Exodus event, this represents God's presence with the people as they wander from Sinai to the promised land (Exod. 13:21-22). However, though perhaps hinting at a meaning on the divine-human level in a general sense, Gerleman takes this connection much too far.

Second, a more widely held approach than the first is the interpretation that 3:6-11 describes an actual historical event — that is, a wedding processional associated with Solomon. The only question for advocates of this approach concerns the identity of the person in the palanquin and that person's destination. Connected to this question is the additional issue of who is speaking. Perhaps the most common view is that Solomon is in the vehicle, and he is going to his beloved's house. In such a view, the woman herself could be seen as the speaker. However, since the occupant of the palanquin is not specifically named, but only its owner, there are some who believe, on the

---

17. See the excellent article on this verse by R. Wakely, "ḥᵃtunnâ," *NIDOTTE*, vol. 2, pp. 328-30, whose survey of interpretive options helped me organize my own survey here. She is here describing Gerleman's approach in his commentary (*Ruth, Das Hohelied,* 2nd ed. [1981]).

basis of the feminine demonstrative pronoun that begins the poem (see v. 1), that the woman is in the palanquin; that the chorus of young women speaks in verses 6-10; and then finally that the woman speaks to them in verse 11 after she arrives.[18] Still others, for instance, J. Balchin, argue that Solomon and the woman are in the palanquin and are together heading for Jerusalem.[19]

Third, throughout the commentary, we have maintained an approach to the Song that appreciates its poetic quality. Here too, we understand that this poem offers not historical description but rather a poetic description that draws upon the traditional opulence of Solomon's life and kingdom in order to celebrate love and marriage. The Solomon/royal fiction is being exploited here, not because of Solomon's reputation in the area of love per se (where he has a dubious reputation!), but rather because of his incredible wealth. In other words, this poem expresses the woman's poetic imagination as she reflects upon the wonders of love and, in the case of this poem at least, marriage.

Because of its connection to marriage, this is the poem that is most like the only other marriage poem in the Bible, Psalm 45. Perhaps in both cases the language used to describe the love and marriage of a king draws on an actual historical person or marriage, but that is not the point. Both the psalm and the poem in the Song can be, and are intended to be, appropriated by other nonroyal couples.

The Woman

6. *What[20] is this coming up[21] from the wilderness*
   like a pillar[22] of smoke,

18. This is the view of Delitzsch, *Proverbs, Ecclesiastes, Song of Solomon*, pp. 60-70.

19. J. A. Balchin, "Song of Songs," in *The New Bible Commentary*, 4th ed. (Downers Grove, IL: InterVarsity, 1994), p. 623.

20. So the NRSV. Some, such as the NIV, translate *mî* as "who." The Hebrew word is more typically translated who, but *what* is also philologically justified on the basis of the Akkadian cognate (also "what" is the force of *mî* in Judg. 13:17 and Mic. 1:5). The word this *(zô't)* is feminine and may refer to the feminine noun *palanquin*. In the context of the parallel line in 8:5, however, "who" is called for. For the argument that the context allows a translation "who" since the focus is on the bridegroom Solomon, see P. B. Dirksen, "Song of Songs III 6-7," *VT* 39 (1989): 219-25.

21. The verb suggests that the object is moving toward Jerusalem. One "went up" *('ālâ)* to Jerusalem, particularly from the wilderness to its east; cf. Keel, *The Song of Songs*, p. 126, with a reference to Ps. 122:4.

22. According to *NIDOTTE*, vol. 4, p. 289, the word *tîmarâ* is derived from the noun *tamar*, which means "palm tree." Thus, *tîmarâ* denotes a palm-shaped column. Besides being in Song of Songs 3:6, the noun also appears in Joel 3:3 (English 2:30) in reference to columns of smoke that will rise up in the last days.

133

> *perfumed with myrrh and frankincense,*
> *from all the scented powders of the trader?*

7. *Look sharp,[23] it is the palanquin of Solomon;*
> *sixty heroes surround it,*
> *Israel's heroes.*

8. *All of them bear the sword;[24]*
> *they are battle-trained.*
> *Each one has his sword on his thigh,*
> *against the terrors of the night.[25]*

9. *The king has made a litter[26] for himself;*
> *that is, Solomon — from the wood of Lebanon.*

10. *Its posts[27] he made of silver;*
> *its canopy[28] of gold;*
> *its riding seat[29] of purple;[30]*
> *its interior[31] inlaid[32] with love[33] by the daughters of Jerusalem.*

11. *Come and look, O daughters of Zion,*
> *at King Solomon with the crown with which his mother crowned*
> *him,*

23. For *hinnēh,* which functions as an attention-getter, cf. *NIDOTTE,* vol. 4, p. 1032.

24. Pope (*Song of Songs,* p. 435) suggests "held fast by the sword," i.e., "skilled with the sword."

25. Literally, "nights" *(lêlôt)* for the use of the plural here; see the analogous situation in 3:1.

26. For an early etymological study of the word *'appiryôn,* see F. Rundgren, "*'prywn:* Tragsessel, Sänfte," *ZAW* 74 (1962): 70-72. He opposes the idea that the word is a Persian loanword and sees it rather as connected to the Greek *phoreion.*

27. From *'amûd,* which means column, pillar, but in this case either posts or perhaps (carrying) poles.

28. From the verbal root *rpd* "to spread out, support." This is the only use of the noun form, but perhaps the Arabic *rifida* "saddle-blanket" provides insight into its meaning.

29. For this meaning of *merkāb* also see Lev. 15:9; 1 Kings 5:6 (English 4:26).

30. According to Pope, *Song of Songs,* p. 444, *'argāmān* "designates cloth dyed with the reddish purpose dye extracted from the murex shellfish. The dye was very expensive and became at an early period the emblem of royalty."

31. Literally, "its midst" *(tôkô).*

32. A *hapax legomenon,* though perhaps the noun *riṣpa* "pavement" is related.

33. G. R. Driver ("Supposed Arabisms in the Old Testament," *JBL* 55 [1936]: 101-20) argued that the word here is not "love" but, based on an Arabic cognate, "leather." This seems an unnecessary and stretched argument, since "love" fits the context well and Arabic cognates are always easy to find. D. Grossberg ("Canticles 3:10 in the Light of a Homeric Analogue and Biblical Poetics," *BTB* 11 [1981]: 74-76) supports Driver's argument but suggests that there is a double entendre here, the poet wanting us to understand both "love" and "leather."

on the day of his wedding,
on the day of his heart's joy!

6   The new poem is introduced by a question that draws our imagination to a cloud of smoke rising in the wilderness. We will see a similar rhetorical strategy through the use of a closely worded question in 8:5. Again, in 3:6, it is clear that a poet and not a historian speaks. All that is seen is the smoke in the distance, but it is described not only by vision but also by smell, which can only be the result of poetic imagination since smells do not cover such a distance. The smell is the sweet smell of perfume, indeed, the finest smells including *myrrh* and *frankincense*. Such scents are not native to Israel but are brought in from far distant places like Arabia and India, a fact that adds to the exotic and luxurious atmosphere of the scene. The question draws our attention and raises our curiosity as to what possibly could be on the horizon.[34]

7   It is not clear who is speaking in this section. Certainly in 3:11 it is the young woman addressing the daughters of Zion again, but should this whole section be ascribed to the young woman (so NIV), or should verses 8-10 perhaps be placed in the mouth of the daughters of Zion (so NLT)? The case is not clear. If it is the former, though, we can imagine that the woman is speaking throughout to the daughters of Zion. Since there are no clear indications of a change of speaker after verse 5, we will side lightly with the NIV and associate the whole poem with the voice of the young woman.

In this verse we get the answer to the question raised in verse 6. Who is it? It is Solomon! The specific answer to the question is "it is the palanquin of Solomon," which is why the NRSV translates the subject in verse 6 as "What" rather than "Who." Yet the real object of attention is the occupant, not the vehicle, though significant attention will be lavished in the following verses on the vehicle. However, even that attention is to accentuate Solomon's wealth and the grandeur of his wedding.

Before proceeding, we should mention the viewpoint that it is the woman who is in the palanquin. A lot of weight is put on the similarly worded rhetorical questions found in 6:10 and 8:5. In those contexts the answer to the question is "the young woman." However, we have to study the local context of the question before identifying the occupant. The only way Gledhill[35] can argue that the woman is the occupant of the question is to treat 3:6 as completely separate from the following verses, which yields an inelegant hypothesis.

---

34. G. Barbiero ("Die Liebe der Töchter Jerusalems: Hld 3,10b MT im Kontext von 3,6-11," *BZ* 39 [1995]: 101) draws our attention to the fact that the description in vv. 6-11 go from outside to inside ("von aussen nach innen").

35. Gledhill, *The Message of the Song of Songs,* p. 148.

The word translated *palanquin (miṭṭâ)* is literally a "bed" or "couch." In other words, it is a piece of furniture on which one reclines. However, from the context we know it is a moveable recliner, and so a palanquin — although the English word is rare it seems a fairly precise equivalent since it denotes "a conveyance, usually for one person, consisting of an enclosed litter borne on the shoulders of men by means of poles."[36] This palanquin is a symbol not only of wealth and luxury but also of power, since it is accompanied by a troop of sixty men, and not ordinary men but distinguished soldiers. It is commonly pointed out that the retinue of sixty men is twice that which accompanied David, according to 2 Samuel 23:18-19, 23.

8 Verse 8 dwells on the heroes who accompany the palanquin of Solomon. Talking about their skills emphasizes the grandeur of the litter and the importance of its occupant. They are battle-ready. They not only have a sword ready-to-hand, but they know how to use it; that is, they are *battle-trained*. The reference to *terrors of the night (pahad balêlôt)* shows that their protection never stops. They are constantly ready for any threat, especially at night, because evil often seeks the cover of darkness. There has been some speculation, based on a reference in Tobit 3:7-17, that the night threat is demons who "were believed to be especially dangerous at nuptial affairs and to lie in wait for newlyweds."[37]

9 The next two verses describe the opulence and beauty of the palanquin/litter. *Litter ('appiryôn)* is the second of the two words to describe this portable bed (see v. 6 for *miṭṭâ*).[38] The word occurs only here in the Hebrew Bible,[39] but from the context we understand it to signify the portable recliner already referred to in the poem. Thus, we choose the English translation *litter*, though sedan chair might also have worked. Solomon is described as its maker, though it is doubtful we are supposed to imagine Solomon with tools in hand. It is rather that he had this beautiful and comfortable vehicle made for him, for his own use.

At this point, we should remark on Solomon's role in this poem (for Solomon's connection with the book as a whole, see the commentary on 1:1 and the Introduction), taking note of the ambiguity of the references. In this poem, I believe it is Solomon's wealth and grandeur that are being applied to emphasize the magnificence of the wedding and, by association, the marriage relationship itself. It is not imparting historical information as such,

36. So *Webster's New Collegiate Dictionary* (Springfield, MA: G. and C. Merriam, Co., 1951), p. 604.

37. Pope, *Song of Songs,* p. 435.

38. We believe the context indicates that the two words are referring to the same vehicular recliner.

39. As Murphy comments (*The Song of Songs,* p. 149), "There is no certainty whether it is originally Greek, Sanskrit, or Persian" in origin.

though it may be built on the remembrance of Solomon's ornate weddings. The Song is not about Solomon as such, though it uses Solomon and his legend both to praise love, as in this poem, and to warn about the dangers of illicit love, as in 8:11-12.

The parallelism of this verse is difficult to understand. Where should we make the break? Is the name Solomon a gloss?[40] Translating the verse while preserving the syntax would result in the following rendering:

A litter he has made for himself the king Solomon from the wood of Lebanon.

We would be tempted to translate the line according to the following poetic format:

King Solomon has made a litter for himself
from the trees of Lebanon.[41]

However, this creates a large imbalance between the first and the second cola, more obvious in the Hebrew where the word count would be five to two. Thus, we have suggested the break between king and Solomon, though the result seems a little awkward in English if judged according to the standards of prose.

It remains to comment on the composition of the litter. It is made from the wood of Lebanon. The wood of Lebanon simply "represented the best quality lumber available."[42] As such, it would be relatively rare and expensive, and thus it is an indication of wealth and opulence. It was used for the temple and the royal palace, for instance (1 Kings 5:13 [English 4:33]; 5:20, 23, 28 [English 5:6, 9, 14]; 7:2; 10:17, 21). During Solomon's lifetime, he imported it through the agency of Hiram of Tyre. Usually cedar was associated with Lebanon, but other types of precious trees were also available, although here perhaps the scent of cedar is also being called to mind.

10   This verse continues the description of the litter begun in verse 9. Different parts of the vehicle are described one by one. We might expect, accordingly, to get a better picture of the litter; however, for the most part rare, apparently technical terms are used whose nuances escape us (see notes to the translation). The overall impression of the description of the litter is nonetheless impossible to miss. This object is luxurious; it radiates wealth and power. It is made out of the most precious of materials: silver, gold, and

40. So suggests the textual note in *BHS*.
41. The Septuagint divides the verse in this manner, as does Murphy (*The Song of Songs*, p. 148), though he transfers *'appiryôn* to the second colon to balance things out.
42. *NIDOTTE*, vol. 4, p. 901.

purple cloth, all associated with royalty. Purple cloth was particularly rare, being made from a pigment from the murex shellfish. According to R. L. Alden,[43] the Phoenicians were the only ones who could make the dye.

The most difficult colon of the verse is the last one. What does it mean that *its interior* is *inlaid with love?* We might expect an inlay of pearl or some other precious object, but an emotion like love? It appears that the emphasis has shifted from the objective qualities of the litter to its subjective qualities. The women are skilled at the craft of decorating the interior, and they do so not out of compulsion but out of affection.

Some commentators unnecessarily resort to changes to make the colon conform more closely to the previous three. Such a view misunderstands parallelism, which actually allows for considerable variation between related cola. One approach is through emendations, most notably that of Gerleman, who prefers *ᵃbānîm* (stones) to *love (ʾahᵃbâ);*[44] the other approach is to retain the word but appeal to an Arabic cognate for the meaning "leather."[45] M. H. Pope understands the word as love but takes it as referring to love scenes that decorated the interior. In his words, "love scenes are an appropriate decoration for a love couch."[46]

11 The poetic structure of this verse is difficult and complicated by the question of its connection to the end of verse 10. Many modern commentators buck the versification and argue that the concluding reference in verse 10 to the daughters of Jerusalem should begin the last verse of the section, and indeed it is true that the result would be a nice chiastic beginning to verse 11:

> O daughters of Jerusalem, come;
> look, O daughters of Zion.

The resulting parallel is so compelling that we cannot rule this out as a possibility, except that the "daughters of Jerusalem" is prefixed by a *mem,* which we have taken in an agentive sense[47] in the previous verse. Pope, R. E. Murphy, and others argue that something else is going on here. For instance, they suggest that perhaps the Masoretes got confused about an enclitic *mem* that was connected with the word "love" and mistakenly prefaced it to daughters.[48] I personally find such an argument all too convenient and overused by scholars who know their Ugaritic perhaps a little too well.

43. R. L. Alden, *"ʾargāmān," NIDOTTE,* vol. 1, p. 498.
44. Gerleman, *Ruth, Das Hohelied,* pp. 139, 142.
45. Driver, "Supposed Arabisms in the Old Testament," pp. 101-20.
46. Pope, *Song of Songs,* p. 445.
47. B. K. Waltke and M. O'Connor, *An Introduction to Biblical Hebrew Syntax* (Winona Lake, IN: Eisenbrauns, 1990), p. 213, example 13.
48. Pope, *Song of Songs,* p. 446; Murphy, *The Song of Songs,* p. 150.

In any case, the *daughters of Zion* only appears here in the Song, but is a suitable and expected alternate for daughters of Jerusalem; in other words, the two phrases refer to the same group of women (see commentary at 1:4). Zion, after all, is the metaphorical center or apex of Jerusalem, the location of the holy place, a metonymy for the city as a whole.

The woman, more experienced in love, urges the younger women to rush out and gaze on Solomon wearing his crown, a crown associated with his marriage. This is "the only unambiguous use of the piel of *'tr, crown*," since its qal meaning is "to surround" and the other piel occurrences could be either.[49] We are uncertain whether this is his royal crown or a special wedding crown. We might think of the former since the latter is unattested elsewhere, but then again so is the idea that the queen mother crowns her son at either his coronation or his wedding.[50] We may be dealing here more with poetic imagination than actual custom. In any case, the reference to the crown serves to add glory to the wedding ceremony, an impulse that we also observed with the description of the palanquin/litter in the immediately preceding verses.

The focus is on the *day of his wedding*. The word *wedding (ḥᵃtunnâ)* occurs only here in the Song, but the verb *(ḥtn)* and another noun *(ḥātān,* meaning son-in-law, fiancé, bridegroom) occurs with some frequency throughout the Old Testament. See the introduction to this section for a survey of different interpretations of Solomon's wedding in this section. The parallel indicates the joyous nature of this day, this ceremony. It is the day that made his heart rejoice.

---

49. *NIDOTTE,* vol. 3, pp. 384-85.

50. Perhaps the mention of the mother here may be explained by the fact that she plays an important role throughout the Song (noted particularly when we observe the absence of the father; see Introduction: Characters).

CHAPTER FOUR

POEM ELEVEN:
FROM HEAD TO BREASTS: THE MAN'S SENSUOUS
DESCRIPTION OF THE WOMAN (4:1-7)

Though we have divided 4:1–5:1 into three separate poems, these three may also be read together. The first seven verses are a description of the woman's physical beauty from head to breasts.[1] Verses 8-9, a unit that could be divided into two parts (see below), are an invitation and statement of arousal over the beauty of the woman. These verses could be the result of the man's growing excitement as he describes the woman's beauty. Then a metaphoric description of the woman's body continues with a focus on the garden, which is followed by an invitation of the woman, a response by the man, and finally a celebration of their union by the chorus. Keeping in mind these connections between the poems of 4:1–5:1, we will nonetheless treat them separately in our description.

The reason why we treat 4:1-7 separately is that it comprises a form-critical unit, which has been called a *wasf* in recent years. *Wasf* is an Arabic term, which simply means description, and its application to biblical scholarship originated with the research of J. G. Wetzstein in the nineteenth century.[2] Wetzstein was not a biblical scholar, but rather a German diplomat living in Syria at this time. As he attended local weddings, he noted similarities between the customs and songs of the day and what he read in the Song of Songs. In correspondence with the eminent biblical scholar Franz Delitzsch, he talked about songs where the groom and the bride would describe one an-

---

1. "Canticle 4 is the only place in Scripture where the naked woman is praised and admired without restriction"; cf. LaCocque, *Romance She Wrote,* p. 36.
2. J. G. Wetzstein, "Die Syrische Dreschtafel," *Zeitschrift für Ethnologie* 5 (1873): 270-302.

other's physical beauty as a prelude to lovemaking. Delitzsch published excerpts of his personal correspondence with Wetzstein in an appendix in his commentary.[3] Since this time, other more ancient analogies to these descriptive songs have been discovered and described,[4] but they have nonetheless retained the name *wasf* in the literature.

Song of Songs 4:1-7 is simply the first of four *wasf*s in the Song.[5] The others are found at 5:10-16; 6:4-6; 7:2-8. Of these, only 5:10-16 is a description of the man by the woman. While some argue that this is less sensual than the man's descriptions of the woman, I will dispute that in my exposition of those verses. All except 7:2-8 follows the pattern of starting at the head and working down the body. The descriptions all stop with the object of the speaker's sensuous attention. In the case of 4:1-7 that would be the woman's breasts. If we allow that verses 10-14 continue the *wasf,* then it is the woman's vagina. In either case, it is clear that this poem is a prelude to lovemaking.

R. N. Soulen raises the question of the purpose of the images of the *wasf.*[6] He raises what I think is a false dichotomy between a physical description and the arousal of emotions.[7] He parodies the first by citing L. Waterman's idiosyncratic view that the metaphors of this chapter, taken literally, describe a very ugly woman. Waterman believes the intention is to ridicule Solomon by showing him to be rejected by an unattractive country bumpkin. However, anyone with an ounce of literary sensitivity recognizes that the metaphors are not to be pressed literally, and while, as with all imagery, there will be debate over the exact terms of comparison, it is not hard to see that the intention is to paint a picture of a most beautiful and sensuous woman. As we will observe below in our verse-by-verse commentary, the *wasf* both describes and expresses emotions in a way that the readers' own emotions will be evoked. We must particularly bear in mind that love poetry in different cultures will articulate its metaphors in ways that might strike us as strange.

3. See now Delitzsch, *Proverbs, Ecclesiastes, Song of Solomon,* pp. 162-76.

4. For instance, Jinbachian, "The Genre of Love Poetry," pp. 123-35.

5. I wonder whether we should consider 4:12-14 a continuation of the *wasf* begun in vv. 1-7. After the interruption of vv. 8-9, these verses describe the woman's vagina in metaphorical language, thus continuing the downward trend of the *wasf.*

6. R. N. Soulen, "The *Wasfs* of the Song of Songs and Hermeneutic," *JBL* 86 (1967): 183-90.

7. He does this in part by appeal to the now largely discredited idea that Hebrew thought is different from Greek thought. Citing T. Boman (*Hebrew Thought Compared with Greek* [London: SCM, 1960]), he claims that "the ancient Hebrew poet . . . was characteristically disinterested in the appearances of person and things; his concern was with his impression of their qualities"; cf. Soulen, "The *Wasfs,*" p. 188.

We can imagine that other cultures might respond incredulously to our images of love as well.

The Man

1. *Behold,*[8] *you are beautiful, my darling!*
   Behold, you are beautiful,
   and your eyes are doves behind your veil.
   Your hair is like a flock of goats streaming[9] *from Mount*
   Gilead.[10]
2. *Your teeth are like a flock of shorn sheep,*[11] *coming up from a*
   washing.
   Each is paired; not one of them is missing.[12]
3. *Like a scarlet thread are your lips,*
   and your mouth is desirable.[13]
   Like a slice[14] *of pomegranate is your temple*[15]
   behind your veil.

8. *Hinnēh* here and in the next colon functions as an attention-getter. It focuses attention on the woman and her beauty. The translation *behold* is a bit heavy but the best English equivalent we can come up with.

9. The Septuagint erred by reading this verb as a form of *glh* "to reveal" rather than *glš*. The Hebrew word is difficult, occurring only in this context, but see Pope, *Song of Songs,* pp. 459-60, for possible Egyptian and Ugaritic cognates. S. S. Tuell ("A Riddle Resolved by an Enigma: Hebrew *glš* and Ugaritic *glṯ*," *JBL* 112 [1993]: 99-104) argues on the basis of the same Ugaritic cognates for a translation of *glš* as "to flow in waves." The meaning is not all that different from streaming, but Tuell's proposed translation does not fit well, in my opinion, with the movement of goats down a mountain. He would argue that, even so, it fits well with hair. Yet the clause seems still to be focusing on the goats, and so we should choose a verb that fits with goats and not with hair.

10. The parallel in 6:5 omits *Mount (har),* and some Hebrew manuscripts as well as the Septuagint do so too. In any case, the meaning of the image does not change.

11. *Shorn sheep* is a translation of a single word *(qᵉṣûbôt),* a qal passive feminine plural participle from the verb *qṣb,* and so literally "shorn ones." Some argue, based on the supposed custom of washing the sheep before shearing them, that the phrase should be translated something like "sheep to be shorn" (e.g., Murphy, *The Song of Songs,* p. 154).

12. Note the interesting sound play on *each* [of them] *(šekkullām)* and *is missing* *(šakkullâ;* from the root *škl* "to bereave").

13. The niphal of *'wh* can mean either "attractive" or "desirable" (*NIDOTTE,* vol. 1, pp. 304-6). In any case, the one usually implies the other.

14. Keel (*The Song of Songs,* p. 146) suggests "slit" not *slice,* with the slit of a pomegranate suggesting the mouth.

15. Or perhaps "brow." The argument that *raqqâ* is "mouth" not "temple" here and in Judg. 4:21-22; 5:26 is not persuasive, as argued by M. Rozelaar, "An Unrecognized Part of the Human Anatomy," *Judaism* 37 (1988): 97-101. He is unable to provide any cognate evidence, and his philological argument, such as it is, is extremely conjectural.

4. *Like the tower of David is your neck,*
   built in courses.[16]
   A thousand shields are hung on it;
   all are bucklers[17] *of heroes.*
5. *Your two breasts are like two fawns,*
   twins[18] *of a gazelle,*
   grazing[19] *among the lilies.*
6. *Until the day breaks and the shadows flee,*
   I myself will go to the mountain of myrrh
   and to the hills of frankincense.
7. *You are totally beautiful, my darling.*
   You have no blemish.[20]

1   This *waṣf,* or description song, begins with a general acclamation of the woman's *beauty.* Typical to the form, after this general description the poet proceeds to speak of the details of the woman's physical beauty from the head down. The repetition of the opening of the poem in 4:7 gives a sense of closure and marks a poetic unit. The first three lines (seven words in the Hebrew) are identical with 1:15, and that part of the commentary should be consulted for the details of the verse, including the significance of the dove metaphor in relationship to the eyes. However, the phrase *behind your veil* is an addition of significance here. As we will see, many questions arise about the nature of the veil, but one thing seems clear. The veil both hides beauty and heightens desire. The glimpse of physical beauty is more evocative than seeing the whole. The view of the part arouses the desire to see the whole.

Yet what are the uncertainties of the *veil?* First, what did it look like? What does it mean to say that the eyes are behind the veil? We cannot be sure, but several possibilities have been put forward. Perhaps it was a trans-

16. Though *talpîyyôt* occurs only in this context, the best understanding of it is as a reference to the courses of stone by which an ancient tower was constructed; see A. M. Honeyman, "Two Contributions to Canaanite Toponymy," *JTS* 50 (1949): 50-52, and Pope, *Song of Songs,* pp. 465-67.

17. The word *bucklers* translates the plural form of *šelet.* That Hebrew word means shield, as does *māgēn* in the previous colon, but from its rarer use we assume that it has a narrower meaning. Unfortunately, we cannot determine its exact nuance (see *NIDOTTE,* vol. 4, p. 125), and thus we simply translate the Hebrew term with a less familiar English word for shield, without arguing that the Hebrew word specifically has the same meaning as the English term.

18. We have seen the root *t'm* already in 4:2.

19. For the verb "to graze" (*r'h*), see commentary at 1:7.

20. Literally, "There is no blemish/defect in you," but this is much too wooden for English translation.

parent veil that covered the entire face, a "diaphanous muslin gauze" as M. Goulder suggests.[21] Perhaps the eyes are above the veil.[22] We cannot be certain, though I lean toward the former, especially since 4:3 will speak to the color of the woman's cheeks as they are seen behind the veil.

Another question, which at this stage is unanswerable, is: What did a veil signify in terms of a woman's status in society. We do not know enough about the history of this custom to say for sure, and our knowledge is so minimal that we cannot speculate on whether the woman is married, about to be married, or unmarried based on the presence of the veil. The veil heightens the woman's mystery; one wants to look behind the veil. However, it seems less certain that J. M. Munro is right in her assertion that the veil denotes "her inwardness, her hiddenness, her reluctance to be drawn out of doors."[23]

After her eyes, the man's attention is drawn to her hair. A primarily visual image is used, that of *goats* streaming down the slopes of *Mount Gilead.* Why Gilead? Perhaps because it is a beautiful part of that world. Gilead refers to the region in the central Transjordan that surrounds the Jabbok River. It was a distant and awe-inspiring site. The goats, black, stream down, likely to give the impression of lush, flowing hair that captures the man's attention. Note the similarity of this last part of the verse with 6:5.

2   After describing the woman's hair, the man comments lovingly on the woman's teeth, again with a visual image. The images strike us as strange and uncomplimentary on first glance, but we must put ourselves in the ancient context to truly understand the nature of the comment.

In a word, dental hygiene was nothing like it is today. To be banal about it, the verse basically has the man saying to the woman, "Your teeth are white, and you even have all of them!" although the flattery is delivered with more of a flourish than that. He evokes a picture of sheep coming up from a washing, probably in a creek or river. They are either shorn or about to be shorn; the point in either case is that they are glistening white.[24] The sheep are seen as coming up with their partner; literally they are twinned (from *t'm*): that is, they are all identical, perhaps signifying not only that they are all there but also that they are even, with no gaps between them. The picture of twinning probably refers to the fact that the upper teeth mirror the lower teeth, just as the sheep's image is reflected in the pool where they were washed.

21. See M. Goulder, *The Song of Fourteen Songs,* JSOTS 36 (Sheffield: JSOT Press, 1986), p. 33. See the article on *ṣammâ* in *NIDOTTE,* vol. 3, pp. 814-15, for a helpful summary of the options on the physical nature of the veil.

22. Pope, *Song of Songs,* p. 457.

23. Munro, *Spikenard and Saffron,* p. 52.

24. Perhaps a reference to teeth glistening with saliva is meant here, but such a statement may press the imagery a little too literally.

Note the similarity between this verse and 6:6.

3 Verse 3 presents similes of the woman's lips and her temple, continuing the loving description of her attractive head that was begun in verses 1 and 2. The similes here reverse the sentence order of the first two similes in that the comparison is given first, followed by the object of comparison.

Verse 3 contains two bicola, and the first focuses on the beauty and desirability of her *lips*/mouth. Two words are used to refer to her *lips*. The first is the common word for lip *(śāpâ)*.[25] The second is rare, indeed a singly occurring word *(midbār* II). The parallel makes its meaning fairly clear, and we can see it is a noun formed from the verbal root *dbr,* "to speak." This connection leads some to translate the word "speech,"[26] but it seems unlikely to me that this *waṣf,* which focuses so consistently on the physical attributes of the woman, would suddenly praise another aspect of who she is.

The first colon compliments the color of her lips. They are a deep red, i.e., *scarlet* or crimson. In other places, *scarlet* is used for symbolic purposes in association with the cult. After all, it is close to the color of blood, which was of great importance to the sacrificial ritual of Israel. Needless to say, this connection has triggered allegorical readings of this passage.[27] Yet the reference is to the redness of the woman's lips that evokes desire. The reference might be to the natural color of the woman's lips but could refer to the fact that they are artificially colored in a way analogous to modern lipstick.[28]

However, in the context of a love poem, the intention of the compliment is obvious. She has lovely lips; he desires to kiss them. Indeed, her *mouth* is desirable; he would like to possess it.

The second simile of the verse is a bit more difficult for us to penetrate and even picture. We have already discussed the ambiguity of the phrase *behind your veil (mibba'ād l^eṣammātēk)* as it occurred in 4:1 (see commentary). What exactly is *pomegranate*-like about her temple? Images are often difficult to unpack since it is of the nature of a comparison like this to really focus on just one aspect of the pomegranate. The difficulty is further complicated for readers in English-speaking countries because the pomegranate, while known, is not a popular fruit; thus few know what it is like. Its dictio-

---

25. Notice that this is a rare use of the plural construct, rather than the usual dual.

26. As early as the Septuagint and Vulgate, but also Murphy, *The Song of Songs,* p. 155.

27. For a sample of which, see Pope, *Song of Songs,* pp. 464-65.

28. Pope *(Song of Songs,* p. 464) cites Egyptian examples and suggests that other neighboring cultures likely had the custom of females painting their lips.

nary definition refers to it as a thick-skinned fruit, but this is probably not a focus of comparison. It likely compliments her complexion. The fruit is a sort of reddish orange.

4 If we had difficulties with the simile at the end of verse 3, they pale in comparison with that of verse 4! We should note that the pattern of word order that we noted in verse 3 continues here. The verse begins with the comparison, which is followed by the object of comparison. The image is that her neck is like the *tower of David.* This does not immediately strike the modern reader as a compliment since the picture that it evokes is of a long, fat neck, perhaps like that of a linebacker on a football team. Yet of course this is ridiculous. One writer helpfully suggests that what we have here is "not visual correspondence but a transfer of value."[29] So it is not that the woman's neck is long, fat, thick, or the like, but that it is grand, strong, dignified, perhaps elegant.[30] Some offer an additional nuance that the tower image also suggests the woman's imperviousness.[31] Elsewhere in the Song, however, she seems to pursue quite actively the relationship. O. Keel offers a mediation point where the woman is a picture both of "proud reticence and provocative liveliness."[32]

Nothing is known outside of the Song of a *tower of David.* Perhaps it did exist at some time, perhaps not. In any case, David's association with the tower lends a further sense of power and dignity to the image. It also fits into a pervasive use of military imagery to describe the woman.

The second bicolon of the verse then refers to *shields* that are hung on the tower. Perhaps this reference describes the custom of hanging the decorated shields of warriors on the outside of the tower.[33] If so, they may refer to necklaces that enhance the beauty and dignity of the woman's neck.

5 Moving down her body, he next focuses on her *breasts,* objects of male erotic interest that need no explanation. Let it suffice to point out the obvious, that such personal reference indicates intimate relationship. Also, the inclusion of a description of her breasts shows that the book is anything but prudish.

While we can easily understand why the man is captivated by her *breasts,* the metaphor he uses is either subtle enough or culturally distant enough that we are left in some doubt as to precisely what he means by the

---

29. *The Dictionary of Biblical Imagery,* p. 881.

30. Though in as literal a translation as the NIV, the rendition of *talpîyyôt* as "elegant" is clearly misleading, even with its footnote that the Hebrew is obscure.

31. Garrett, *Proverbs, Ecclesiastes, Song of Songs,* p. 405.

32. Keel, *The Song of Songs,* p. 147.

33. Ezek. 27:11 witnesses to the custom of hanging shields on the exterior of city walls.

comparison. How are her breasts like *two fawns,* like *gazelle* twins (see also the similar reference in 7:4 [English 7:3])?[34]

The *fawn/gazelle* was known for a variety of qualities, including speed, sleekness, and sensuality. Speed hardly seems a fitting comparison with a woman's breasts, but certainly an attractiveness of form is. The *fawn* is a youthful deer, and so perhaps the breasts of a young, recently matured woman are being described. The emphasis on the *twin* nature of her breasts seems to point out the obvious, but perhaps he is struck by their symmetrical nature. Most interesting, and less often commented upon, is the posture of the animals of the imagery. They are grazing among the *lilies.*[35] Are we to picture them from the rear then? That is, as they stick their heads into the sweet smell of the flowers, their rounded rumps with their small tails may remind the poet of breasts with their protruding nipples. Perhaps we carry the image too far, but then again there are no formulas for knowing when to stop (see Introduction: Reading Imagery).[36]

6   In the previous verses he has described the physical beauty of the woman from her head down to her breasts. He now breaks away from the description and states his desire to be with her. He begins with a temporal phrase, identical to the one that opens 2:17 *(Until the day breaks and the shadows flee).* The reader can consult the commentary at that point to see the ambiguity inherent in the phrase. Is he talking about all night or all day? While the answer to that question is unclear, there is no doubt about his desire to be with her. She is the *mountain of myrrh;* she is *the hills of Lebanon.* We saw something similar in 2:17, where the woman asks the man to come and be like a gazelle on the mountains of Bether. There we saw that the root of Bether meant "to cut in two" and suggest cleavage of some sort. Perhaps, we saw, it was a reference to her breasts, or perhaps the vagina (the *mons veneris*). In the present verse, the sweet-smelling mountains of myrrh, a fragrant resin, and the mountains of Lebanon, also sweet smelling because of its association with the cedar tree, refer in some way to the sensual body of the woman. At the least, the woman as a whole is meant. Here he subtly and tastefully describes his desire to be intimate with her.

7   The first part of the *waṣf* concludes with a general statement of the woman's beauty. The term translated *totally (kullāk)* is a combination of the word for "all" *(kōl)* with the second feminine singular pronominal suffix.

---

34. For the Hebrew terms for fawn *('ōper)* and gazelle *(ṣᵉbîyyâ),* see the commentary at 2:9 (also 2:17). See also 4:5 and 7:4 (English 7:3).

35. For a discussion of the word *lilies* (singular *šôšannâ),* see 2:1.

36. Note Murphy's *(The Song of Songs,* p. 159) criticism of this understanding: "Many excellent commentators betray an insensitive literalness here, as when the breasts are compared to a vision of the backsides of fawns nuzzling among flowers." Again, what formula does he use to rule out this reading of the imagery?

147

Verse 7a parallels verse 1a to a large extent and creates a kind of envelope structure or inclusio, which gives a sense of closure to this part of the poem. It asserts positively the physical beauty of the woman. Verse 7b follows the positive assertion of her beauty with a second assertion of her beauty that is cast more negatively. She has no *blemish* or defect *(mûm)*. The Hebrew word refers to physical imperfection. It is usually used of animals, and those animals with a defect of some sort — and the term can refer to a wide range of imperfections — are ineligible for use in the sacrificial ritual (Lev. 22:20-21, 25; Deut. 17:1). However, here the phrase is used in a nonreligious sense, similar to the reference to Absalom (2 Sam. 14:25) and Daniel and his three friends in the court of Nebuchadnezzar (Dan. 1:4). It is true that the Hebrew word *mûm* can have the sense of a moral defect[37] (and thus its negative, that of moral purity), but, as M. H. Pope points out, there is no indication in this poem or throughout the book of explicit interest in anything but her physical beauty.[38]

POEM TWELVE:
THE INVITATION (4:8-9)

As mentioned in the introduction to 4:1-7, there is a close relationship here with the preceding poem. The invitation may be consequential to the description of the woman's beauty and then lead to the description of the woman's garden (4:10-14). Verse 8 is clearly an invitation. The man wants the woman to come to him. She is described as being in a wilderness area, a frightening place where there are lions and leopards. Dramatic approaches to the Song assign a measure of reality to this description, as if the woman is literally in the mountains of Lebanon. Those who believe the woman is a country lass being unsuccessfully wooed by Solomon understand the words to be spoken by Solomon in his attempt to get her to leave her country setting (and her shepherd lover) and join his harem. However, again, the poetic quality of the Song must be recognized, and the wilderness scene must be appreciated for what it is: a trope of alienation that the lover wants the woman to overcome so that they may be united in intimate bliss.

Verse 9 is a further expression of his admiration for the woman. It is an expression of an overwhelming passion for her.

---

37. The Septuagint seems to have understood it this way by translating *mûm* with a word that sounds the same *(mōmos)* but means "blame."

38. Pope, *Song of Songs*, p. 473.

The Man

8. *With me*[39] *from Lebanon, (my)*[40] *bride;*
    with me, from Lebanon, come!
 Come down[41] *from the top of Amana;*
    from the top of Senir and Hermon,
    from the dens of lions,
    from the heights of leopards.
9. *You drive me crazy, my sister, my bride!*
    You drive me crazy
 with one glance[42] *from your eyes,*[43]
    with one jewel from your necklace.

8   The man expresses his desire to the woman by an invitation to come to him. It is important to remind ourselves again that this is poetry and not a narrative. We are not to think that the woman is literally roaming the wilderness crags of the northern mountains. She is not living with the animals. The distant, dangerous location signifies her present distance from the man. He wants her to join him in a place of safety, namely, his embrace. The emphasis of the verse is on *with me.*

Hermon, of course, is the well-known mountain at the northernmost reaches of Israel. It is an imposing, often snow-capped mountain that is also the southernmost in a range of mountains that extends up into *Lebanon.* The other peaks are *Amana* and *Senir.* According to Pope, both of these peaks are in the Lebanon range.[44]

39. With the MT. The versions read *'ittî* as *'etî,* which is "come" (the imperative feminine singular of the verb *'th*). See O. Loretz, "Cant 4,8 auf dem Hintergrund ugaritischer und assyrischer Beschreibungen des Libanons und Antilibanons," in *Ernten, was man sat: Festschrift für Klaus Koch zu seinem 65. Geburtstag,* ed. E. R. Daniels, U. Glessmer, and M. Rosel (Neukirchen-Vluyn: Neukirchener, 1991), p. 136, for the suggestion that here the preposition means "to" *(zu).*

40. The pronoun is added; it is not represented in the Hebrew.

41. Understanding the root to *šwr* II "to come down, descend," not *swr* I "to gaze."

42. Literally, "with one of your eyes." The word "glance" is supplied from the context to communicate with a modern audience.

43. M. Malul ("Janus Parallelism in Biblical Hebrew: Two More Cases (Canticles 4:9.12)," *BZ* 41 [1997]: 246-49) suggests that *'ayin,* here translated "eyes," is a Janus parallelism, where *'ayin* is to be read with a second meaning "bead" with the last colon of the verse. First, the evidence for Janus parallelism is debatable; second, Malul has to argue here for a hitherto unattested meaning of *'ayin.*

44. According to Pope (*Song of Songs,* pp. 474-75) in regard to Amana, "it is generally assumed to be the same as the river name Abanah (*Qere* Amanah), II Kings 5:12, which issues at the foot of the Anti-Lebanon and flows through Damascus under the name

The point of the poet seems to be that these peaks are distant, and he wants her close. They are also the habitat of wild animals such as the dangerous *lion* and *leopard,* and he wants her in a safe place. The verse as a whole is an invitation to union.

In this verse, he calls her his bride (*kallâ;* see also vv. 9, 10, 11, 12; 5:1). This reference clearly places the poem in the context of marriage. Some scholars object that some uses of the noun appear in a nonmarriage context; thus, e.g., Snaith makes the outlandish claim that "the term bride seems here to bear no connotations of marriage but stands rather as an emotionally charged term of affection."[45] Contexts like Isaiah 49:18; 61:10; 62:5, and Jeremiah 2:32 are often cited as support for this view. Close examination of these texts, however, shows that they are weak support since if the couple in mind is not already married, then they are at the ceremony. To say that it has no connotation of marriage is clearly wrong.

The famous linguist Roman Jakobson analyzed this verse from a poetic point of view.[46] His close analysis noted that the preposition *min* is repeated six times in the verse and causes it to cohere; that a noun occurs in the second position in every colon; and that there are a large number of nasal phonemes in the verse. It is doubtful that all of the details that Jakobson catalogs were consciously intended by the author or actually noticed by readers,[47] but in the unconscious minds of the readers they may provide a coherence to the verse.

9 In this verse the man expresses the strength of his desire for the woman. In the first bicolon, he twice uses a verb formed from the noun "heart" *(lēb).*[48] The verb is a piel, which we may understand in the tradi-

Barada. The modern name of the mountain at the source of the Barada is Jebel Zebedani. Akkadian inscriptions mention the mountain in variant forms of the name Umanum, Ammana, and Ammun." In regard to Senir, Pope summarizes by saying, "According to Deut 3:9, Senir is the Amorite designation of Mount Hermon which the Sidonians called Sirion. . . . It is not clear whether the two terms are completely synonymous or whether Senir properly designates only part of the Hermon range, the southern section north of Damascus which the Arab geographer Abulfeda termed Sanir." See also 1 Chron. 5:23, where both names are mentioned; it is unclear whether they are two different mountains or peaks or one name for both ("Senir, even Mount Hermon").

45. Snaith, *Song of Songs,* p. 65.

46. In his article, "Grammatical Parallelism and Its Russian Facet," *Language* 42 (1966): 399-529.

47. See the critique by Z. Zevit, "Roman Jakobson, Psycholinguistics, and Biblical Poetry," *JBL* 109 (1990): 385-401.

48. N. M. Waldman ("A Note on Canticles 4 9," *JBL* 89 [1970]: 215-17) offers an alternative explanation by referring to the Akkadian verb *labābu* and Late Hebrew *lbb.* He then posits a "semantic development . . . from a sense of 'rage' to 'be aroused to fury' to one of 'be aroused sexually.'" In either case, the meaning is basically the same, but the de-

tional sense as a verbal stem that intensifies, or perhaps one that "causes a state rather than an action."[49] According to its use in the Hebrew Bible, the noun *lēb* refers to one's inner life. Sometimes the emphasis is on one's mental processes, but not in this context. Here, the focus is on the emotions, and the word refers to the man's excited emotional state as he thinks of the woman. A more colloquial translation of the verb would be "you drive me crazy!"[50] Pope describes the sensual sense of "heart" in Mesopotamian literature, particularly in reference to the so-called ŠÀ.ZI.GA (Akkadian *nīš libbi*), "rising of the heart" texts. These rituals are designed to increase male sexual interest.

The man refers to the woman by means of two epithets, both of which raise interesting issues. We have dealt with the epithet *bride* in the commentary on the previous verse, but here she is also his *sister.* In today's context, this epithet raises eyebrows. Indeed, the New Living Translation chose to render the word "my treasure" to avoid any interpretation of the verse as an approval or example of incest. On the contrary, it is now well established that the use of sister as a term of endearment between an intimate couple was common in the Near East, particularly in Egypt.[51] It is clearly unnecessary to invoke the sexual relationships of the gods and goddesses of the Near East to understand this epithet, though it is true that often the sexual relationships among the deities were between gods and goddesses who were also siblings.

It does not take much to set the man off in a frenzy of excitement over the woman: a mere *glance* of the eyes or one *jewel* from her necklace. Anything about her or associated with her brings him to his knees in adoration. The term "jewel" occurs here in the singular; often it appears in the plural and is translated necklace (Judg. 8:26; Prov. 1:9).

---

velopment from the Hebrew noun *lēb* seems a more elegant hypothesis. In addition, Pope (*Song of Songs,* p. 479) disputes Waldman's suggestion that the Hebrew verb is not related to "heart" but rather is cognate with the Akkadian *labābu.* He believes that the development of the Akkadian sense of arousal of anger to the Hebrew sense of sexual arousal can be argued for on the basis of the Greek *orgē* "wrath" and *orgaō* "swell with lust."

49. Waltke and O'Connor, *An Introduction to Biblical Hebrew Syntax,* p. 400.

50. This is the way Keel (*The Song of Songs,* pp. 162-63) translates. He points out that the piel could (and has been) taken as privative ("you have stolen my heart") or intensifying ("you make my heart beat faster") and suggests that his proposed translation incorporates both aspects.

51. Westenholz, "Love Lyrics from the Ancient Near East," p. 2474.

POEM THIRTEEN:
EATING IN THE GARDEN OF LOVE (4:10–5:1)

While it is possible to treat this poem as a separate composition (as I am here), we must also acknowledge its close relationship with the preceding two poems. Certainly 4:1-7 is a complete *wasf*, which is marked off by an inclusion indicated by the use of "beautiful" (*yāpâ*; cf. vv. 1 and 7). Verses 8-9 are not a part of a *wasf* but rather an invitation and further statement of the man's passion for the woman. However, now the metaphorical description of the woman's body continues — and not insignificantly is introduced by a phrase that includes the word "beautiful" (*yāpû*). The metaphor is that of a garden, which, as we will explain below, is not only the place of lovemaking but a metaphor of the woman's most private and intimate part. The same is true of the fountain imagery. The man notes that the garden and fountain are sealed, private, and closed, but when the woman responds to his speech, she opens them to him. He enters the garden and partakes of its pleasures, while the chorus celebrates their union.

This section has proven to be a major stumbling block for the three-person drama view (see Introduction). F. Godet, e.g., describes Solomon as giving the ecstatic speech to the beautiful shepherd girl that he wishes to bring into his harem.[52] She, it will be remembered, remains loyal to her country boyfriend. In order to account for the woman's affirmative response to the man's speech, Godet asserts that she is in a trance ("an almost lifeless body"), and that while Solomon dares apply her words to him, she is really thinking about her absent lover so many miles away. When one thinks about this proposed scene, one can hardly blame Solomon for his confusion!

The Man
10. *How beautiful your love, my sister, my bride!*
    How much better your love than wine
    and[53] the scent of your oils[54] than spices!
11. *Your lips drip honey, O bride.*
    Honey and milk are under your tongue.
    The scent of your garments is like the scent of Lebanon.

---

52. F. Godet, "The Interpretation of the Song of Songs," in *Classical Evangelical Essays in Old Testament Interpretation,* ed. W. C. Kaiser (Grand Rapids: Baker, 1972), pp. 151-82.

53. With "how much better" understood from the first part of the verse. In other words, it is an ellipsis.

54. The Septuagint reads "your garments" (*himatiōn sou* = *salmōtayik*), based on the parallel with v. 11.

12. *You are a locked garden, my sister, my bride.*
     You are a locked garden,[55] a sealed fountain.
13. *Your "shoots" are a garden of pomegranates*
        with choice fruits,
     henna and nard,
14.   *nard and saffron,*
     calamus and cinnamon,
        with every kind of incense tree,
     myrrh and aloes,
        with all the chief spices.
15. *You are a garden fountain,*
        a well of living water,
     streaming down from Lebanon.

The Woman
16. *Wake up, north wind,*
        and come, south wind!
     Blow on my garden
        and let its spices flow forth.
     Let my lover come into his garden
        and eat its choice fruit.

The Man
5:1. *I have come into my garden, my sister, my bride.*
        I have gathered[56] my myrrh with my spices.
     I have eaten my honey comb with my honey.
        I have drunk my wine with my milk.

The Women of Jerusalem[57]
     Eat, friends, drink!
        Be intoxicated, lovers!

10 In this verse, which begins a section that picks up the physical description of the woman that began the chapter, he again starts with a general com-

---

55. MT has *gal* ("wave"? perhaps "pool"; cf. Pope, *Song of Songs,* pp. 488-89). However, we follow about fifty Hebrew manuscripts plus the Septuagint, the Vulgate, and the Peshitta in reading *gan* "garden."

56. The verb *'rh* occurs only here and in Ps. 80:13 (English 80:12) in the sense of pluck or gather.

57. To be sure, the young women of Jerusalem are not here mentioned by name. In the context of this individual poem perhaps it would be safer to refer to an anonymous chorus.

pliment concerning her beauty and his relationship with her. Her beauty is unsurpassed and her love is unsurpassed. Indeed, her scent is also wonderful, far better than the fragrance of one of the finest spices known to humans. The spice (*bōśem*, also mentioned in 4:14, 15; 5:10 as a spice and in 5:13; 6:2; 8:14 as a plant) to which her scent is compared is the spice that is used in the anointing oil associated with the tabernacle (Exod. 25:6); it is one of the gifts that the queen of Sheba brought to Solomon (1 Kings 10:2, 10, 25). This spice was also part of the beautification process undergone by Esther as she prepared to spend a night with the king of Persia (Esth. 2:12).

11 With this verse, the man returns to a metaphorical description of different parts of the woman's body that attract his sensual interest. He begins with her *lips,* which he has already described as an inviting place in 4:3. There her lips were scarlet and her mouth was pleasant. In this verse he uses a metaphor of taste to describe her lips and *mouth.* The taste is sweet and sensual. Two words for *honey* are used in the verse (*nōpet* in colon a and *d^ebaš* in colon b). They both refer to honey, though the first is used for honey from the comb, while the second can also refer to honey made from fruits like grapes, dates, or figs. In this case, the variation may be simply for poetic purposes, but we should also note the addition of the word *milk* in the second colon (*ḥālāb*). This is particularly noteworthy because *d^ebaš* and *ḥālāb* are frequent pairs elsewhere in the Bible, particularly in reference to the land of Palestine, which is a land "flowing with milk and honey." These two liquids seem to indicate luxury, wealth, and abundance. They are thick, sensual liquids, which leave a strong aftertaste in the mouth. It is doubtful in the extreme that the reader is to think of Israel as they read this description of the woman's mouth. On the contrary, this delicious metaphor of taste anticipates the man's partaking of its sweetness.[58]

Her lips are said to *drip (nṭp)* honey. The slow dripping rather than pouring also evokes a sensual picture. Too much honey would also sicken the one who consumed it. In addition, we should point out that looks are sometimes deceiving, not in the present context, but certainly according to Proverbs 5:3-6:

> The lips of an immoral woman are as sweet as honey,
>   and her mouth is smoother than oil.
> But the result is as bitter as poison,
>   sharp as a double-edged sword.
> Her feet go down to death;
>   her steps lead straight to the grave.

---

58. I think it doubtful that the image here refers to the speech of the woman, as suggested as a possibility by Snaith, *Song of Songs,* p. 66.

For she does not care about the path to life.
She staggers down a crooked trail
    and doesn't even realize where it is.

Our present poem, on the contrary, has no hint of this deception, and anticipates a wonderful union. The description of these sensual liquids under the
tongue invites deep exploration with a kiss.

The verse describes not only the sense of taste but also that of smell.
Her *garments* smell inviting, like the smell of *Lebanon*, by which we are to
understand the cedar trees of Lebanon. The pleasant smell both invites and
motivates physical intimacy.

12   The next three verses will describe the woman as a *garden* and a
fountain. In the ancient Near East[59] and elsewhere in the Bible (Prov. 5:15-
20), these are highly erotic images. The images of fountain and garden probably are to be visualized together since a garden would need a water supply.
The focus may well be on the ultimate place in the act of lovemaking, the
woman's vagina. Two of the images are in the present verse, garden and
fountain. She is not a garden or fountain open to every passer-by; she is
rather a *locked* garden, a *sealed* fountain.[60] These images describe her inaccessibility. However, as we will see soon, she will open up her treasures to
the man who will enter her garden ("enter" often has the overtones of sexual
intercourse). With the image of sealing and locking, we would be hard
pressed to miss the idea of virginity (at least up to now).[61] However, O. Keel
remarkably and without argumentation simply asserts: "contrary to frequent
claims, the locking and sealing have nothing to do with chastity or with exclusive rights of usage and ownership."[62]

13   The garden of the previous verse is now described in more detail,
and it turns out to be a most exotic garden indeed. Perhaps the most problematic aspect of the two verses that detail the garden is found in the first word,

---

59. For the garden, see S. Paul ("A Lover's Garden of Verse: Literal and Metaphorical Imagery in Ancient Near Eastern Love Poetry," in *Tehillah le-Moshe: Biblical
and Judaic Studies in Honor of Moshe Greenberg*, ed. M. Cogan et al. [Winona Lake, IN:
Eisenbrauns, 1997], pp. 99-110), who comments that the garden "functions not only as a
favorite assignation (with its esthetic and sensual delights and hideaways) for lovers'
trysts and afresco amour, but may simultaneously allude to female sexuality and fertility
in general and to the pudenda in particular," with examples from Sumerian, Akkadian, and
Egyptian love poetry.

60. For the use of this image in Egyptian literature, see Fox, *The Song of Songs
and the Ancient Egyptian Love Songs*, pp. 283-87.

61. Remember that this poem, as part of an anthology, should not be read as part
of a broader narrative. That earlier poems have already suggested intercourse (as early as
1:4!) says nothing about the sexual status of the woman in our present context.

62. Keel, *The Song of Songs*, p. 174.

which we have translated *your shoots ($š^e$lāhayik)*. The word is composed of a plural noun from *šelah* II with the second person feminine pronominal suffix. The noun is a rare nominal form from the common verb *šlh*, which means to send or to stretch out. The verb, when used in a botanical context, can indicate the sending out of roots (Jer. 17:8) or branches (Ps. 18:12 [English 18:11]), and a related noun form *(š^elāhôt)* also indicates shoots or tendrils of a plant. It thus seems clear from the philological evidence that the word, when it appears in a garden setting like the present one, means something like a shoot. But then to what does the "shoot" metaphor refer? The *wasf* context indicates that it would refer to a part of the woman's physical makeup. Above, we have suggested that the garden, as well as the well/fountain/spring, symbolism indicates the woman's vagina. If so, then perhaps the shoots refer to her pubic hair. Another suggestion is that the shoots refer to her legs, and still a further suggestion, understanding the linguistic argument in a different way, is that the reference is to what Pope calls "her groove."[63]

Her shoots compose her *garden*. Here we have the use of a special word for garden, not *gan* but *pardēs*. We must be careful not to read too much into the choice of this word, but it is the Hebrew word (originally a Persian loanword) that leads to our English term "paradise." It occurs rarely in the Old Testament (Eccles. 2:5; Neh. 2:8, and here). Specifically, this garden paradise is one composed of many *choice*[64] *fruits* like the *pomegranate* (see 4:3), but also other fruits as well as spices, many of which are then listed. The list, which continues into the next verse, simply accentuates the abundance of exotic and precious fruits and spices, which of course also accentuates the abundance of pleasure to be associated with the woman. F. Landy puts it well when he says, "the list persuades us that there is no spice tree, or perhaps fruit tree that is omitted, that it is a Noah's Ark of the vegetable kingdom. Like the garden of Eden, in it all species are represented, in a confined place."[65] It obviously expresses the man's intense desire for union and intimacy with the woman. The specific spices and fruits mentioned include:

> *Henna (kōper):* a shrub with white flowers. Its leaves provide a reddish brown dye that even today is used to color hair.
> *Nard (nērd):* a fragrant oil from the plant *nardostachys jatamansi.*

---

63. Pope, *Song of Songs,* pp. 490-91, though we judge his argument as tenuous at best, tortured at worst. The same may be said for Keel, *The Song of Songs,* pp. 175-76. Keel *(The Song of Songs)* suggests that the word should be translated "canals"; cf. the discussion in M. Gorg, "'Kanäle' oder 'Zweige' in Hld 4,13?" *BN* 72 (1994): 20-23.

64. A word used only in the Song (see also 4:16; 7:14 [English 7:13]) and Deut. 33:13-16.

65. Landy, *Paradoxes of Paradise,* p. 192.

The plant is found in India, China, and Japan, and the oil gives off a sweet, woody, and spicy odor.

14   Verse 14 continues from the previous verse the list of fragrant plants that make up the woman's exotic garden. Note that the list begins with a repetition of *nard,* which ended the previous verse, and which we understand not to be a mistake but rather the result of poetic piling on and connection with the previous colon. The new exotic plants that appear in this verse include:

> *Saffron (karkōm):* a type of crocus that has purple flowers and produces an oil that gives a sweet, spicy, floral scent. The flower is native to western Asia, Asia Minor, and the eastern Mediterranean. The word is from Sanskrit.
>
> *Calamus (qāneh):* literally, the "cane," but in this context it is likely a reference to sweet cane oil, which has a warm, woody, spicy odor.
>
> *Cinnamon (qinnāmōn):* refers to the aromatic bark of any of a number of trees. The English word is derived from the Hebrew via the Greek, although the substance comes from the far East, Ceylon, or India. In the Hebrew Bible we find it used in the oil of anointing (Exod. 30:27) and in the bed of the adulteress (Prov. 7:17).
>
> *Incense tree ('aṣê lᵉbônâ):* a word that does not denote a certain kind of tree but rather a type of sweet-smelling tree.
>
> *Myrrh (mōr):* as defined in 1:13, an aromatic gum from the bark of the Bulsamadendron tree from Arabia, Abyssinia, and India. The word also occurs in Song of Songs 1:13; 3:6; 4:6; 5:5, 13).
>
> *Aloes ('ᵃhālôt):* a fragrant wood of an east Indian tree.
>
> *Spices (bōśem):* or perhaps "perfumes" in this context; see 4:10.

15   The man ends his description of the woman's *garden* with this exclamation that now focuses on the metaphors of *fountain* and *well.* The words seem to be used in parallelism to refer to a single water source, but we have to be careful about making such assertions due to the fact that parallel cola do not automatically set up equations of similarity.[66] In any case, this water source is in the garden, and so we have not yet left that metaphorical field. The term "fountain" as well as "garden" has been discussed above (4:12); the new term introduced here is *well (bᵉ'ēr).* The well, a deep watery

---

66. J. Kugel (*The Idea of Biblical Parallelism* [New Haven: Yale University Press, 1981]) has shown that the proper way of understanding the relationship between the first colon and those that follow is as one of sharpening or intensifying (A, what's more B) rather than simple synonymity (A = B).

pit, suggests an association with the woman's vagina (see also Prov. 5:15; 23:27), the focus of male sexual interest. The well is abundantly watered. It is not a stagnant well, but one that constantly flows with new water. This is the contribution of the second two cola of the line, most notably the phrase *living water (mayim ḥayyîm)*. Then, in the third colon of the line the author associates this water with *Lebanon*, already seen to be a place of beauty and natural freshness. Lebanon contains a range of high mountains whose melting snow would provide streams of water to the valley below.

16 The man has ended his long (for the Song), passionate speech. He has expressed intense desire for the woman and for intimate union. She now speaks positively in response to his longing, but she is subtle, not direct. She addresses not him but the *north* and *south winds*.[67] Remember that she has been described as a locked garden, a sealed fountain in 4:12. Now, however, she invites the winds to blow on her garden, suggesting an opening to the outside world. The winds are here obviously personified, which is one reason why I translate the imperative verb ʿwr as *wake up* rather than stir up, which is also a possibility. We should further note the connection between the use of the verb ʿwr here and in the refrain where we first saw it (2:7; see also 3:5 and 8:4). In the refrain, she warns the daughters of Jerusalem not to awaken love until the right time. Here she awakens the winds to blow on her garden. Presumably, the time is right for her.

The winds are to *blow* on her garden with the result that the *spices* of her heretofore private garden will now become public, at least to the man. The verb *blow* in reference to the wind is also used in 2:17 and 4:6 in a romantic setting. She then issues a direct invitation to the man to enter her garden and *eat* its fruit. It is problematic to know how literally to take the verb *eat*, but there is no doubt about the fact that she invites him to sexual union of the most intimate type.[68]

5:1 *The Man.* The man responds as we would expect him to in the light of the woman's (his *sister,* his *bride,* for which epithets see vv. 8 and 9) invitation. Metaphorically he describes how he follows up on her invitation for sexual union. He enters the garden and enjoys all of its delights. He has *gathered, eaten,* and *drunk* in the garden. The verbs all speak of his partaking of the good things in the woman's garden. The delights are represented by the

---

67. The simple words *north (ṣāpôn)* and *south (tēmān)* stand here for the winds that emanate from those directions (see also Prov. 25:23; Ps. 78:26; Zech. 9:14 for the directions north and south referring to winds). I take north and south winds as a merism meaning that she opens herself up completely to the man.

68. As J.-J. Lavoie ("Festin érotique et tendresse cannibalique dans le Cantique des Cantiques," p. 145) puts it, "on peut affirmer que manger (ʾkl: Ct. 4,16; 5,1) et boire (šth et škr: Ct. 5,1; cf. šqh en Ct. 8,2) est un couple de totalité qui exprime bien l'union sexuelle entièrement réalisée."

myrrh, spices, honeycomb, honey, wine, and *milk.* The double objects of each of the final three cola indicate the totality of his experience. He hasn't just had her wine, but also her milk, not only her honey but also her comb. He has possessed her completely, a fitting image of sexual intercourse.

The Women of Jerusalem. The poem concludes with the chorus pitching in their word of celebration at their union. We saw this kind of dynamic already in the first poem of the book (see 1:4). The chorus is the voice of those outside the relationship who put their imprimatur, as it were, on the relationship. They encourage them in their union. They command them to *eat* and *drink,* indeed drink so much that they get *intoxicated* because of their union. Love, and the act of love, sometimes acts like a little too much alcohol, making the head reel and causing one to lose touch with reality.

CHAPTER FIVE

POEM FOURTEEN:
TO SEARCH AND (NOT) FIND, ONCE AGAIN (5:2–6:3)

This lengthy poem is clearly demarcated from what precedes and what follows. Instead of the joyful and intimate union that we find at the conclusion of the previous poem, this one starts out with isolation and alienation. However, although they have a rocky start, the couple once again find themselves in a close embrace by the end of the present poem, thus bringing closure before the raucous, though admittedly ambiguous, scene that follows in poem fifteen.

Song of Songs 5:2–6:3 is a unity that has clearly defined subunits. The poem opens with the woman speaking. She is telling a story, an account of an experience. At the start, it is not at all clear that she is speaking to anyone, but 5:8 records her charge to the chorus, so perhaps it is best to understand the first verses as addressed to the chorus. Certainly the experience of 5:2-7, which details why her lover is absent from her, leads to the charge to the women to help her find her lover. They then respond to the woman's request by asking her for a description (5:9), and this sets up the woman's *wasf*, or descriptive poem, extolling the physical beauty of her lover.[1] While there are three other *wasf*'s (see 4:1-7; 6:4-7; and 7:2-8) in the Song, this one is the only one where the woman describes the man.[2] Finally, the woman tells the women of Jerusalem where to find the man: in the nut grove, a place that sug-

---

1. For more on the *wasf* as a genre, see the introduction to poem thirteen (Song of Songs 4:1–5:1).

2. D. C. Polaski (" 'What Will Ye See in the Shulammite?' Women, Power and Panopticism in the Song of Songs," *Biblical Interpretation* 5 [1997]: 75) points out a difference between the lover's descriptions of her and this female *wasf*: while she is with him when he describes her beauty, he is not with her in this *wasf*; rather, she speaks to the other women.

gests intimacy. She finishes off her speech with a climactic statement of mutuality.

The actions of the characters in the poem seem odd if judged by standards of everyday life. The man comes to the door, but she demurs at first. By the time she changes her mind and opens the door, he is gone. She sets out in hot pursuit, searching for him in public places. She does not find him and instead gets beaten by the city patrol. In real life, such abuse is traumatizing, but the next verse finds her unfazed and enlisting the aid of the chorus in her search. The point is that this poem, like all the other poems in the Song, are not focused on a real-life occurrence.[3] They are creating moods and sensations. We can debate whether the poem intends for us to understand this as the woman's dream or not, but we cannot insist that these are real experiences. They are dream-like and poetic.

This poem, especially the first part, utilizes some of the most erotic imagery in the Bible, but it does so very tastefully, through the use of double entendre. We will point these out in our verse-by-verse exposition.

The situation of the first part of this poem is reminiscent of the Chester Beatty Papyrus I, Group C, no. 46, which reads:

As for what she — (my) sister — did to me,
    should I keep silent to her?
She left me standing at the door of her house
    while she went inside,
and did not say to me "Welcome,"
    but blocked her ears in my night.[4]

Recently, C. E. Walsh has argued that the poem describes a woman's self-pleasuring.[5] Her reading of the poem is (overly) ingenious and perhaps tells us more about present desires than past intentions. Her interpretation is that this poem is ". . . a biblical wet dream of a woman, and an allusion to autoeroticism with her hands and fingers involved, and the man vanishing." However, a close examination shows that she reads the poem selectively and does not account either for the woman's search for the man who has vanished or for the implication that she finds him at the end.

Provocatively, A. Feuillet has read Song of Songs 5:2 in the light of Revelation 3:20: "Here I am! I stand at the door and knock. If anyone hears

3. Goulder (*The Song of Fourteen Songs*, p. 41) seems to think otherwise and takes it as a real scene the night after the wedding.
4. Cited from Fox, *The Song of Songs and the Ancient Egyptian Love Songs*, p. 75.
5. C. E. Walsh, "A Startling Voice: Woman's Desire in the Song of Songs," *BTB* 28 (1998): 129-34.

my voice and opens the door, I will come in and eat with him, and he with me."[6] Feuillet is driven by his overall approach to the Song, which preserves elements of the old allegorical approach. The metaphor of the door in the Song has a clear sexual meaning that it lacks in Revelation, so in the final analysis we cannot agree with Feuillet.

The Woman

2. *I was sleeping, but my mind[7] was alert.*
    The sound of my lover knocking![8]
"Open for me, my sister, my darling,
    my dove, my flawless one.[9]
My head is full of dew;
    my locks[10] with the drizzle[11] of the night."
3. *"I have taken off my clothes,[12]*
    should I get dressed again?
I have washed my feet,
    should I get them dirty?"
4. *My lover sent his hand through[13] the hole,*
    and my innards roiled toward him.[14]

6. A. Feuillet, "La double insertion du Cantique des Cantiques dans la vie de la communauté chrétienne et dans la tradition religieuse de l'Ancien Testament," *Divinitas* 35 (1991): 18.

7. Literally "heart," but here certainly referring to mental alertness.

8. The root *dpq* means to "drive hard, push, knock." It is used three times, twice of knocking at a door (the third occurrence is Gen. 33:13 and concerns driving flocks). In Judg. 19:22 it refers to the men of Gibeon who knock at the host's door to demand sex with the traveling Levite who is his guest.

9. "Flawless" *(tam)* denotes moral wholeness in many other contexts (Job 8:20; 9:20-22), but in the Song (see also 6:9) it most likely indicates physical perfection.

10. *Qᵉwuṣṣôt* is a rare word for "hair" (see its use also in 5:11); the more common word is *śeʿar*.

11. Or "wetness." The root *rss* means "to moisten" in this context as well as Ezek. 46:14 (cognate with Arabic and Syriac). In Amos 6:11 it means "to crush" (cognate with Old Akkadian, Mishnaic Hebrew, and Aramaic). See *NIDOTTE,* vol. 3, p. 1133.

12. According to *NIDOTTE,* vol. 2, pp. 742-43, *kuttōnet* "is a more specific item of clothing than those described by the root *lbš.* It is often a fine garment, a dressy robe, or something worn for show." Keel suggests it is an undergarment (*The Song of Songs,* p. 189).

13. The preposition *min* here with *šlḥ* has perplexed commentators since the combination would suggest a meaning of "from" for the preposition, which does not work well with the broader context. Pope (*Song of Songs,* p. 518) provides the details of the evidence that allows for a meaning of *through* or into.

14. A number of Hebrew manuscripts read "toward me" *(ʿly),* but there is no reason to accept this as a superior text (but see the NLT).

5. *I[15] stood up to open to my lover,*
   and my hands dripped myrrh
   and my fingers liquid myrrh
   on the handles of the lock.

6. *I[16] opened to my lover,*
   but my lover had gone away;[17] he had left.[18]
   My spirit had gone out at his speaking.
  I sought him, but did not find him.
   I called him, but he did not answer.

7. *The guards found me,*
   those who make their rounds in the city.
  They struck me; they bruised me.
   They lifted my garments from me,
   those guards of the walls.

8. *I adjure you, O daughters of Jerusalem,[19]*
   if you find my lover, what should you say to him?
   That I am sick with love!

The Women of Jerusalem

9. *How is your lover better than (another) lover, O most beautiful of*
   women?[20]
   How is your lover better than (another) lover, that we should so
   swear?

The Woman

10. *My lover is radiant and ruddy,*
   distinguished among ten thousand!

11. *His head is pure gold.*
   His locks are wavy, black like a raven.

12. *His eyes are like doves by water streams,*

---

15. Note the pleonastic use of "I" (*ˀănî*) in this colon.

16. As at the beginning of v. 5, note the use of the pleonastic first-person pronoun.

17. The verb *ḥmq* occurs only twice in the Hebrew Bible, here and in Jer. 31:22, where it occurs in the hithpael (not the qal as in our verse) with the meaning of moral and spiritual wavering. A noun form occurs in Song of Songs 7:2 (English 7:1).

18. The Septuagint has only one verb for the lover's abandonment at the end of the clause, not two. Either the verb was missing from the *Vorlage* of the Septuagint or else the translator treated it as a hendiadys.

19. For a discussion of the *daughters*, their identity and their function in the Song, see the Introduction as well as the commentary at 1:4, 5, where they make their first appearance.

20. For this epithet of the woman, see the commentary at 1:8.

> *bathing[21] in milk,*
> *sitting by pools.[22]*

13. *His cheeks are like spice beds[23]*
    growing[24] aromatics.[25]
    His lips are lilies
    dripping with liquid myrrh.

14. *His arms[26] are bars[27] of gold,*
    set[28] with Tarshish-stones.
    His member is an ivory tusk,
    ornamented[29] with lapis.

15. *His legs[30] are pillars of marble,[31]*
    founded on gold pedestals.
    His appearance is like Lebanon,
    choice like the cedars.

16. *His palate is sweet.*
    He is totally desirable.

21. The Septuagint has "bathed" *(lelousmenai)*.

22. The MT *yōšᵉbôt 'al-millē't* literally means "sitting on fullness." Here we follow the lead of the Septuagint *(kathēmenai epi plerōmata hydatōn)* and the Vulgate *(et resident juxta fluenta plenissima)*, which render "sitting by the fullness of water."

23. Reading as plural (ending with *-gôt* instead of *-gat*), which fits the context better and also the parallel in 6:2. This is further supported by some Hebrew manuscripts as well as the versions.

24. The MT *migdᵉlôt* "towers" is often (as here) emended to *mᵉgadᵉlôt*, the piel feminine participle of *gdl*, with the support of the Septuagint *(phyousai)* and the Vulgate *(consitae a)*. Keel (*The Song of Songs*, p. 196) stays with the MT and translates "His cheeks are like beds of [balsam], (like) towers of ointments."

25. Note the related word *reqaḥ* in 8:2.

26. *Yad* usually means hand but can mean the arm (Gen. 24:30, 47; Jer. 38:12). Ancient Near Eastern evidence also indicates that it can denote the male member, but this meaning is unlikely in the present context because it is plural.

27. *Gālîl* has an uncertain meaning in the present context. It occurs in two other contexts. In 1 Kings 6:34 (twice) it refers to the hinge of double doors. In Esth. 1:6 it is a silver rod or rings from which curtains hang. The meaning *rods* or *bars* is appropriate for these contexts, and it is fitting to the meaning of the root verb *gll* "to roll."

28. The pual feminine participle of *ml'* has this meaning according to *NIDOTTE*, vol. 2, pp. 939-41.

29. The pual feminine participle of *'lp* (see grammatical parallelism with v. 14a).

30. *Šôq* can refer to the leg or the thigh, usually the latter when in reference to a sacrificial animal (*NIDOTTE*, vol. 4, p. 70).

31. Or perhaps "alabaster"; see *NIDOTTE*, vol. 4, pp. 258-59. The word occurs only here and in Esth. 1:6, where it refers to the marble or alabaster of Ahasuerus's courtyard.

This is my lover and this is my darling, O daughters of
Jerusalem.[32]

The Women of Jerusalem
6:1. *Where did your lover go, O most beautiful of women?*[33]
   Where did your lover turn,[34]
   that we may search for him with you?

The Woman
2. *My lover went down to his garden,*
   to the bed of spices,[35]
to graze in the gardens,
   to pluck the lilies.
3. *I belong to my lover,*
   and my lover belongs to me —
   he grazes among the lilies.

2   The mental state of the woman in the first clause of this verse has been much debated. One's determination of this question could affect the understanding of the whole poem. The question is, Was she asleep and awakened by the knock on the door, or was she sleeping lightly and dreaming the contents of the poem that follows?[36] The language is ambiguous, but I would like to suggest that this question is really not as important as it appears to be. The question is most pressing if we are dealing with a real historical situation, but the action that follows this introduction is almost surreal and, later, when the woman is abused by the city guards (5:7), somewhat sadistic. The approach taken by this commentary, as we noted in the Introduction (see Introduction: Genre), is that the couple and the action are fictional. We are moving in the world of poetry with its associated themes, motifs, and images.[37]

   The action of the poem begins in earnest when the woman hears a *knocking* at her door. This sound is followed by the voice of her lover, who

32. I am treating this last line as a climactic monocolon.
33. For this epithet of the woman, see 1:8.
34. The Septuagint wrongly rendered *pānâ* as "look away" *(apeblepsen).*
35. See the similar construction in 5:13.
36. *The Message* makes the latter interpretation explicit when it freely translates, "I was sound asleep, but in my dreams I was wide awake."
37. S. Israelit-Groll ("Ostracon Nash 12 and Chapter 5 of Song of Songs," in *Proceedings of the Tenth World Congress of Jewish Studies* [Jerusalem, 1990]) notes that a parallel with language in the Egyptian Ostracon Nash suggests that 5:1 indicates "to be in a state of dreaming" (p. 134). The parallel does not seem to be as close as she suggests.

asks her to *open*. In the context, it is clear that the door is meant. He wants her to open the door so that he can be with her. However, this is not the only level of meaning. Throughout this poem we have the use of double entendre, not only a surface meaning for the action but also the use of sexual euphemism, and part of that double entendre is that he is asking her to open up to him sexually. After all, the door, unmentioned but implied in his request, is a long-standing symbol for entry into a woman's body.[38] We might note first Gilgamesh's charge to the promiscuous Ishtar that she is a "back door [which does not] keep out blast and windstorm."[39] More recently, the rock group Led Zeppelin sings, "I wanna be your backdoor man." The door is clearly a euphemism for a woman's vagina, and an open door denotes a sexually available woman. In the context of the Song and the intimate, exclusive relationship described here, there is no question of promiscuity, just sexual openness (see also Song of Songs 8:9).

In the process of inviting her to sexual union, he pours on the complimentary epithets, most of which we have already seen. She is his *sister* (see 4:9, 10, 12; 5:1), his *darling* (1:9, 15; 2:2, 10, 13; 4:1, 7; 6:4), and his *dove* (2:14). Yet here he caps it off by referring to her as his *flawless one*. She is perfection itself (see also 6:9).

In the last bicolon of the verse, the man, still outside, describes the condition of his hair as wet. I feel less confident suggesting that there is sexual euphemism here. The man, though, has braved uncomfortable conditions to be united with his beloved. This again is a story of desire, of yearning for union, but the next verse suggests a less than happy outcome.

3 The woman here responds to her lover's request that she open up to him. She does not respond with enthusiasm. Are we to suspect coyness here?[40] If so, it fails since her reaction sends him away (see v. 6). More likely her response suggests her lack of readiness for union. She is undressed and does not want to get *dressed again* (does she really suspect that that is what her lover wants?). She has *washed her feet*, and she doesn't want to walk across the floor and *dirty* them again. The first colon has obvious sexual overtones, but what about the second? Perhaps again we are justified in suggesting double entendre. After all, *feet* are a well-known euphemism for genitalia, both male (Exod. 4:25; Judg. 3:24; 1 Sam. 24:4 [English 24:3]; Ruth

38. See also the commentary at 8:9 and the comment by Bergant, "'My Beloved Is Mine and I Am His' (Song 2:16)," p. 31.

39. Tablet VI, line 33, in *ANET*, p. 84. The theme is also found in earlier Sumerian literature and is probably part of marriage ritual, as pointed out by Sefati (*Love Songs in Sumerian Literature*, p. 104), who writes: "after the bride bathes, adorns herself, and opens the door for the groom, who knocks at it, which constitutes the major symbolic act of marriage, comes the sexual union of the couple."

40. So Murphy, *The Song of Songs*, p. 170.

3:4, 7) and female (Deut. 28:57; Ezek. 16:25),[41] in the Old Testament. If this is double entendre, then she is expressing her reluctance to engage in physical intimacy at this point.

4 Undeterred by his beloved's apparently cool reception to his arrival, the man tries to force his way in. On the surface, he tries to undo the lock on the door, which is alluded to by the word *hole* (*ḥōr;* the lock [*man'ûl*] is mentioned explicitly in the next verse). However, nowhere else does the word "hole" indicate a lock on a door, which may be a clue to the reader to look for additional significance to the word. Since we have observed above the presence of double entendre, which will continue in what follows, we are justified in asking the question of whether "hole" has some kind of sexual meaning. In the commentary to 5:2 we noted the potential sexual overtones of the door, and when we think about a hole in a door in such an erotically charged context, I believe we are led to the conclusion that this verse implies a sexual overture on the part of the man. We might add that the noun *hand,* said to be thrust through the hole itself, is used occasionally in Hebrew for the male penis (Isa. 57:8-10). M. H. Pope also describes at length the Ugaritic evidence, particularly the extended discourse about El's hand in the myth "The Birth of the Beautiful Gods."[42]

This viewpoint is supported by the woman's reaction. The term *innards (me'ah)* has the broad connotation of the interior or exterior abdominal area, but most commentators recognize that the woman's lower erogenous zone is the referent here. In response to the man's thrust of his *hand,* these innards roil or, as Pope translates, "seeth"[43] toward him. It is true that the exact meaning of the combination of innards *(me'ah)* and roil *(hmh)* will depend on its context. They appear also in Jeremiah 51:39 in the relationship between a mother and a son (metaphorically of God and Israel), expressing an intense emotional desire or longing.

5 In response to her lover's overture, she gets up and moves to the door. She indeed will *open* to her lover. She moves toward him with anticipation of union. That anticipation is underlined by the image of dripping *myrrh,* implied in the second colon and made explicit by the adjective in the third colon. Myrrh can come in a solid form or be liquefied. The debate has centered over the issue of where the myrrh came from. Was it the man who left it on the lock, or was it left there by the woman who quickly grabbed some myrrh with which to anoint her lover? The issue is really unimportant; the mention

41. See *NIDOTTE,* vol. 3, p. 1048, where it is also noted that urine is described as "water of feet" in 2 Kings 18:27//Isa. 36:12.

42. Pope, *Song of Songs,* pp. 517-18. See earlier M. Delcor, "Two Special Meanings of the Word *yd* in Biblical Hebrew," *JSS* 12 (1967): 230-40.

43. Pope, *Song of Songs,* p. 519.

of the sweet-smelling ointment and the sensuous description of a thick-dripping liquid certainly add to the erotic atmosphere of this section.

6 The moment comes when, on one reading of the text, she opens the door of her house to her lover, but the result is disappointment. With the other equally valid reading, she opens herself up to her lover's intimacies, where too she experiences disappointment. He is not there any longer. He has *gone away, left*. We are not explicitly told why he has left, but perhaps it is a natural inference from the woman's verbal response to her lover's request to open up to him that he has gone because of her initial reluctance. Perhaps the double verb at the end of the second colon is a hendiadys, but we have chosen to translate them as two verbs in order to capture what we take to be her emphatic disappointment, perhaps even her disbelief.

The third colon of the verse gives expression to her emotions. However, we must acknowledge some ambiguity in the colon, and for that reason we have chosen to translate the Hebrew rather woodenly as *my spirit had gone out at his speaking*. We have more than one option for understanding this line, and we find it difficult to adjudicate the issue. The first decision we must make is how to understand the prepositional phrase that ends the colon (*bᵉdabbᵉrô*). We have understood the base verbal stem of the phrase to be the common *dbr* II "to speak," but it is also possible that it may be related to *dbr* I "to turn away, drive away."[44] That is, her spirit went out at his abandonment. It fits the context well, but *dbr* I occurs much less frequently than *dbr* II, and a number of its attestations are disputed.[45] Our decision on *dbr* has an effect on our understanding of the rest of the colon. The going out of her spirit could conceivably indicate either longing or disappointment.[46] We are suggesting by our translation an interpretation of the phrase that indicates her reaction when she heard him speak. At first she was reluctant, but his voice filled her with longing that moved her to open up to her lover. The other interpretation implies that her spirit left her when she discovered his absence. Of course, both interpretations make psychological sense in the context.

Her discovery of his absence sends her out in hot, but futile, pursuit. She did not find him, but she herself was found, unfortunately, as we will learn in the next verse.

7 In the previous verse, the woman had set out in pursuit of her absent lover. This search took her from the private intimacies of her bedroom out into the cold public gaze of the city. The *guards* represent the public

---

44. Murphy (*The Song of Songs*, p. 165) and Pope (*Song of Songs,* p. 526) understand it this way.

45. See *NIDOTTE*, vol. 1, pp. 912-15, for discussion of both *dbr* I and II.

46. Notice the use of the combination of *nepeš* and *yṣ'* in Gen. 35:18, where it indicates death.

gaze that treats the woman brutally (see also Song of Songs 3:3).[47] On a literal level, it is not too harsh to speak of their treatment of the woman as physical and sexual abuse. They hit her hard enough to leave bruises. They remove some of her clothing. The word that we translate generally as *garments (rᵉdîd)* is more specific than that, but since we are not quite sure exactly what type of clothing it is, we leave it more general. Two of the leading contenders for the specific nuance of *rᵉdîd,* based on Arabic and Syriac cognates, respectively, are "cloak" and "veil." Whatever the specific item of clothing, the city guards treat her with harshness. Some speculate that she is being taken and treated as a prostitute, but, even so, the treatment is inappropriate in its Old Testament cultural context. Some press the fact that this is a dream sequence, a view that we have questioned above. We must admit, however, that the movement of this part of the poem is better understood as a dream than as an actual event. Otherwise, the motivations are difficult to understand. After all, as we will see, this beating and abuse gives the woman little pause. She continues in her search and actually adopts a very upbeat attitude, as is evidenced by her upcoming description of the physical attributes of her lover. We understand the poem as a poem, not as a dream or an event. As such, we are not driven to provide motivations as much as to understand the symbolic function of the guard's treatment of the woman, which we have already taken as the unfriendly urban-public gaze versus the private intimacies of the couple.

8   The woman's search continues. With no apparent effects from her beating by the city patrol, she turns now to the *daughters of Jerusalem* to aid her in her search. The daughters seem to appear out of thin air, but this is only a problem for those who want to treat the poem as a narrative of an actual event. She begins by making them swear to a promise *(I adjure you).* This phrase has already been encountered in 2:7 and 3:5, where the fuller formula is "I adjure you by the gazelles or the deer of the field." The shorter formula is used here, but note that the Septuagint adds the concluding phrase. What is it that she makes them promise? She makes them promise to give her lover a message if and when they find him. That message is *I am sick with love.* She used this exact phrase *(kî-ḥôlat 'ahᵃbâ 'anî)* in 2:5, but there, we would argue, with a slightly different nuance. In chapter 2, she was physically spent from the exercise of love. She needed the sustenance of food, of aphrodisiacs, to carry on. In other words, he is present in the poem in chapter 2. Here, however, he is absent, and so here the translation "sick" rather than "faint" is appropriate. She pines for him. She needs him desperately. Her message is an exclamation of desire and a plea for union.

---

47. For the contrast between the city and private settings in the Song, see Falk, *Love Lyrics in the Bible,* pp. 139-43.

9 The woman's speech to the daughters of Jerusalem elicits a question from them *(How is your lover better than [another] lover?).* This question looks back to her request to look for her man but also will introduce the following section of the poem. In effect, their question will evoke a poem that describes the physical attributes of the man (a *wasf*)[48] delivered by the woman. This verse and the preceding provide a neat little segue from the first part of the poem, where the woman is initially reluctant to present her passionate description of the lover.

The daughters of Jerusalem simply ask her, "What's so special about this man?" This gives her the opportunity to answer in verses 10-13. The question is given in a repetitive bicolon, where the first part repeats. We have translated that first part as *"How is your lover better than another lover?"* As R. E. Murphy points out,[49] it is literally "What is your lover from (= more than) a lover?" The idea is, how does your lover stand out from others, and the *wasf* that follows will answer that question.

10 The question by the daughters of Jerusalem provokes the woman to present a *wasf* extolling the physical beauty of the man. It begins with a general statement on his body. He is *radiant (ṣaḥ),* a word that denotes the healthy hue of his skin. The related verb *shh* is used for healthy-looking skin in Lamentations 4:7; in our context we have the adjective. His skin is also *ruddy ('ādôm),* a noun related to the verb *'dm* "to be red." Esau, we might remember, was associated with this word, and considered "very red" at birth. Esau was the patriarch of the Edomites, another name associated with the root. David too was ruddy, according to 1 Samuel 16:12; 17:42. Murphy and Pope wonder whether this redness should be associated with cosmetics.[50] However, the word signifies a rather broad swath of the color spectrum and includes brown or brownish red, which could signify the color of skin rather than cosmetics.[51]

The woman also begins her description by stating up front that this man is like few others. He is one in *ten thousand.* Certainly, this is an idiom that means he is like no other in her estimation. The meaning of the word *distinguished (dagul)* has caused consternation among commentators since the root occurs with an apparently different meaning in 2:4; 6:4, 10. The Septuagint and Vulgate renderings help us with what appears to be a *hapax* use of the verb *dgl* I, cognate with an Akkadian root "to look."

11 She now proceeds to specify different parts of his body, working her way from top to bottom. She begins with his *head,* which is described as

48. See pp. 140-42.
49. Murphy, *The Song of Songs,* p. 165.
50. Murphy, *The Song of Songs,* p. 165. Pope, *Song of Songs,* pp. 531-32.
51. Cf. *NIDOTTE,* vol. 1, p. 262.

pure gold.[52] Pope points out that the closest analogue in the Bible is to Nebuchadnezzar's statue in Daniel 2, and, outside the Bible, to statues of idols. Perhaps she is saying he is "God-like" in appearance, but certainly this is a description of a human male, not a divine being. She next compliments his hair. The second part of the description is clear. His hair is *black* like the feathers of a *raven*. Ravens indeed were and are a deep black. The problem with the description of his hair (the relatively rare word *locks* [*qewûṣṣôt*] is used here; cf. 5:2) is with the first compliment and, in particular, with the word that we have taken with not a great deal of confidence as *wavy (taltalîm)*. The Akkadian and Arabic cognates point to the date cluster or palm frond.[53] Pope, however, calls to our attention the rabbinical Hebrew use of the word as curly.[54]

12 Her praise of the man's physical beauty continues with a description of his eyes. There is some debate over whether the entire verse is devoted to the topic of his eyes. Murphy,[55] citing A. Vaccari,[56] puts forward a strong case for the dropping of a reference to the teeth in the second half of the verse. He translates:

> His eyes, like doves
> by the water streams.
> (His teeth) washed in milk,
> set in place.

He presents three arguments in favor of this view. First, the description is appropriate for the teeth. However, we wonder whether this is true. He understands the milk metaphor as a reference to glistening teeth, the result of a coat of saliva. However, the liquid is not really white, and thus milk is not really appropriate here (of course recognizing that Murphy would say that it is the teeth that provides the whiteness). Furthermore, the usual explanation of the metaphor in relationship to the eyes is quite reasonable. That is, the pupil, represented by the dove (see 1:15), is awash in the whiteness of the rest of the eye. The two other arguments that Murphy marshals in support of the teeth have to do with the structure of the *waṣf*. Second, Murphy argues that if we read both bicola as referring to the eyes, then this would be the only place where a part of the body has two parallel lines; the rest have only one. Third, and closely connected to his second argument (indeed, perhaps a repeat of it),

---

52. The poet uses two words for gold *(ketem pāz),* which seems to be an indication of the special nature of the gold, thus *fine gold.*

53. Thus, Murphy's translation *(The Song of Songs,* p. 164), "his hair, palm fronds." Exactly what this signifies is ambiguous.

54. Pope, *Song of Songs,* p. 536.

55. Murphy, *The Song of Songs,* p. 166.

56. A. Vaccari, "Note critiche ed esegetiche," *Bib* 28 (1947): 399-401.

he mentions that, again, if both bicola refer to the eyes, then this would be the only place where a part of the body does not begin a line. The argument(s) from structure have some force, but do they perhaps impose too rigid a requirement upon the poet? Just because this is the only variant from the pattern, does that mean that we must squeeze it into the expected structure? This represents a rather rigid application of form criticism that needs to be avoided.[57] In the final analysis, the Vaccari-Murphy proposal is a conjectural emendation; the versions apparently do not have a problem with the MT. For these reasons, we stay with the text as we find it in the MT.

Nonetheless, we do recognize that we are left with some uncertainty as to the force of the compliment. As mentioned in the commentary at 1:15, the connection between the eye, in this case specifically the pupil, and a dove is uncertain. Does it denote color? That perhaps is doubtful since the color of a dove is not particularly striking. Perhaps it is the softness of the dove, or simply its beauty in the eyes of the ancient poet. More likely, the fluttering of the eyes is being compared to the fluttering wings of a dove.[58] The extended metaphor of doves by streams of water, bathed in milk, and sitting by pools (if the latter is the correct interpretation) seems to emphasize the glistening nature of the eyes. It is interesting to note that the image of bathing or bathed in milk applies awkwardly to the doves, although this image is by no means beyond the practice of the biblical poet. While the first and second images are appropriate to doves "literally," the same is not true of bathing in milk. Nonetheless, the poet is playing with reality here in his creation of an image that describes the pupil highlighted by the eye's whiteness.

13 Next comes the woman's description of the man's *cheeks* and *lips*. Or is the first half of the verse really speaking of the man's beard? I think this likely, especially considering the fact that as far as we can tell men in all periods of Israel's history wore beards. Indeed, there were laws that prohibited clipping beards (Lev. 19:27; 21:5), and to shave was embarrassing (2 Sam. 10:4; Isa. 15:2).[59] The description of the cheeks as growing a bed of spices also seems to fit with the view that this half verse is really about a beard (which, after all, also grows). Interestingly, though, the emphasis that the poet places on the beard has nothing really to do with its looks, but rather its smell. The man's beard is a veritable garden of spices. Again, the olfactory images imply a certain physical closeness, as well as a desire to get even closer.

---

57. See T. Longman III, "Form Criticism, Recent Developments in Genre Theory, and the Evangelical," *WTJ* 46 (1985): 46-67.

58. So Goulder, *The Song of Fourteen Songs,* p. 5.

59. Thus, we disagree with Keel's interpretation (*The Song of Songs,* p. 201) that refers this description to a beardless cheek.

The second half of the verse describes the man's *lips*. They are like *lilies* (see also 2:1, 2, 16; 4:5; 6:2), but again the comparison is somewhat unclear. Is this a reference to color, shape, or simply, as Keel[60] (who along with Pope takes the noun as a reference to the lotus rather than the lily) suggests, to the "enlivening effect of their kisses"? There is no question that his lips arouse desire in her. They drip with liquid myrrh (5:5). While his lips drip myrrh, her lips, as we previously saw, drip honey (4:11).

14   The woman's description of the man's physical beauty continues with her praise of his arms and, then, his sexual organ. Both parallel lines of this verse have difficulties of interpretation. What does it mean to picture his arms as bars of gold, set with gems? Perhaps the description in verses 14-15 pictures the man as a statue. I do not believe that this should be taken as evidence that the man is really an idol, even though some of this language could be used to describe the statues that represented gods in the ancient Near East. Perhaps, however, she is using god-like language to describe the man. He has taken on larger-than-life proportions to her. Her vision is the vision of love.

It is also possible that her language reflects a physical reality. Perhaps his arms are covered with gold bracelets that have gems set in them. Perhaps it is just a way of speaking about how precious each of his physical attributes are to her. His arms are like gold, and not mere gold but bejeweled gold. We do not know the exact identity of *Tarshish* gems. We assume that they are gems that originate in Tarshish, but even if we are right in identifying Tarshish with Spanish Tartessos, this would only narrow down the identity of the gems. The two leading candidates, according to Zimmerli,[61] would be black jet or golden topaz (see also Exod. 28:20; 39:13; Ezek. 1:16; 10:9; 28:13; Dan. 10:6).

I will admit up front that I am being more adventurous than usual in my translation and interpretation of the second part of the verse. It is conceivable that the verse simply is referring to the fact that his stomach is as smooth as a slab of *ivory*. However, the words are too suggestive for me to settle on that approach. When one thinks of ivory, one thinks of a tusk of ivory, an object that could easily have erotic connotations. The decoration with *lapis,* a precious stone blue in color, simply would highlight the object's preciousness. In such an erotic poem, the line at the least is suggestive of, if not explicitly referring to, the man's member, and thus it is to be compared to the well-garden imagery in 4:12-13. The word that we are here translating as member *(me'eh)* also had an erotic sense in regard to the woman in 5:4.

15   The woman has been steadily working down the man's body,

60. Keel, *The Song of Songs,* p. 201.
61. W. Zimmerli, *Ezekiel 25–48,* trans. J. D. Martin (Minneapolis: Fortress, 1985), p. 83.

proclaiming it delectable. She lowers her gaze below his hips and comments on his *legs*. They are like marble pillars with gold pedestals. We have already noted that this language at least vaguely reflects a description of statues of gods in the ancient Near East. We have rejected Pope's idea that this means that the lover is really a deity, but we have affirmed that this insight does indicate the high nature of the praise. With this verse and the next, we note that the language reflects a description of materials and resources utilized by the temple. Again, we resist using this fact to allegorize the text, but again we suggest that it associates her description with something exalted, even holy. In a word, her description of the man is extravagant, which makes public her strong desire for him.

Indeed, the term for *leg* (or thigh, *šôq*) is used predominantly to describe the thigh of an animal that is sacrificed in the temple. Of course, *pillars (ʿammûd)*, most notably the two named pillars, Jachin and Boaz (cf. 7:15-22; also 1 Kings 7:6) form a significant part of the temple structure. Furthermore, if *šayiš* is related to *šēš*, as Pope believes, then it is interesting that the former is mentioned in 2 Chronicles 29:2 as being collected for use in the temple. The word for *pedestals (ʾdn)* is used often in the description of the tabernacle (Exodus 26–27; 35–36; 38–40), and *gold (pāz)* is found especially in the more holy places. The connections are too numerous to be simply haphazard; at the least, we should note that two extremely precious objects (the tabernacle/temple and the man) are described using similar terms.

As with most imagery, the exact significance of the comparisons are difficult to pin down. His legs are like *marble*. Perhaps that signifies strength and/or smoothness and/or complexion. They are set on *gold*. Is this simply to differentiate the feet from the legs? Certainly it indicates that the whole is bounded by the most precious of metals (cf. 5:11).

The verse concludes with a general compliment to the man to the effect that his whole *appearance*[62] is like *Lebanon*. The line then gets more specific in its metaphor by picking out the most precious commodity of that region, namely, its cedars. Lebanon with its mountains denotes beauty and grandeur. The cedars do as well, being among the most majestic of trees. The latter also evoke the sense of smell, since that tree is among the most fragrant of trees. The cedars of Lebanon too were used in the construction of the temple.

16 The woman has now described his body from head to feet, concluding with the general statement concerning his physical beauty. However, she is not yet done. She concludes with a comment about his mouth, indeed, his inner mouth or *palette (ḥēk)*. The reason appears to be that this anticipates her desired action. The inside of his mouth is described as *sweet* (the root is *mtq;* see also 2:3 and 4:11). The implicit message is that she wants to taste

62. *Mar'ēh;* see its use in reference to the woman in 2:14.

him. Her comments anticipate a deep kiss. Of course, she has to find him first.

Again, she concludes with a general comment, this time with a statement of her intense desire for him. The word *desirable (maḥᵃmaddîm)* derives from the root *ḥmd*.[63] "All the derivatives of *hmd* refer to outward appearance. They also emphasize more the attractiveness of an object, with some emphasis on the value of the object."[64]

The *wasf* ends with a definitive proclamation to the women, the daughters of Jerusalem, to whom she has been speaking. They asked in 5:9 for a description of her lover, and she has given it to them. For daughters of Jerusalem, see the comments at 1:4; 2:7, and the Introduction. For her epithets of the man, see 1:14 for lover *(dwd)* and 1:15 for darling *(re'a)*.

6:1   As mentioned in the introduction to this section, the chapter division is not felicitous. The poem continues, though now the women of Jerusalem respond to the woman's description of the man. Note the similarities in structure to the question in 5:9. There they asked what was it about the man that should stir them into the action of searching for him. Now they are more than persuaded. As T. Gledhill comments, ". . . now the girl's companions are convinced that this paragon of masculine beauty, this almost god-like figure, is worth finding, and they want to catch a glimpse of him."[65]

The questions of the daughters of Jerusalem serve as a catalyst to the speeches of the woman, and so in the next verse she begins to describe the place where the man fled.

2   The logic of this section is strange. The lover is lost to the woman, and she has enlisted the aid of the women of Jerusalem to find him. Yet then in answer to their question in 6:1 she responds with her lover's location. He is in the *garden*. However, what our initial confusion demonstrates more than anything is the problem of applying logic to the scene as if it is a real occurrence rather than a poetic reverie. The theme of seek and find, which characterizes this poem, expresses the desire of the woman for the man. He has never really left her, but the struggle for union finds consummation here only at the end of the poem.

The themes and images of this verse have found expression elsewhere in the Song. The *garden*,[66] for instance, is a symbol both for the woman herself as well as for the place where love is made (4:12, 15; 5:1). Here the two merge. He has *gone down to the garden;* that is, he is intimately united with

---

63. Most notable for its use in the tenth commandment. See its previous use in the Song (2:3).

64. *NIDOTTE,* vol. 2, p. 168.

65. Gledhill, *The Message of the Song of Songs,* p. 185.

66. Similar to the vineyard theme.

her. The garden is no ordinary garden, but a garden of sweet-smelling *spices* (so the intensification in the second colon).

Pope and others in the school of cultic interpretation have overread the verb *yārad (go down)* to signify a descent into the netherworld.[67] If one accepts the overall premise of a cultic reading, which we do not, then perhaps there is some justification for such an interpretation. We have described and criticized this approach to the book in the Introduction (see pp. 44-46).

The theme of grazing (from *r'h*) to express intimacy has been observed in 2:16 and 4:5; the former is especially appropriate to the meaning of the present verse (see also the conclusion of 6:3). Here the theme is expanded. In the other occurrences the phrase is simply to graze among the *lilies*. In the present verse, colon a speaks of grazing in the garden in general, whereas colon b specifies plucking or gathering the lilies. For the significance of lilies, see the commentary at 2:1.

3 This lengthy poem climaxes with a formula of mutual affection. We have here the same formula, though in reverse order, as we saw in 2:16 (see also 7:11). I do not believe we can attach much significance to the reversal of order, but we can find significance in the fact that a poem that begins with the problem of alienation between the man and the woman ends with an affirmation of togetherness.

67. Pope, *Song of Songs,* pp. 554-55.

CHAPTER SIX

POEM FIFTEEN:
AWESOME AS AN ARMY UNDER BANNERS (6:4-10)

The previous poem (5:2–6:3) left the woman telling the daughters of Jerusalem that her man was in the garden. Her speech may imply that she would journey to be with him there. Poem fifteen is in large part the man's speech as he describes the unique beauty of the woman. Nothing in the poem itself, however, leads us to believe that the man is present in the nut grove and speaking to the woman there. We, therefore, treat it as a separate song. The end of this poem is marked by an inclusio. The man starts by proclaiming that the woman is "awesome as an army under banners" (v. 4), and the unit ends with a group of women giving the identical affirmation (v. 10).[1] While some commentators add 6:11, 12 to the end of this poem,[2] this works against the inclusio. In addition, there are no strong semantic connections between the two sections. We have thus decided to treat 6:11-12 as a separate poem.

Poem fifteen is another example of a *wasf,* or descriptive poem (see also 4:1-7; 5:10-16; 7:1-5). This is the second *wasf* in which the man describes the beauty of the woman, and there are some repetitions of imagery from the first. Nonetheless, there are innovations as well. This *wasf* is in the context of arguing that the woman's beauty is superior, even unique, compared to the beauty of others — represented by the sixty queens, eighty concubines, and countless young women. At the conclusion, even they will join in their enthusiastic assessment of her beauty (6:10). The woman's beauty is so great that it shakes the man to the very core (v. 5). She is surrounded by

1. See the commentary at 6:4 for the debate over the exact translation of this repeated phrase.
2. See Goulder, *The Song of Fourteen Songs,* pp. 48-52, and LaCocque, *Romance She Wrote,* pp. 127-50.

mystery. Geographical, military, floral, and faunal imagery are all evoked to give a sense of her hold on the man's affections.

The Man

4. *You are beautiful, my darling, as Tirzah,*
     attractive as Jerusalem,
     awesome[3] as an army under banners.
5. *Turn your eyes away from me;*
     for[4] they unsettle me.
   Your hair is like a flock of goats,
     streaming from Gilead.[5]
6. *Your teeth are like a flock of ewes, coming up from the washing.*
     Each is paired; not one of them is missing.
7. *Like a slice of pomegranate is your temple*
     behind your veil.
8. *There may be sixty queens*
     and eighty concubines,
     even countless young women,
9. *but my dove, my flawless one — she is unique!*
     She is the only one of her mother;
     she is favored of the one who bore her.
   The daughters saw her and called her blessed!
   Queens and concubines praised her!

The Women of Jerusalem

10. *Who is this who looks down like the dawn,*
      beautiful as the moon,
      bright as the sun,
      awesome as an army under banners?

4 This poem is a second *waṣf* of the man describing the woman's beauty. Indeed, it contains allusions and even exact repetitions from the first description found in 4:1-7. The *waṣf* starts, e.g., with a general affirmation of the woman's beauty. However, in the present poem he begins with metaphor. The woman is compared to two cities, *Tirzah* and *Jerusalem. Jerusalem,* of

---

3. From *'āyōm,* occurring only three times: here, Song of Songs 6:10, and Hab. 1:7 (in reference to the Chaldean threat). There is a *Nebenform,* however, *'ēymâ,* that occurs much more frequently.

4. Understanding the *še* to have a causal sense; cf. Pope, *Song of Songs,* p. 564.

5. The parallel text in 4:1 has the fuller expression "from Mount Gilead," making the mountain *(har)* explicit.

course, is well known; *Tirzah* is not, though it had its moment of fame as the capital of the northern kingdom from the time of Jeroboam (1 Kings 14:17; 15:21, 33; 16:6, 8, 9, 15, 17, 23) until Omri moved the capital to his new city of Samaria (1 Kings 16:24, 28). Archeologists have identified Tirzah with Tell el-Farah, which is six miles north of Shechem. To be honest, we cannot be sure what guided the poet to compare the beauty of the woman to the city of Tirzah. Perhaps this particular poem was written during the heyday of this city, but most scholars judge that to be unlikely since at that time the north and south were bitter enemies. However, if the city was renowned for its beauty, the poet may have transcended political enmity to make the comparison, thus evoking not only two beautiful cities but also two powerful cities. After all, as we learn at the next half verse, her beauty arouses not only desire but also fear. Perhaps the choice of Tirzah is as simple as the connection between the city's name and the Hebrew verb *rṣy* "to be pleasing." All of these factors may indeed be operative. It is totally unnecessary to suggest that the city of Tirzah is not meant here. Indeed, it may be that the author was avoiding a reference to Samaria, precisely because of the political hostilities between the north the south.[6] As O. Keel has rightly pointed out, if cities can be compared to women, then women can be compared to cities.[7] M. H. Pope seems more driven by an interesting comparison to an Ugaritic grammatical construction than to the sense of the text when he provides a convoluted argument that the word is not a reference to the city of that name but rather is a nominal form of the verb *rṣy*.[8] He further argues that the reference to Jerusalem must be a mistake as well, and then he argues for an unusual meaning of the word *nidgālôt* to reach the following translation of the verse:

> Fair you are, my darling, verily pleasing,
> Beautiful as Jerusalem,
> Awesome with trophies.

Pope seems to understand that his suggestion for this verse is unlikely to find acceptance,[9] and he is right in that regard.

The reference to Jerusalem seems natural and obvious in this context once we grant the appropriateness of the comparison between a woman and a city. After all, Jerusalem is "the perfection of beauty" (Ps. 50:2). It is "mag-

---

6. J. H. Walton, V. H. Matthews, and M. W. Chavalas, *The IVP Bible Background Commentary: Old Testament,* p. 579.

7. Keel, *The Song of Songs,* pp. 212-13; contra Pope, *Song of Songs,* pp. 558-60.

8. Though the Septuagint does support reading the word as a nominal form of *rṣy* rather than as a city name *(eudokia).*

9. Pope offers his interpretation "with diffidence and without expectation of instant acceptance" *(Song of Songs,* p. 560).

nificent in elevation — the whole earth rejoices to see it!" The sight of Jerusalem excites joy and evokes awe (Psalm 122).

The beauty of the woman is so overpowering that it arouses fear as well as joy. This *wasf,* as the one in chapter 4, begins its specification of the beauty of the woman with her eyes, and here and in the first half of verse 5 we see that they overwhelm the man. It is the face, particularly the eyes, that bring us into the most intense contact with another person. There is a division over the precise nuance of the last phrase of verse 4. We have understood the word *dgl* as *dgl* II, which means "to carry [or set up] a banner or standard." It is a niphal participle that is used as a noun. Others, however, take it from *dgl* I, which means "to look," or "behold."[10] In the latter sense, R. E. Murphy[11] translates "awe-inspiring as visions," and N. Snaith[12] renders "splendid as the heavenly phenomena." More recently, G. A. Long has argued from this latter meaning for the translation "overwhelming like the[se] sights [i.e., Tirzah and Jerusalem]."[13] However, these suggestions are put forward in the first place because it seems odd to have military metaphors in a love poem. Yet in many places the Song uses military images, and it makes sense from a psychological point of view because the presence of one who is loved can cause one to be paralyzed with fear.[14]

5 In the previous *wasf* (see 4:1), the poet compared the woman's eyes to doves. Here, instead of description he requests that she turn her gaze from him. They overwhelm him. The verb *rāhab* occurs only four times in the Old Testament. According to a recent article on the word, "the translation of the verb is dictated by context. . . . It is impossible to offer a single lexeme to translate this verb."[15] The context in our verse would lend itself to one of the following glosses: "overwhelm, excite, overpower, *unsettle.*" Her gaze is too much for him; he asks her to avert it from him.

10. Gordis, "The Root *dgl* in the Song of Songs," pp. 203-4.
11. Murphy, *The Song of Songs,* p. 175.
12. Snaith, *Song of Songs,* p. 88.
13. G. A. Long, "A Lover, Cities, and Heavenly Bodies: Con-Text and the Translation of Two Similes in Canticles (6:4c; 6:10d)," *JBL* 115 (1996): 703-9. See the commentary below for his suggestion on the analogous colon there.
14. See the study of C. Schroeder, "'A Love Song': Psalm 45 in the Light of Ancient Near Eastern Marriage Texts," *CBQ* 58 (1996): 417-32, who does not address the Song but points out the mixing of military and marital language in Psalm 45. C. Meyers ("Gender Imagery in the Song of Songs," *HAR* 10 [1986]: 215) also recognizes the military imagery throughout the Song as applied to the woman and concludes, "its use in the Song in reference to the woman constitutes an unexpected reversal of conventional imagery or of stereotypical gender association."
15. *NIDOTTE,* vol. 3, p. 1063.

The second part of the verse comments on her *hair.* With only minor variation, the metaphor is the same as that in 4:1 (see commentary there).

6 The poet praises the woman's *teeth* in language nearly identical to that found in 4:2 (see commentary). The only variation is that instead of "shorn sheep" *(qᵉṣûbôt),* the poet compares the whiteness of her teeth to *ewes (rᵉḥēlîm)* coming up from a washing.[16] The reason for the change is not obvious, since the meaning does not seem affected. In both cases, the teeth are characterized by glistening whiteness in the first part of the verse and by the fact that none are missing in the second.

7 One might expect the man to turn his attention to the woman's lips as he did in 4:3, but that line is missing from the present *wasf.*[17] He rather passes on to a description of her *temple,* which he describes using the same terms as in 4:3b (see commentary).

8 The *wasf* concludes with an exclamation of the uniqueness of the woman in verses 8 and 9. Verse 8 sets up the context for the man's statement of incomparability, and apparently he bases his statement on extensive experience. He describes three classes of women in this verse: *queens, concubines,* and *young women.* These three categories may reflect different levels within the royal harem; certainly that is true of the first two. In any case, we see that royal fiction is at play again here. To argue, with F. Delitzsch and others,[18] that this text reflects an early period in Solomon's life since the numbers are only a portion of his final tally of 700 wives and 300 concubines (1 Kings 11:3) seems quite stretched. The numbers are not to be taken literally since they are a clear example of a numerical parallelism.[19] The numbers that increase from *sixty* to *eighty* to infinity are not to be pressed literally but rather are to be taken all together as a reference to an unbelievably large number of women of all types.[20] The three classes of women in the court range from most important in terms of status to less important. First, he mentions *queens (mᵉlākôt).*[21] These would be the king's primary wives, the ones who would bear potential heirs to the throne. The next in status would be the

16. Snaith *(Song of Songs,* p. 90) is wrong to say that there is a variation in the word translated *is missing;* they are *šakkulâ* in both.
17. However, not from the Septuagint, which adds the reference to the lips.
18. Delitzsch, *Proverbs, Ecclesiastes, Song of Solomon,* p. 111.
19. For which see W. F. Albright, "Archaic Survivals in the Text of Canticles," in *Hebrew and Semitic Studies Presented to Godfrey Rolles Driver,* ed. D. Winton Thomas and W. D. McHardy (Oxford: Clarendon, 1963), pp. 1-7, and Pope, *Song of Songs,* p. 568.
20. Note the use of this type of parallelism in Amos 1 and 2, where the progression "three, yea four" sins also seems to indicate "many" rather than a literal number, since usually fewer than four sins are listed as concrete examples.
21. Notice the use of the third person masculine pronoun *(hēmmâ)* with queens here, a "rarity" in the words of Murphy, *The Song of Songs,* p. 175.

concubines (pîlegšîm),[22] secondary wives. The third group is simply called *young women (ʿlāmôt,* singular *ʿalmâ).* The term is not restricted to the court, and the status of these women is much less clear. After extensive discussion,[23] John Walton concludes "that a woman ceases to be an *ʿalmâ* when she becomes a mother — not when she becomes a wife or a sexual partner." Thus, in this context, these women may be associated with the court but have no formal marital status. However, Snaith goes too far when he understands these women to be prostitutes.[24]

The man thus evokes all the women of his royal experience for a comparison to the object of his poetical affections.

9 Among all these women, this woman is *unique.* She is different from all the others. He calls her by the same combination of epithets *(my dove, my flawless one)* that he used in 5:2. He continues by specifying that she is unique to her mother. Perhaps this is a way of saying that "they broke the (maternal) mold" when she was born. The term *"favored" (bārâ;* from the root *brr)* combines the ideas of chosen and pure.[25] This woman is indeed special.

The man goes even further in his praise. He not only proclaims her the best of all the women of his experience, but he also has the women concede her excellence. Three classes of women are mentioned in this verse as well. Two are repetitions, namely, *queens* and *concubines.* We are probably to see that the *daughters (bānôt)* are the equivalent to the young women in the previous verse.[26] All the women extol the unique one of the poem.

10 There is some uncertainty about who speaks this line. Yet if it is connected with the preceding verses, which seems likely, then it is most fitting to think that this is the praise that the above-mentioned women give to the beautiful, unique one.[27] The form of the verse is that of a rhetorical question similar to 3:6 and 8:5 *(Who is this . . . ?).* There is no question as to the answer; it is the woman, the unique one. The women then provide a description mostly in astronomical imagery, which is appropriate because it places

22. The word has no Semitic cognate and certainly does not look like a Semitic word. It seems similar to the Greek *pallakē,* and speculation has it that it was perhaps borrowed from the Philistines, who had Indo-European roots (*NIDOTTE,* vol. 3, pp. 618-19).

23. *NIDOTTE,* vol. 3, pp. 415-19.

24. Snaith, *Song of Songs,* p. 92, citing A. Schoors, "Two Notes on Isaiah XL–LV," *VT* 21 (1971): 503-5.

25. The Septuagint renders *bārâ* as *eklektē,* and the Vulgate, as *electa.*

26. It is possible that the *daughters* are the daughters of Jerusalem and that young women and daughters of Jerusalem are the same group (see 1:3).

27. Long ("A Lover, Cities, and Heavenly Bodies," p. 707) notes the ambiguity but leans toward the idea that the man continues to speak here, though he believes that the man represents the perspective of the women. In this light, it really makes little difference to the meaning of the verse.

her in the heavens as she looks down on everyone and everything else. Indeed, the verb "looks down" (niphal participle from *šqp*) is used elsewhere of God looking down from heaven (Ps. 14:2) or someone looking down from a window (Prov. 7:6). The first comparison is with the dawn *(šāḥar)*. It is interesting to note that the dawn (Shahar) is a deity in Canaanite mythology (see "The Birth of the Beautiful Gods," where Shahar, the dawn, is paired with Shallim, the dusk). Perhaps intentional mythological allusions are again used here to emphasize the extraordinary beauty of this woman. She is also as beautiful as the moon. The term for *moon* here *(lᵉbānâ)* is used only three times in the Hebrew Bible. It is found two times in Isaiah (Isa. 24:23; 30:26). The first is used to characterize the glory of God's rule over Jerusalem, and the second, God's future work of redemption. The word *lᵉbônâ* is always, including here, in parallel with the word *ḥammâ (sun)*. Here the woman is said to be as bright as the sun. "Bright" is a translation of the Hebrew word *bārâ*, which we rendered "favored" above in verse 9. The contexts drive our translation. However, the ideas of pure and of choice are operative in both contexts. The last phrase is repeated from 6:4. We have translated the phrase the same way, though the context may support the idea that here the reference is to the starry hosts, not the military hosts.[28]

POEM SIXTEEN:
A SURPRISE IN THE NUT GROVE (6:11-12)

In the discussion of the preceding poem, we noted that there is disagreement over the independence of these two verses. However, though it is always possible to construct a relationship, there is no clear connection with what precedes and what follows. We thus treat this as an independent, short poem.[29]

In this section, the woman recounts an experience. The setting is the cultivated countryside, a setting that we now associate with intimacy. It is springtime, a time of love. As she goes to the garden to investigate the spring growth, something unexpected happens to her. What that is, unfortunately, is not clear, since verse 12 is one of the most difficult passages in the entire book.

---

28. So NEB, "majestic as the starry heavens." Long ("A Lover, Cities, and Heavenly Bodies," p. 709) renders this phrase "breathtaking like the[se] sights [i.e., the moon and sun]." See his slightly variant rendition of 6:4. In this translation tradition, also see S. D. Goitein, "*Ayumma Kannidgalot* (Song of Songs VI.10): 'Splendid Like the Brilliant Stars,'" *JSS* 10 (1965): 220-21.

29. With this conclusion, we agree with Murphy, *Wisdom Literature*, p. 119.

The Woman

11. *I went down to the nut*[30] *grove,*[31]
    to see the new growth[32] *in the valley,*
    to see[33] *the budding of the grapevine,*
    the bloom[34] *of the pomegranates.*[35]
12. *I did not realize that my desire had placed me*
    in[36] *a chariot*[37] *with a noble man.*

11 It is somewhat difficult to ascribe this speech to either the man or the woman with certainty. It probably should be associated with the following verse, which is one of the most difficult verses in the Song, but which most likely belongs in the mouth of the woman. The NLT associates this verse with the woman; the NIV with the man.

In any case, the imagery of the verse implies a tryst between the two. The word *grove (ginnat)* is a construct of a biform for the more frequently occurring word that we have been translating "garden" *(gan; gannâ);* both (along with vineyard) describe the body (particularly of the woman [which may be why the NIV associates the speech with the man]) and also the place where the couple join together in intimacy. Pope has provided an exhaustive study of *nut* imagery.[38] Much of what he says is irrelevant to the context and is driven by his particular cultic interpretation of the book (see Introduction). However, he has interestingly pointed out the connection between the nut and the genitalia of both men and women. The whole nut represents the male gland (even down to contemporary English slang), and the open nut, the woman's vulva. In any case, the verse as a whole is a coy suggestion of intimate relations between the man and the woman. When she talks of exploring

---

30. *'egôz:* Perhaps more specifically the walnut tree *(Juglans regia).* The word occurs only here in the Hebrew Bible, but frequently in the Talmud.

31. *Ginnat* is the construct of *ginnâ* (cf. also Esth. 1:5; 7:7-8), which is a biform of the more commonly occurring *gannâ/gannat* (cs), which occurs in a number of places.

32. The word *'ēb* refers to plants that are still growing on the ground. It occurs only twice in the Hebrew Bible, the other occurrence being Job 8:12.

33. Often rendered, "to see *whether/if* the vines had budded," but I see no reason to add the italicized portion.

34. The hiphil of *nṣṣ* (see *NIDOTTE,* vol. 3, p. 147).

35. *Pomegranates* were used as aphrodisiacs in the ancient world. The Septuagint adds here, "there I will give you my breasts" *(ekei dōsō tous mastous mou soi).*

36. The Hebrew does not provide a preposition here. Our rendition is based on the context and the need for some kind of link between the verb and the object.

37. The word is grammatically a plural *(markᵉbôt),* but we have taken it as a plural referring to a "complex inanimate noun," a category discussed in Waltke and O'Connor, *An Introduction to Biblical Hebrew Syntax,* p. 120.

38. Pope, *Song of Songs,* pp. 574-79.

the grove, she means that she will be exploring the man's body. Thus, whether we understand the imagery to refer to the place of lovemaking or the lover's private parts, or perhaps both, we understand the speaker to say that intimate union is in mind.

12   Commentators agree on the incredible difficulty of the text.[39] The meaning of the words is ambiguous and the syntactical connections are dubious; they do not allow the interpreter to get a firm foothold in order even to guess about the meaning of the whole verse with much confidence at all. As we will see, this exegetical confusion extends back at least to the time of the earliest known translations.

Even a literal translation is variously expressed. Pope renders, "I do/ did not know my soul (it) set me chariots of my princely people."[40] Snaith translates, "I did not know my soul set me chariots of my willing people."[41] We can see why people have detected all kinds of problems in this verse. Whatever interpretation is adopted, it should be held very lightly.[42]

Note the confusion that is found in the main ancient versions. The Septuagint and Vulgate understood the last part of the verse to refer to an individual named Amminadib (or variant spelling). The Septuagint took the verse as "my soul did not know; it made me chariots of Aminadab" *(ouk egnō hē psychē mou: etheto me harmata Aminadab)*. The Vulgate rendered, "I did not know; my soul disturbed me because of the chariots of Aminadab" *(nescivi anima mea coturbavit me propter quadrigas Aminadab)*.[43] The other Greek versions, however, did not take the last part of the verse as a reference to an individual named Amminadib/Aminadab.

Note the variation among the most widely used modern English translations:

---

39. As noted by K. Froehlich, "'Amminadab's Chariot': The Predicament of Biblical Interpretation," *Princeton Seminary Bulletin* 18 (1997): 262-78, who also reminds us that "Amminadab's chariot" was considered a four-horse chariot or quadriga during the Middle Ages, and it became a cipher for the fourfold meaning and interpretation of Scripture.

40. Pope, *Song of Songs,* p. 584.

41. Snaith, *Song of Songs,* pp. 95-96.

42. Another possibility (but it is no more than that) is S. M. Paul's suggestion that *lo' yadatî napšî* should be translated "I am beside myself with joy." However, the Mesopotamian parallel that he bases his suggestion on simply denotes the loss of consciousness and is found in medical texts. See his "An Unrecognized Medical Idiom in Canticles 6,12 and Job 9,21," *Bib* 59 (1978): 545-47.

43. See the discussion and translation of the Septuagint and Vulgate provided by Murphy, *The Song of Songs,* p. 176.

NIV:

> Before I realized it,
>> my desire set me among the royal chariots of my people.[44]

NLT:

> Before I realized it, I found myself in my princely bed with my
> beloved one.[45]

NRSV:

> Before I was aware, my fancy set me
> In a chariot beside my prince.[46]

The opening clause (*I did not realize* [*lō' yādatî*]) expresses confusion or ignorance on the part of the speaker, whom most people — including myself — understand to be the woman. One of the first ambiguities of the verse is the role and sense of *napšî*, which we have rendered *desire*. The word can mean *desire* or *appetite*, or it can simply be the way the speaker refers to herself ("my soul" = "myself"). We have taken it as the former, for no better reason than it feels right in this context. Besides the uncertainty over its meaning, it is not at all clear whether it is an intensifier of the subject of the main verb or whether it is the subject of the subordinate clause. We have adopted the latter view.

While the first part of the verse is difficult, the last part has seen the most variety in rendition. In the first place, there is no marker indicating the relationship between the two parts of the verse. We have understood the relationship to have the force of the preposition *bet*. Second, the main question concerns the translation of *'ammî-nādîb*. Some have taken it as a construct phrase consisting of the word "people" (*'am*) and *nādîb*, a word often rendered "prince," but more appropriately taken as *noble*, generous, or willing.[47] Many have understood the word to be a proper name, Amminadib, taken as a variant of the more frequently attested Amminadab. This rendition certainly is possible, and, if correct, the figure of Amminadab would have a similar function to Prince Mehi in Egyptian love poetry. The latter is a well-known lover, who is also associated with chariots.[48] However, two factors speak

---

44. With footnoted variants for the last part of the verse, including "among the chariots of Amminadab" and "among the chariots of the people of the prince."

45. Words put in the mouth of the man and with the following footnote: "Or 'among the royal chariots of my people,' or 'among the chariots of Amminadab.' The meaning of the Hebrew is uncertain."

46. With the note that the meaning of the Hebrew is uncertain.

47. *NIDOTTE*, vol. 3, pp. 31-32.

48. See Keel, *The Song of Songs*, p. 226, who follows Gerleman here. Note also the discussion provided by Fox, *The Song of Songs and the Ancient Egyptian Love Songs*, pp. 64-66, where he says "He [Mehi] is a Cupid-figure who embodies the power of love."

against this view. One, it is something of a last resort to appeal to a proper name in a difficult text. Second, the Amminadab of the Bible has no special connection with love, and there are no other tales or evidence to suggest that another Amminadab had those connections. We, along with Pope, understand the 'ammî to be a corruption of the preposition 'im "with"[49] and nādîb as meaning a noble man and referring to the one who is the object of the woman's attention.[50]

Thus, we can agree that the translation of this verse is full of pitfalls. No one can speak with much certainty about its rendition or its interpretation. The most definite point we can make about this verse is that it expresses strong passion, most likely of the woman for the man. Her passion has so overwhelmed her that she is "caught up" and discovers herself transported into the man's chariot. Perhaps the chariot ought to be compared with the "palanquin" (miṭṭâ) of 3:7 and the "litter" ('appiryôn) of 3:9.

In a recent article, M. J. Mulder[51] argues that it is the man who speaks this verse and that the chariot is a reference to chariot (merkābâ) mysticism, which he argues is a late Old Testament phenomenon, even though its clearest expressions are postbiblical. Thus, he concludes that the verse describes that the man's love for the young girl "had unconsciously passed the boundary between this world and the divine," i.e., a kind of love trance. While interesting and possible, this interpretation is too speculative to accept. Most troubling is the connection between the chariot and merkabah mysticism.

49. So Pope, Song of Songs, p. 589.

50. G. Barbiero takes the 'ammî as a reference to "my people" and translates "mein edles Volk" ("my noble people"). For his extensive discussion of this verse, see G. Barbeiro, "Die 'Wagen meines edlen Volkes' (Hld 6,12): Eine structurelle Analyse," Bib 78 (1997): 174-89.

51. M. J. Mulder, "Does Canticles 6,12 Make Sense?" in The Scriptures and the Scrolls: Studies in Honour of A. S. van der Woude on the Occasion of His 65th Birthday, ed. F. G. Martinez et al. (Leiden: Brill, 1992), pp. 104-13.

CHAPTER SEVEN

POEM SEVENTEEN:
A DESCRIPTION OF THE DANCING SHULAMMITE
(7:1-11 [ENGLISH 6:13–7:10])

The delineation of this poem is filled with all sorts of questions. It is conceivable that 7:1 (English 6:13) stood alone, but we take the reference to gazing at the Shulammite as the motivation for the description of her physical charms that follow, and such an analysis in particular explains why this *wasf* begins with her feet and works upward. It is also possible that 7:11 (English 7:10), the refrain of mutual affection, is separate, but it more than likely is the climax of the poem. The largest question pertains to the relationship between 7:1-6 (English 6:13–7:5) and 7:8-11 (English 7:7-10). An argument could be made that these are two separate poems, the first a *wasf* and the second an admiration poem. However, we understand the relationship as causal. The man's description of the woman's physical charm leads him to express his admiration and his desire for sexual union. The woman then responds with the refrain of mutual affection. Form critically, the unit begins with a *wasf*, as we have stated. It is the third of four (see 4:1-7; 5:10-16; and 6:4-8) and arguably the most erotic. For a fuller discussion of the *wasf* as a genre, see the introduction to 4:1-7.

In summary, poem seventeen begins with a call for the Shulammite to return, which leads to her questioning why they want to look at her. At this point, the man, presumably in answer, describes her physical charms and then proceeds to express his desire for her by means of the metaphorical narrative of climbing the palm tree. The woman expresses her affirmation by means of the refrain, already seen in 2:16 and 6:3, of their mutual love.

I find that I cannot agree with A. Brenner in her analysis of the following *wasf* as a parody of the previous two. She manages this interpretation by arguing that it is signaled by a reversal of direction from the previous *wasf*

188

poems. That is, instead of starting with the head, the man starts with a description of her feet. Yet, as she herself suggests, this reversal has more to do with the fact that it begins with her dancing, when all attention would be on her feet. She also, in my opinion, reads the images in ways that the somber and celebratory tone of the poem militates against. For instance, in 7:3 (English 7:2), she takes the "belly" as a heap of wheat and as a reference to a woman who is so fat that her stomach rolls as she dances. She sees the image of the breasts as a rather grotesque image of quivering that would be unpleasing, not exciting, to the man.[1]

The Women of Jerusalem[2]
1. (English 6:13)   *Return, return, O Shulammite![3]*
                     Return, return, and let us look at you!

The Woman
                     Why should you gaze at the Shulammite,
                     as[4] the dance of two war camps?[5]

The Man
2. (English 7:1)   *How beautiful are your feet[6] in sandals, O noble*
                    daughter!
                    rounded are your hips like rings,
                    the work of the hands of a craftsman.

---

1. So A. Brenner, "Paradox and Parody in the Song of Solomon: Towards a Comic Reading of the Most Sublime Song," in *On Humour and the Comic in the Hebrew Bible,* ed. A. Brenner and Y. T. Radday (Sheffield: Almond, 1990), pp. 251-76. Since I do not find myself in agreement with this reading of Brenner, I certainly find objectionable the extension of her idea to the other *wasfs* put forward by W. Whedbee, "Paradox and Parody in the Song of Solomon: Towards a Comic Reading of the Most Sublime Song," in *A Feminist Companion to the Song of Songs,* ed. A. Brenner (Sheffield: JSOT Press, 1993), pp. 266-78.

2. Munro (*Spikenard and Saffron,* p. 31), without evidence but based on her understanding of the context, takes this as a sole occurrence of a "Male Chorus."

3. *Shulammite* has a prefixed definite article. This is to be understood as having the same force as a vocative particle (see Pope, *Song of Songs,* p. 600, who cites W. Gesenius, *Hebräisches und Aramäisches Handwörterbuch* (Leipzig: Vogel, 1915), 137-38; GKC (*Gesenius' Hebrew Grammar,* ed. E. Kautzsch, trans. A. E. Cowley, 2nd ed. [Oxford: Clarendon, 1910]) 126e, note [e].

4. So Leningradensis. Some Hebrew manuscripts have *bet* instead of *kaph.* However, Septuagint, Syriac, and Latin all support L.

5. The NIV takes this as a reference to the city of Mahanaim, but the connection seems dubious. The term means camp, but, as we learn from *NIDOTTE,* vol. 2, p. 918: "most often the camp is a war camp and indeed can be correctly translated that way."

6. Not *regel,* but *pa'am,* which is relatively rare for the meaning *foot.*

189

3. (English 7:2)   *Your "navel" is a rounded[7] bowl,*
               which does not lack mixed wine.
               Your "belly" is a heap[8] of wheat,
               bordered with lilies.

4. (English 7:3)   *Your two breasts are like two fawns,*
               twins of a gazelle.

5. (English 7:4)   *Your neck is like an ivory tower.*
               Your eyes are pools in Heshbon,
               by the gate of Bat-rabbim.
               Your nose is like the tower of Lebanon,
               keeping watch toward Damascus.

6. (English 7:5)   *Your head (on you)[9] is like Carmel*
               and the hair of your head like purple.
               The king is ensnared by your tresses.[10]

7. (English 7:6)   *How beautiful you are, and how pleasant,*
               O love[11] with (your) delights.[12]

8. (English 7:7)   *This — your stature — is[13] like a palm tree,*
               and your breasts are like fruit clusters.

9. (English 7:8)   *I said,[14] "I will climb up the palm tree;*
               I will grasp its date blossoms!"
               May your breasts be like clusters of the vine,
               and the smell of your breath be like apples.

10. (English 7:9)   *May your palette be like fine wine,*

---

7. A *sahar* is a *hapax* in Hebrew; cf. *NIDOTTE*, vol. 3, p. 227.

8. The noun is derived from the verb *'rm*, "to dam up." As Ruth 3:7, Neh. 13:15, and Hag. 2:16 indicate, the word is often used of grains (and fruits).

9. *"On you"* is in the Hebrew (*'ālayik*) and makes sense in the context, but it appears awkwardly redundant in English translation.

10. *R^ehāṭîm* is a *hapax* with the meaning "tresses." Pope (*Song of Songs*, p. 630) describes how it may have developed from a root *rhṭ* (known from Aramaic) with the sense of "to run" and used in connection with water in Gen. 30:38, 41; Exod. 2:16, but here the coursing of water evokes the idea of flowing hair (note the similar use of the term *glš* in 4:1). This etymology explains the Septuagint translation of our verse as "in courses" (*paradromais*) and the Vulgate as "in canals" *(canalibus)*.

11. This is an abstract use of the term love (*'ah^abâ*) to refer to the concrete person.

12. Murphy (*Song of Songs*, p. 180) follows the Septuagint in the second colon of this verse and understands that a *taw* fell out by haplography. Thus in Hebrew he reads *bat ta^anûgîm* (for Greek *thygatēr tryphon*) = "O loved one, delightful daughter."

13. The syntax here is unusual in the Hebrew. Snaith (*Song of Songs*, pp. 106-7) rightly describes it in this way: "*zō't qômātēk dām^etāh* . . . both completes the nominal sentence, 'this is your stature,' and provides the subject for the verb *dām^etâ*, 'your stature is like . . .' — the word *qômātēk*, points both ways." He calls this a Janus structure.

14. This use of *'mr* may well indicate not oral expression but rather thought.

> running straight to me,[15]
> flowing over my lips and my teeth.[16]

The Woman

11. (English 7:10)   *I belong to my lover,*
and his desire is for me.

1 (English 6:13)   The problems with which we left off at the end of the last chapter persist as we encounter 7:1 (English 6:13). In the first place, it is not obvious who is speaking. It seems a fair conclusion to suggest that the first and second halves of the verse are spoken by different parties as we move from an imperative directed at the *Shulammite* to a sentence that seems to question the command. In the first parallel line, noted by the fourfold repetition of the verb *return (šûbî)*, the speakers are plural and request that the Shulammite come back into their presence so that they may get a close look at her. The verse does not closely identify the plural speakers of this command. However, up to this point the only plural speakers are the women of Jerusalem,[17] and so the most elegant explanation is that these women, acting as a kind of chorus (see Introduction), are in view here. The speaker of the second half of the verse is also ambiguous. However, it seems likely that it is the young woman herself who is speaking. To be sure, this view implies that she speaks of herself in the third person, but this is not a large obstacle. The content of her reply indicates either her lack of self-consciousness or her humility. Perhaps she is playing coy, but it does set up the *wasf*, or descriptive poem, which follows in 7:1-9 (English 7:2-10).

The women, if that is who they truly are, call on the young woman to *return (šûbî)*. This verb seems a little out of place in the context. Unless we are to imagine her transport to the chariot of the previous verse to be in mind here, then we do not get a clear sense where she went and to where she is being called back. Some have suggested a simple emendation to a form of the verb *sbb* "to turn around," which, it is suggested, fits in better with the dance context that follows.[18] The answer may be as simple as recognizing that *šûb*

---

15. MT has "to my lover," which does not fit the context well. After all, it seems odd for the lover (the man) to request that the wine run straight to "my lover." We posit *to me (lî)*. We should point out that Murphy (*Song of Songs*, p. 187) and others believe that the woman bursts in here temporarily, and so they retain the MT.

16. MT has "sleepers" (*yᵉšēnîm*). We follow the Septuagint text *(kai odousin)* by emending to *and my teeth (wᵉšinnāy)*.

17. It is true that later (see 8:8-9), the woman's brothers will speak, but the context makes it impossible that they are in view here.

18. Pope (*Song of Songs*, p. 595) suggests the meaning "leap," which involves a slight emendation but also an appeal to an Arabic cognate of dubious connection; see

can have the meaning of turn or turn around. It is not specifically a technical dance term but may just indicate a request that the woman turn, so that the speakers can get a good glance at her.[19]

The term *Shulammite* is clearly some kind of epithet for the woman. As is often the case with the term Qohelet in the book of Ecclesiastes,[20] Shulammite appears with a definite article. However, its meaning presents yet another conundrum, and most commentaries list three major proposals for the meaning of the term. Two, in my opinion, are unlikely, while the third, though not certain, is the best explanation available. Some, like M. H. Pope[21] and W. F. Albright[22] before him, associate the term with the name of the Mesopotamian goddess of love and war named Sulmanitu. The persuasiveness of this connection depends on one's previous commitment or lack thereof to a cultic approach to the book (see Introduction). The second suggestion is to note a connection between Shulam and the city of Shunem. No one doubts the possible philological connection between the two, since an *l/r* interchange is well attested in Semitic. Often, this hypothesis goes further by suggesting a connection with one of the two women known in the Old Testament as associated with the city of Shunem: Abishag (1 Kings 1:1–4:15), the woman who played the role of heating blanket to the aging David.[23] However, it is quite a stretch to understand why Abishag should play a role in the Song where, we have argued, the main players are poetic types and not historical personages. The third explanation is the most reasonable. The name Shulammite is a feminine form of the name Solomon (*šᵉlômô*). Solomon, though not a consistent character in the book, plays a prominent role in two places, 3:6-11 and 8:11-12, and of course 1:1. The name Shulammite thus is an appropriate name for the female of the Song. It may also reflect its root

---

R. E. Murphy, "Dance and Death in the Song of Songs," in *Love and Death in the Ancient Near East: Essays in Honor of Marvin H. Pope,* ed. J. H. Marks and R. M. Good (Guilford, CT: Four Quarters, 1987), p. 117.

19. See *NIDOTTE,* vol. 4, p. 55.

20. T. Longman III, *The Book of Ecclesiastes,* NICOT (Grand Rapids: Eerdmans, 1998), pp. 1-9.

21. Pope, *Song of Songs,* pp. 598-99.

22. W. F. Albright, "The Syro-Mesopotamian God Šulman-Ešmun and Related Figures," *Archiv für Orientforschung* 7 (1931-32): 164-69.

23. The other woman is the older lady who interacts with Elisha in 2 Kings 4:8-44. This woman is married and has a child, and for these reasons identification with the Shulammite in the Song of Songs is unlikely. In a recent article, S. Frolov ("No Return for the Shulammite: Reflections on Cant 7,1," *ZAW* 110 [1998]: 256-58) uses torturous exegesis and the assumption of a historical background to the text to argue that the reference to *maḥᵃnāyim* reveals that the Shulammite is none other than Bathsheba and that this episode follows the wedding scene of Solomon's marriage, since it mentions his mother, who of course is Bathsheba.

meaning of peace or wholeness. She is one who brings peace to the one who loves her (8:10).[24] Now, of course, this is the only place in the book where this name appears, so it is dubious to refer to the woman in the Song as Shulammite throughout.

Ambiguities persist in the second part of the verse, but I think the general tenor is relatively clear. The half-verse is a question introduced by the interrogative particle *ma*, usually translated "what," but the context here leads us to render *why*. The speaker, whom we identify as the Shulammite, questions their desire to look at her. What is so special about her that they want to gaze at her so intently? Indeed, their gaze is fixed in amazement. Watching her is as mesmerizing as watching two armies battling with one another. That is how we understand the colorful expression *the dance of two war camps*. Imagine the scene of battle from a point overlooking the battlefield. As the two armies encountered one another, who could turn their eyes from the scene as they watched the strategic moves and countermoves of attack and defense? The beauty of the Shulammite draws the same kind of awestruck attention. Her appearance has already been described in military terms earlier in the poem (6:4).

Again, this verse is difficult, but the emotions it expresses are clear. In the first place, the chorus articulates desire and longing for closer intimacy. This is met by an answer from the woman that reflects the riveted attention of her onlookers. The view, occasionally still cited, that this is a sword dance performed at a wedding is dependent on anachronistic near modern Arabic wedding practices.[25]

2 (English 7:1)   From the context, we suggest that the man begins to speak again. Form critically verses 2-7 (English vv. 1-6) are another *wasf* (cf. 4:1-15; 5:10-16; 6:4-8), and the third one focused on the woman. A descriptive poem of the woman's physical beauty is most appropriately understood in the mouth of the man, and this conclusion is strengthened by the highly erotic nature of this particular poem and the verses that follow, which suggest his movement toward sexual intimacy.

This *wasf* is different from the previous ones, however, in that it begins with the *feet* and works up the body rather than vice versa. The reversal was most probably compelled by the previous verse, which remarks on the woman's dance, which would focus attention on her feet. Indeed, that may be why her feet are specifically mentioned as sandaled, in that she is involved in a dance. However, appropriate footwear can enhance the erotic at-

---

24. Or perhaps *šālôm* should here be translated, "the perfect one"; thus Walton, Matthews, and Chavalas, *The Bible Background Commentary*, p. 580.

25. For the connection, see Delitzsch, *Proverbs, Ecclesiastes, Song of Solomon*, p. 171, who cites Wetzstein.

traction of the female foot,[26] and this may be the reason why the *sandal* is mentioned.

The woman is called *noble daughter.* For the adjective, consult the commentary at 6:12, where the word *nādîb* is also found. It is a term of respect and endearment. It does not necessarily imply that the woman is noble by blood, but even if the term did imply this, we would understand the appellation in the same way we understand "king" in reference to the man, although he is not royal. They are regal in each other's eyes.

The poet-lover then proceeds to describe her *yārēk.* The term refers to the upper thigh or *hip.*[27] We have chosen to translate the term as "hip" because it seems the most appropriate of the two for one to describe as *rounded* or curved *(ḥammûq)*[28] — yet the term is not incompatible with her thigh either, especially the inside of her thigh. The poet adds a simile to get his point across: he likens her *hip*/thigh to an ornament. The Hebrew term is *ḥl',* which is a biform of *ḥly.* It occurs only here, in Proverbs 25:12, and in Hosea 2:15 (English 2:13). In the latter, it is parallel with earring, which suggests a piece of jewelry. M. J. A. Horsnell suggests that the term is specifically a *ring* in its postbiblical usage,[29] and ring would certainly be appropriate in the present context. Even further, it is a work of extraordinary craftsmanship, being the product of an *'āmman (craftsman).* The term's only other definite appearance in the Hebrew Bible is in the debated context of Proverbs 8:30. It is likely related to Akkadian *ummānu,* which refers to the famous wise men who lived before the Flood.

Thus, the man describes the sensuous beauty of her feet and hips. As she dances, he is fixated on her moving body.

3 (English 7:2) Working up from the thigh, the poet next pauses over the attraction of the woman's *"navel"* and *"belly."* These words are in quotation marks because we believe that they are euphemisms for the woman's vulva. Some scholars, notably Pope, try to identify these Hebrew words *(šōr* and *beṭen)* with the woman's genitalia by means of philology. Pope argues that the word *šōr = šurr* is related to a similar Arabic word *sirr,* which means "secret" and "pudenda." However, as R. E. Murphy has pointed out, there is an Arabic word *surratu,* which means "navel," and the Hebrew word clearly has this meaning in its only other undisputed attestation found in Ezekiel 16:4. However, I am driven less by philology and more by the comparison. The poet says that her *"navel"* never lacks *wine.*[30] The

---

26. Snaith (*Song of Songs,* p. 100) mentions Judith 16:9, where in Judith's seduction of Holofernes "her sandal ravished his eyes."

27. *NIDOTTE,* vol. 2, p. 543.

28. Related to the verb *ḥmq* "to turn/go away," found in 5:6.

29. M. J. A. Horsnell, *"ḥᵃlî,"* *NIDOTTE,* vol. 2, p. 543.

30. Specifically, the Hebrew word (*mezeg,* a *hapax legomenon*) indicates a special

navel is not a particularly moist location, whereas the vulva is, at least when sexually excited. I would further argue that males are attracted to the female navel because of its proximity to the vulva and also because it is a near, but not actual, aperture; it thus reminds the male of the vulva. This indirect reference to the vulva is in keeping with the poet's strategy of tasteful, though erotic allusions to the woman's body. Whether literally navel or vulva, the image evokes a comparison that is based on taste. The description of the woman's aperture as containing wine implies the man's desire to drink from the sensual bowl. Thus, this may be a subtle and tasteful allusion to the intimacies of sex.

The verse goes on to describe her "belly" as a heap of wheat. Some commentators, such as Murphy and O. Keel, suggest that here the image is not visual but one of fertility. Wheat (*ḥiṭṭâ*) is one of the main foodstuffs of ancient Israel. Yet if fertility is meant, then the allusion is more than to her belly as such. It is to her womb, again a reference to her genitalia. The heap of wheat calls to mind vaginal hair. It is a work of art to the man, framed or bordered by lilies.

4 (English 7:3)   The verse is identical[31] to 4:5.

5 (English 7:4)   Three body parts are praised in this verse, the *neck*, the *eyes,* and the *nose*. The parallelism is not symmetrical. The verse has one colon describing the *neck* and two each describing the *eyes* and the *nose*. It is a dubious matter to try to "fix" the parallelism, though, so we treat the verse as three separate poetic lines.[32]

The woman's *neck* is likened to an *ivory tower.* Note again (especially 6:4, 10) the use of a martial image in reference to the woman. In the first female *wasf,* her *neck* was described as a *tower* (see commentary at 4:4). There we suggested that the image was "not a visual correspondence, but a transfer of value."[33] It is not that the woman's *neck* is long, fat, thick, or the like, but that it is grand, strong, dignified, and perhaps elegant. In 4:4, the *tower* is described as the tower of David; here it is an ivory tower. *Ivory,* of course, is precious material. It too suggests strength, and the tusk is an apt image for a long, elegant neck.[34]

---

kind of wine (*yayin* is the generic word for wine). Most understand it as mixed, spiced, or blended wine. It has cognates in Aramaic, Syriac, and postbiblical Hebrew (cf. *NIDOTTE,* vol. 2, p. 908).

31. With the exception that the word *twinned* (here spelled *tā'ōmê*) is spelled defectively, whereas it has its plene spelling in ch. 4.

32. Contra Murphy, *Song of Songs,* p. 182, who suggests bringing 7:6a up to this point in the text.

33. *The Dictionary of Biblical Imagery,* p. 881.

34. I find dubious Snaith's (*Song of Songs,* p. 102) suggestion that the ivory image represents a pale complexion.

Her *eyes* are compared to *pools* of water, a similar, though not identical, image to that of the man's eyes in 5:12. The woman's moist eyes are as attractive as the pools in a particular location, specifically those of *Heshbon,* particularly those near the gate of *Bat-rabbim.* The reference seems proverbial from its context, but we have no similar references to support this idea. Heshbon, located at the east side of the Dead Sea, is a beautiful area, but we cannot be more specific than this in our exposition. Brenner, however, argues that the reference is to Rabbah, an Ammonite city near Heshbon. However, her suggestion is a conjectural emendation that has no basis in ancient manuscripts, and she uses this identification to support her mistaken theory that the *wasf* is a parody, in this case associating the woman with the Ammonites and Moabites who were hated by Israelites and linked to sexual perversities.[35]

The woman's *nose,* like her neck, is tower-like. The image seems to imply a prominent nose, certainly considered attractive (otherwise why the comment?) to the original audience of the poem. Its grandness and dignity are underlined by its reference to *Lebanon* and its prominent role in protecting the important city of *Damascus.* There could be no more important tower with which to compare her nose.

6 (English 7:5)   The culmination of this *wasf* is the *head* and its *hair.* The poem has completed its journey from her feet to her *head.* The comparison here is with *Carmel.* Carmel is the range that juts out into the Mediterranean, just south of Acco. In this context, the reference to Carmel likely refers to the fact that she stands tall and dignified.[36]

Royal imagery comes back into play in the second colon, where her hair is said to be *purple.* Purple was the most expensive dye at the time and reserved for both human (Judg. 8:26) and divine (Exodus 25–39) monarchs. She is queen-like and fit for a king. Indeed, according to the third colon, her hair (a metonymy for her whole being) ensnares or entraps a king. Her stunning beauty cannot be resisted.

7 (English 7:6)   The *wasf* ends, typically, with a general affirmation of the woman's beauty. Here the roots *yph* (to be beautiful) and *n'm* (to be pleasant) are used as near synonyms. We have already encountered them together in 1:16 in reference to the woman. *Yph* is also found as a general acclamation in the first *wasf,* as seen in 4:10. Here we have the second person

---

35. A. Brenner, "A Note on *Bat-Rabbîm* (Song of Songs VII 5)," *VT* 42 (1992): 113-15.

36. *NIDOTTE,* vol. 4, pp. 464-65, lists three symbolic values for Carmel: "(a) a symbol of fertility, (b) a symbol of height, and (c) a sacred place." It also lists Jer. 46:18 and Amos 9:3 as other examples where Carmel is symbolic of a kind of dignified height.

feminine singular verbal form used. To call her beautiful and pleasant is a high compliment.

The last phrase of the verse, *O love, with your delights ('ah'bâ batt'"nûgîm)*, seems awkward in the Hebrew and has led to some proposed emendations. It may be simply a cry of ecstasy as the man contemplates a joyous union with the woman. The noun "delights" comes from the verbal root *'ng* "to be delicately brought up" (pual), "to delight in" (hitpael). The verb occurs ten times and the noun five times in the Hebrew Bible. It can be used both in a theological sense of delight in God, and in a human sense of enjoyment, including, as here, sensual enjoyment.

8 (English 7:7)   The relationship of this verse and the following verses to the preceding is ambiguous. Certainly the man takes a new tack here, but it may well flow from the preceding *waṣf*. He has described her beauty, and now he continues that description, but with another image — one that also implies action on his part.

He likens her to the *palm tree (tāmār)*. The palm tree has a tall, slender trunk, and since he mentions her height *(qômâ)*, that seems to be the reference here. The palm is a slender tree, so it probably also indicates that the woman is slim. The palm, however, explodes with leaves (fronds) and fruit at the top. He likens her *breasts* to the *fruit* of the palm, which may well in this case be the date palm.[37] The fertility of the palm tree is represented by its fruit, and the sensuousness of this reference will be exploited in the next verse. Murphy's opinion that the palm tree image represents "grace and elegance"[38] does not seem to take into account its use in the next verse.

Two notable women have the name Tamar *(palm tree)* in the Bible. First, there is Tamar, the daughter-in-law of Judah, in Genesis 38. Second, there is the Tamar who attracts the illicit attention of her half-brother Amnon (2 Samuel 13). Both women are enmeshed in stories of a sexual nature. The name, in the right context, may suggest a kind of sensual woman.

9 (English 7:8)   The man now plays with the image of the *palm* tree. If the woman is a palm tree, then he will *climb* her. It does not take much imagination[39] to note the suggestive sexual language as the man figuratively describes shinnying up the woman's slender body (i.e., "mounting" her), but he confirms his sexual intent when he proclaims his intention to grasp the *date blossom cluster (sansinnâ)*[40] of the palm, which we have just

37. Even though the term *'aškōlôt* usually refers to grapes, here it must refer to the *date* since grapes do not grow on palms. In 1:14 it refers to a cluster of henna blossoms.

38. Murphy, *Song of Songs*, p. 186.

39. Though Snaith (*Song of Songs*, pp. 107-8), at this point at least, seems to lack it.

40. The *sansinnâ*, a *hapax legomenon* in Hebrew but cognate with Akkadian *sisinnu*, is either the branch or the *date blossom cluster*, according to *NIDOTTE*, vol. 3, p. 685. If it is the former, then it is figurative for the woman's hair or arms. The context,

seen in the preceding verse is a metaphor for her breasts. This then leads him to bless her *breasts*. It is interesting that he appears to mix his metaphors when he expresses his hope that her breasts will be like the *clusters of the vine (haggepen),* since this suggests the grape, not the date. The fact that her breasts are like clusters of grapes implies that his wish is that the woman be well endowed. He goes on to express his desire that her *breath*[41] smell like apples. The *apple* has a pleasant scent, and that is a good enough reason for its appearance in the present context. He desires to get intimate with her, and sweet smells often enhance the experience. However, as we already observed in connection with the appearance of the word *apple (tappûaḥ)* in 2:3 and, especially, 2:5, the apple functions as an aphrodisiac as well (see also 8:5).

10 (English 7:9) The *palate (ḥēk)* is the inner mouth. He continues his blessing on the woman, which is very expressive of his own desires, by asking that her palette be like *fine wine.* The simile makes public his desire to kiss her. This wine is a wine he wants to taste, and so we have a tactful expression of a deep kiss. That this verse asks for a deep kiss becomes clear in the next two cola as he proclaims his desire that she share the wine with him.

11 (English 7:10) This verse is a variation of what we have already seen in 2:16 and 6:3. It is an expression of mutual affection, and the similarities among these three verses suggest that they function as a kind of refrain in the Song (see the Introduction). See the commentary at 2:16 for a discussion of this verse as an expression of mutual ownership.

The unique feature found in this verse is the appearance of the word *desire (tᵉšûqâ).* It appears only three times in the Bible. Besides this context in the Song, it appears twice in Genesis. It is clear that Genesis 4:7 talks about a desire, which is negative. Sin desires to dominate Cain. The third occurrence is in Genesis 3:16 in the context of the curse on the woman, which

---

especially the very next colon, suggests that the date blossom cluster is meant, representing the woman's breasts.

41. The word translates *'ap,* which normally indicates smell or nose or nostril. Here such a meaning makes no sense ("the scent of your nose be like apples"). In spite of the fact that *'ap* in the sense of breath is not attested elsewhere as far as I am aware, it seems the best meaning for the context. It is conceivable that the "scent of her nose" specifically refers to the breath from her nose, and thus this phrase indicates a "nose kiss"; see Snaith, *Song of Songs,* p. 108. M. Dahood ("Canticle 7,9 and UT 52,61," *Bib* 57 [1976]: 109-10) cites only one example from Ugaritic to support the reading of *'ap* as "nipple," with the resultant reading "the fragrance of your nipples like apples." While nipple creates a closer parallel to breast in the previous colon (a stronger argument when the old Lowthian view of parallelism was in favor), the blessing of a good-smelling nipple seems odd.

describes how her desire will be for her husband. The debate rages about the force of desire in this context. Is it positive as in the Song or negative as in Genesis 4?[42] I believe that context argues for negative, but the important matter for its meaning in the Song, where the positive nuance cannot be challenged, is that all three occurrences express a strong desire, urging, longing.

POEM EIGHTEEN:
I WILL GIVE YOU MY LOVE
(7:12-14 [ENGLISH 7:11-13])

The form of this poem is that of a love monologue — more specifically, an invitation from the woman to the man. She desires that he join her in the vineyard to see the awakening of nature. Thus, we have the evocation of a spring setting that calls to mind all the fresh smells and pleasant temperatures of that season. It is a time of love and lovemaking. We have already observed (see commentary at 1:6) that the vineyard, like the garden, is a locus of lovemaking, as well as a symbol of the woman herself. She twice states her desire to give him her love: the first time literally (7:13 [English 7:12]) and the second time symbolically (7:14 [English 7:13]).

According to Murphy, some scholars[43] separate 7:14 (English 7:13) from the preceding verses since verse 14 (English 13) mentions mature fruit rather than newly blossoming plants. He is right to respond that "v. 14 can be understood symbolically of herself, especially after her statement in v. 13b."

The Woman
12. (English 7:11)   *Come, my love.*
                     Let's go out to the field,
                     let's spend the night in the villages.
13. (English 7:12)   *Let's go early to the vineyards;*
                     let's see if the vine has budded,
                     the bud[44] has opened,
                     the pomegranates[45] have bloomed.[46]
                     There I will give my love to you!

42. See the helpful study by Susan Foh, "What Is the Woman's Desire?" *WTJ* 37 (1974-75): 376-83.
43. Murphy, *Wisdom Literature,* pp. 120-21, cites Rudolph, Loretz, Krinetzki, and Gerleman.
44. For *sᵉmādar,* see 2:13.
45. For *pomegranate,* see 4:13.
46. For the verb *nṣṣ,* see 6:11.

14. (English 7:13)   *The mandrakes give forth their scent,*[47]
                             and on our entrance[48] *is every precious gift.*
                      The new as well as the old,
                          I have treasured up for you, my love.

12 (English 7:11)   The woman[49] now invites her lover to a tryst in the countryside. We have already observed the motif that the city is a place of alienation, due to lack of intimacy (5:2-7), but the countryside is a location of intimacy. Thus, the invitation to the countryside is an invitation to lovemaking.
The commonly occurring word *field (śādeh)* could indeed be understood and
translated as the word "countryside." There is some ambiguity over the
meaning of its parallel in the prepositional phrase of the last colon of the
verse. Is *kᵉpārîm* from *kāpār* "village" or *kōper* "henna"?[50] The dilemma is
rendered more difficult as well as less important by the fact that both meanings fit the context well. If the term is village, as we have translated here, the
parallelism clearly leads us to understand these as villages in the countryside.
If the word refers to henna, the poet in this way evokes a natural setting. In either case, we have the city/country opposition at play here.

Her purpose is to spend some time in the countryside with her lover
for the purpose of physical intimacy; indeed, the most propitious time for romance is the nighttime.[51]

13 (English 7:12)   She continues her invitation to the man by urging
him to rise early (the verbal root is *škm*) and go into the countryside. Perhaps
the early rise is simply a way of emphasizing the fact that she desires to
spend as much time as is possible in his presence. Perhaps the early morning
is a time of relative calm and privacy in the vineyard setting. It is hard to be
more than suggestive.

The country/nature setting resonates through the verse. It begins with
a reference to the *vineyards.* As early as 1:6, we encountered the vineyard
and explained how the vineyard is a sexually charged metaphor in the Song.
It can be used to refer both to the woman's body and to a place of lovemak-

---

47. The term *scent* (or smell; *rēaḥ*) is used a number of other times in the Song for
the good smell of the woman (4:10) and her garments (4:11). Sometimes, as here, it is
used in reference to the good smell of spring fruits (2:13).

48. The Hebrew word is a plural, "entrances," but as Murphy (*Song of Songs*,
p. 184) and others point out, it functions here as a so-called plural of generalization
(P. Joüon, *Grammaire de l'hebreu biblique* [Rome: Pontifical Biblical Institute, 1947],
#137j).

49. That the woman is speaking here is suggested by the use of the epithet "*my
love/*my lover" *(dōdî)*, which is her favorite way of referring to the man.

50. In 1:14 and 4:13, the reference is clearly to henna.

51. The verb *lwn* ("to lodge, to spend the night") suggests a night tryst.

ing, perhaps at times echoing with both meanings. The woman then reveals three reasons to go to the vineyard. The first colon *(let's see if the vine has budded)* is explicitly conditional, and we are to understand the next two as conditional as well. In all three cases, she wants to explore the progress of the vegetation of the vineyard. This language suggests the springtime as fertility springs back to life. The sights and smells of a springtime vineyard make for a pleasant fantasy setting for romance.

I treat the last sentence of the verse *(There I will give my love to you!)* as a climactic monocolon, where the woman[52] clarifies her intention to explore the vineyard. She will give her love to him; the vineyard again is a place of lovemaking.

14 (English 7:13)   The poem concludes with a two-line verse. The first line talks about the sweet smell of their home (presupposed by the reference to *our entrance*). Mandrake *(dûdāʾîm)* may be mentioned more for its putative power as an aphrodisiac than for its actual smell. That the mandrake was thought to be an aphrodisiac is implied by Genesis 30:14-16.[53] Rachel, who was having difficulty conceiving children, received some mandrakes from Leah in exchange for a night with Jacob. The narrative reports that Rachel soon gave birth to a son, though it does not relate the mandrakes directly to that result. The Hebrew name of the plant *(dûdāʾîm)* is very close in spelling and pronunciation to a common word for love or lover in the Hebrew of the Song of Songs *(dwd),* and this may also explain its presence in the love poem and the superstition that it is an aphrodisiac. Indeed, apparently the drug made from the plant is more likely to put one to sleep than get one excited.[54] Yet the poet is interested more in literary effect than pharmacological accuracy. The second colon of this line states that there are many *precious gifts* (from *meged*) at the *entrance (peʾtāḥ)* to their home. This colon is admittedly ambiguous to us. We know of no specific custom from antiquity where a married couple will have the entrance to their domicile festooned with fruits or anything else. To suggest that the entrance has reference to the

---

52. I acknowledge the difficulty of the pronominal reference "to you" *(lāk)* at the end of the verse since it appears to be *"to you"* (feminine) in the context of a speech that is marked at its beginning by an epithet that is to be understood as addressing the man *(my love/lover [dōdî]).*

53. See the discussion by G. Wenham, *Genesis 16–50,* Word Bible Commentary 2 (Dallas: Word, 1994), pp. 246-47.

54. So Pope, *Song of Songs,* p. 649, who states that the "mandrake is actually more of a soporific and narcotic than a stimulant." However, a physiological reaction may not be in view here — at least it may not be what generated the belief that the mandrake was an erotic stimulant. The roots of the mandrake have the appearance of genitalia; the analogy today may be with the ginseng plant, an oriental aphrodisiac that is becoming increasingly popular in the West.

woman's genitalia is stretching the point to the extreme. Perhaps the most provocative interpretation is the citation of a Talmudic reference to the practice of hanging fruit in a wedding tent.[55] In any case, the context does suggest that the precious gifts are sweet smelling, since we assume that colon b somehow enhances the thought of colon a. The understanding that the precious gifts are fruits or plants is supported by the references in 4:13 and 16 (see commentary there) as well as in Deuteronomy 33:13-16.

The second poetic line of the verse is also ambiguous in large measure.[56] She has saved or treasured up the *new* and the *old* for her man. This begs the question, New or old what? The immediately preceding context might suggest new and old sweet-smelling plants, but why old plants? I suspect that the terms "new" and "old" here are used as a merism. W. G. E. Watson defines a merism as "when a totality is expressed in abbreviated form."[57] Specifically, this merism is one defined by "polar word-pairs."[58] Other examples include sky/earth to mean all of creation and Dan/Beersheba to mean the entire land of Israel. Old and new things might mean all things. She has stored up or *treasured* (from *ṣpn*) everything near and dear to her for her man. She gives him everything.

55. Cited by Pope, *Song of Songs*, p. 650.

56. "New" and "old" are used as a pair in Lev. 26:10 and Matt. 13:52, but these contexts throw little light on the present one.

57. W. G. E. Watson, *Classical Hebrew Poetry* (Sheffield: JSOT Press, 1984), p. 321.

58. Watson, *Classical Hebrew Poetry,* p. 321.

CHAPTER EIGHT

POEM NINETEEN:
YEARNING FOR LOVE (8:1-4)

The woman expresses her yearning for union with the man by wishing that he were her brother, a wish that is difficult to understand given our ignorance of biblical customs. We can infer from the passage that brothers could show public affection, but why couldn't the lover and the beloved? Were they not married? We can only speculate that their public union would not be acceptable for one reason or another. Certainly this is another example where the Song speaks of a love that resists cultural restraint.

The passage ends with the repetition of two refrains: 8:3 states that the couple is in an embrace (see also 2:6), and 8:4 has a shortened form of the refrain that warns about the arousal of love (see also 2:7 and 3:5). These refrains also indicate that the woman satisfied her desire for intimacy with the man.

The Woman
1. *Oh, that you were like my brother,*
    who sucked at the breasts of my mother!
   Then I would find you in public and kiss you,
    and they would not shame me.
2. *I would lead you; I would bring you*
    to the house of my mother who taught me.
   I would make you drink spiced[1] wine,
    from my own pomegranate wine.
3. *His left hand is under my head,*
    and his right embraces me.

---

1. Notice the related word *merqāḥ* in 5:13.

203

> 4. *I adjure you, daughters of Jerusalem,*
>   *do not awaken and do not arouse love until it desires.*

1 The verse opens with a grammatical construction that expresses a wish. *Mî yittēn* (here with the second-person masculine pronominal suffix) occurs twenty-five times in the Hebrew Bible.[2] The woman's wish sounds strange to our modern ears. It seems odd, perhaps even a bit perverse, that she would want her lover to be her *brother* so that they could share intimacies in public. I suspect that the poet is playing a bit on the brother/sister terms that are used for epithets of endearment in the Song and other Near Eastern love poetry (see, e.g., 4:10). However, the verse likely reflects some kind of cultural norms for public intimacy. That is, it might be permitted to touch, hold hands, and kiss a brother, but not a lover (or perhaps even a husband) since the latter, as opposed to the former, would have erotic implications, likely thought unseemly in public. The problem, however, is that we must infer this custom from the verse since we do not know in any kind of detail the customs of the day (or, for that matter, have great certainty about the time of the poem).

This verse is a nearly insuperable problem for those who want to read the Song as a logical plot from courtship to wedding and then early marriage. Here the relationship is best understood as a secret one; at least it is highly unlikely that they are married at this time.

The second colon *(who sucked at the breasts of my mother)* is a descriptive way of referring to the brother. We should not lose sight of the fact that this particular description heightens the erotic nature of the poem by using the term "breasts." It also is a very intimate way of referring to one's brother.

The second line of the verse explicates the reason for her desire that he were her brother. She could kiss him in public without *shame*. The term shame is what shows us that a matter of cultural delicacy is at issue here.

2 This verse continues the expression of the woman's desire begun in 8:1. She fantasizes, perhaps the result of frustrated desire, about an intimate rendezvous with her lover. The opening two verbs indicate that she is the initiator of the relationship *(I would lead you; I would bring you)*. These two verbs (*'enhāgᵃkā* *ᵃbî'ᵃkā*) could be treated as a hendiadys, translated something like "I would compel you." However, according to the MT this stands as a single colon, and for balance we translate both verbs in our English rendition.

---

2. Literally, "who will give." For this grammatical construction, see *NIDOTTE*, vol. 3, p. 209. The same expression may be found with a strong optative sense in Num. 11:29; Deut. 28:67; 2 Sam. 19:1; Jer. 9:1, 2.

Another interpretive difficulty occurs in the next colon as well and is related to the verb *taught me (tᵉlammᵉdēnî)*. We have taken this verb in connection with the mother (but see below). She has taught her child, the woman, in the home where she now leads the man. From the context, we would assume that the mother taught her daughter the art of intimacy. Already in 3:4 we observed this motif of the mother's home as a place of privacy and security, and we dealt with what is to us the odd desire to bring her lover to that place. We noted the possible function of the mother in the arrangement of the marriage of her daughter.[3] The similarities between 8:2 and 3:4 have led to attempts to emend the verse, beginning at least as early as the Septuagint. The latter omits the idea of the mother teaching the woman and substitutes the idea found in 3:4 that the mother is the one who conceived her *(kai eis tamieion tēs syllabousēs me = wᵉ 'al-ḥeder ḥôrātî)*. This emendation is a possibility,[4] but the MT as it stands is understandable and appropriate to the context. The sense is roughly the same in both cases. There is a further ambiguity, however: the possibility that *tᵉlammᵉdēnî* should be taken as the second-person masculine rather than the third feminine.[5] In other words, it is not the mother who has taught her daughter but the lover who will teach the woman in the privacy of the bedroom. I think this is less natural to the context and may be a way of unnecessarily lessening the woman's role as initiator of the relationship.

The second line of the verse utilizes the by-now-well-attested theme of drinking intoxicating liquids to signify physical intimacies (1:2; 5:1; 7:9). Sexual activity is both sensual and intoxicating, and so is drinking *spiced wine* and *pomegranate wine*.[6] Notice the woman's subtle touch by adding the first-person pronominal suffix to the end of pomegranate wine. She is asking him not just to taste the wine but to taste her own sweet juices. There is also an interesting word/sound play between "I would make you drink" (*'ašqᵉkā* from *šqh)* and "I would . . . kiss you" (*'eššāqᵉkā,* from *nšq)* in 8:1.

3 This verse repeats 2:6 with minor variation.[7] See the commentary at that point for the details of the verse. It serves as one of the refrains of the Song that bind the whole together (see Introduction: Structure).

4 This verse repeats 2:7 and 3:5 with some variation. It, like the refrain in the immediately preceding text, binds the whole Song together (see Introduction: Structure). There are two significant changes from the previous

---

3. For details, see the commentary at 3:4.

4. Or perhaps instead of the verb *hrh,* we should omit the *mem* in the MT verb to produce *tēlᵉdēnî* ("who bore me"), as Pope, *Song of Songs,* p. 659.

5. So Murphy, *The Song of Songs,* p. 180.

6. *Pomegranate wine* is composed of the construct of *ʿasîs* (grape juice or new wine) and *rimmon* (pomegranate).

7. There is no *lamed* prefix to *rôʾš (head)* as there is in 2:6.

two attestations of the refrain. First, the oath "by the gazelles and the deer of the field" is missing. Second, we have the *mah* of negation[8] rather than the *'im*. Both of these changes make the warning stronger and more urgent by respectively shortening the command and using a stronger form of negation.

POEM TWENTY:
LIKE A SEAL (8:5-7)

This poem is arguably one of the most powerful in the whole book. Indeed, it is hard not to think of the remaining two poems as somewhat anticlimactic. Some, like M. H. Pope, take it as the high point and even the defining poem in the collection.[9] Of course, for him (see Introduction), the association of love and death supports what he sees as the main theme and religious background of the text.

As we will explicate in the commentary proper, the poet here uses striking imagery that has Near Eastern mythological overtones. It is the only place in the Song that really steps back and reflects on the nature of love itself.

The unity of the section is open to doubt, and R. E. Murphy is a good example of someone who would create a separate section for 8:5.[10] However, it seems clear to me that at least 8:5b belongs with verses 6-7 as an address by the woman toward the man. Murphy further questions the attribution of the speech in verse 5b to the woman; however, his reasoning is not persuasive to the point that we would go against the Masoretic pointing of the second-person singular suffixes, which make it clear that they understand the speech to be addressed to the man.[11]

The section begins with a rhetorical question similar to the one in 3:6, but in a context where the same answer is not expected. Only the context leads us to think that this question is spoken by the chorus. The function may be in part to provide a poetic echo with 3:6 as well as to introduce the woman who then speaks in verses 5b-7. In her speech, she directly addresses the

8. Murphy cites *Gesenius' Hebrew Grammar* #144h and R. J. Williams, *Hebrew Syntax: An Outline*, 2nd ed. (Toronto: University of Toronto, 1976), #128, 428; cf. Murphy, *The Song of Songs*, p. 184.

9. Pope, *Song of Songs*, pp. 661-78.

10. Murphy, *Wisdom Literature*, pp. 121-22.

11. Murphy (*The Song of Songs*, p. 191) argues that there has been no "previous reference to the woman arousing the man to love under the apple tree." Yet this seems specious, as does his argument that elsewhere the reference to the mother is to the woman's mother.

man. First she declares (vs. 5b) that she aroused him under the apple tree (an erotic image), and then she asks him to proclaim his ownership of her (v. 6). This gives her the occasion to talk about the power of love with a series of profound and compelling metaphors (v. 7). She ends the section by proclaiming the value of love over money, reminiscent of the frequent claims in other wisdom books that wisdom itself is more precious than fine jewels or precious metals (cf. Job 28).

The Women of Jerusalem
5. *Who is this that comes up from the wilderness,*
   leaning on her lover?

The Woman
   Under the apple tree, I aroused you.
      There your mother conceived[12] you.
      There the one who gave you birth conceived you.
6. *Set me like a seal on your heart,*
      like a seal on your arm.
   For stronger than death is love,
      tenacious like the grave is jealousy.
   Its flame is an intense fire,
      a god-like flame.
7. *Many waters are not able to extinguish[13] love,*
      nor rivers flood it.
   Even if a person gave all the wealth of his house for love,
      he would be completely despised.[14]

5 The verse reminds us of 3:6, which follows an exhortation to the daughters of Jerusalem with a question:

What is this coming up from the wilderness . . . ?

---

12. According to *NIDOTTE*, vol. 2, p. 12, it is not clear whether the verb *ḥbl* refers to conception or to "travail in childbirth." The verb also occurs in Ps. 7:15 [English 7:14], and a noun, almost always indicating the travail of childbirth, is used eight times. In the context of a love poem, it seems to me that the moment of conception (sexual intercourse) is more appropriate than the pain of giving birth.

13. The word *kbh* is used here (as frequently in the Old Testament) metaphorically, though literally it has to do with extinguishing a fire (Prov. 31:18; Isa. 34:10).

14. The grammar is literally "they would completely (the infinitive absolute used as an intensifier) despise him." The sense is better rendered in English by the active rather than the passive state (cf. Murphy, *The Song of Songs*, p. 192, who also points out that *bwz* is repeated from 8:1, perhaps as a kind of catchword).

Both verses begin with the interrogative *mah,* but in 3:6 we translated it "what" rather than the more typical "who" because the section continued and identified Solomon's palanquin as the answer to the question. It is on the basis of the analogy with 3:6 that we assume that the present question opens a new unit, because otherwise there is not much connecting the question with what follows. We assume that it is the chorus, elsewhere identified as the women of Jerusalem, who ask this question. After all, what is seen in the distance is the lover and the one who is leaning on him, a fact that rules out the man and the woman as speakers.

As in 3:6, we assume that the couple is leaving the *wilderness* for the city, where they are being greeted by the chorus.[15] The countryside, in this case the wilderness, is a locale associated with privacy and intimacy in the Song, a place where they enhance their togetherness fostered by the retreat. Now they return to the city.

The verb *leaning* is a hitpael participle from the verb *rpq,* which occurs only one time in the Hebrew Bible. The posture of the woman leaning on her lover denotes intimacy and mutual dependence and alludes to what they were doing in the wilderness.

The woman starts speaking in the next poetic line, perhaps implicitly answering the question that they ask.[16] It is the woman who is coming up from the wilderness. However, she does not address the women but rather the man. She connects the apple tree with the place of sexual excitement and arousal. We have already encountered the *apple* in erotic contexts before (2:3, 5; 7:9 [English 7:8]). The apple tree, being a fruit tree with a sensuous scent, evokes an appropriate atmosphere for the act of love, which may itself bear fruit. In a recent edition of Sumerian love songs, Y. Sefati translates a poem that he calls "Among the Apple Trees," which shows the long history of this poetic motif:

> The brother b[rought me] into his garden,
> I stood with him among his standing trees,
> I lay down with him among his lying trees,
> He laid me down . . . ,
> The dates . . . my . . . ,
> The wild-bull speaks with me among the apple-trees. . . .[17]

15. See 3:6 for the view that *'lh* may more specifically assume that they are headed out of the wilderness and toward Jerusalem.

16. Keel (*Song of Songs,* p. 267) believes that the transition is too abrupt here, and thus that this is a separate poem from the preceding question and was placed here only because of the repetition of the verb *'wr* from 8:4.

17. Sefati, *Love Songs in Sumerian Literature,* p. 321.

Again (see 8:2), the woman speaks of the *mother,* but in this case the man's mother,[18] in an intimate way. It seems that she stands in the tradition of his mother by making love to her man in the same erotic locale as his mother did. Perhaps the emphasis on the place of conception may give a hint of her hopes of becoming pregnant.

6 This verse is arguably the most memorable and intense of the entire book. M. Sadgrove remarks on this verse and the next that "this is the only place in the Song where any attempt is made to probe the meaning of the love that is its theme; everywhere else it is simply described."[19] The woman beseeches the man to take full possession of her. Indeed, as N. J. Tromp points out, the exclusivity of the relationship as expressed in this verse and the next militates against the idea that the Song concerns "free love."[20] The *seal* in mind here is the seal of ownership and personal identification.[21] These seals would come in two types, stamp and cylinder, but the function of both is the same. We have numerous examples of both that have survived from ancient Mesopotamia and Syro-Palestine. The stamp seal, the most common type found in Palestine, would simply be pressed down on soft clay to make an impression. That impression would include some kind of personal inscription or picture to identify the person who owned the seal. The cylinder seal, more common in Mesopotamia, was rolled across the clay to leave an impression. In either case, a seal signified an association with, even an ownership of, the object being sealed. As W. W. Hallo points out, a seal "was a symbolic representation of the individual and served to commit him as well as to identify him."[22] J. M. Sasson further

18. I see no good reason to emend the pronominal suffixes, as Murphy does (*The Song of Songs,* p. 191), so that this refers to the woman's mother rather than the man's mother.

19. M. Sadgrove, "The Song of Songs as Wisdom Literature," *Studia Biblica 1978* (Sheffield: JSOT Press, 1978), p. 245.

20. N. Tromp, "Wisdom and the Canticle: Ct., 8, 6c-7b: Text, Character, Message and Import," in *La sagesse de l'ancien testament,* ed. M. Gilbert (Leuven: Leuven University Press, 1990), p. 94, where he goes on to write concerning 6c-7b that "its somewhat isolated position, its extraordinary beauty, and its profound insight serve to reinforce the idea that the sage who composed, rewrote and edited the collection of love-songs, added the passage under discussion in order to show what kind of love all this poetry is about: an irresistible and quasi-fatal factor, a dynamic and vital force, a creative, divine power which unites a man and a woman in an exclusive and lasting relationship."

21. Gaster ("What 'The Song of Songs' Means," p. 322) mentions and supports the argument of A. Kaminka that the image rather indicates finality since the seal was put at the conclusion of a document, stating the force as "Let me be the last to be loved by your heart or embraced by your arms!" While unpacking images is inherently ambiguous, I do not believe this is the comparison implied by the verse.

22. W. W. Hallo, "'As the Seal upon Thy Heart': Glyptic Roles in the Biblical World," *BR* 1 (1985): 22.

suggests that the seal might well have a special connection with death since "seals were often deposited in tombs so that the deceased could take them to the afterworld."[23]

The woman is asking the man to allow her to "own" him, but not in some kind of cheap commercial sense; she wants him to willingly give himself to her. She asks him to mark her on his *heart* and *arm*. Perhaps the first refers to his inner being,[24] his personality, what makes him tick; and his arm refers to his actions. Taken together, heart and arm signify the whole person.

The woman gives a motive for her request to the man. It is a very strong statement of her desire for him, although she proclaims it in the form of a general principle: love is stronger than death. Death is an irresistible and inevitable force. Nothing can stop death, as the book of Ecclesiastes makes clear:

> Then I turned and observed something else under the sun. That is, the race is not to the swift, the battle not to the mighty, nor is food for the wise, nor wealth to the clever, nor favor to the intelligent, but time and chance happen to all of them. Indeed, no one knows his time. Like fish that are entangled in an evil net and like birds caught in a snare, so people are ensnared in an evil time, when it suddenly falls on them. (Eccles. 9:11-12)[25]

Furthermore, in the ancient Near East, *death* is personified as a god of great power. In Ugaritic mythology that god's name is Mot ("Death"), whose power is such that he at least temporarily defeats and swallows Baal, who represents fertility, the power of life. Here the woman boldly asserts that love, her love, is even stronger than death.[26] It is, in other words, irresistible, resolute, and unshakable.

23. J. Sasson, "Unlocking the Poetry of Love in the Song of Songs," *BR* 1 (1985): 14. A point also made by Hallo in his just cited article as well as in "For Love Is Strong as Death," *JANES* 22 (1993): 45-50.

24. Keel (*Song of Songs,* p. 272) wrongly understands *leb* to refer to the breast or chest of the man. *Leb* almost always refers to the internal component of what makes us human. This faulty understanding leads him to see the seal imagery as a matter of the man wearing the seal rather than the seal making an impression (at least metaphorically) on the man. G. Scholem (*Zohar: The Book of Splendor* [New York: Schocken, 1963], p. 70) seems closer to the truth when he quotes the Zohar, the main work of Jewish kaballah, "'Set me as a seal upon thy heart.' For as the imprint of the seal is to be discerned even after the seal is withdrawn, so I shall cling to you."

25. For translation and commentary, see T. Longman III, *The Book of Ecclesiastes,* p. 132.

26. W. G. E. Watson ("Love and Death Once More (Song of Songs VIII 6)," *VT* 47 [1997]: 385-86) cites a line from the Gilgamesh epic (Tablet X vii, lines 11-12), which he translates "the fine young man, the beautiful girl when making love, together they confront death."

She continues in the corresponding b colon to make this thought even more specific. Here, instead of love she speaks of *jealousy (qin'â)*. Jealousy in this context denotes a single-minded devotion to something. In common speech, jealousy is almost always seen in a negative fashion, as narrow-minded and self-seeking. This may be a legitimate reason to substitute a word like passion for *qin'â* in this context. The NRSV, e.g., renders this colon "[its] passion fierce as the grave," and the REB, "[its] passion cruel as the grave." However, I think it is important to understand that the Bible affirms a proper type of jealousy, a desire for someone else that tolerates no rivals. After all, God himself is characterized by this jealousy. The prophet Nahum begins his work with the following:[27]

> The LORD is a jealous *(qannô')* God and an avenger;
> the LORD is an avenger and exceedingly angry;
> the LORD is an avenger against his foes,
> and rages against his enemies. (Nah. 1:2)[28]

Or, in a more positive context, consider Zechariah 1:14-17:

> Then the angel who was speaking to me said, "Proclaim this word: This is what the LORD Almighty says: 'I am very jealous for Jerusalem and Zion, but I am very angry with the nations that feel secure. I was only a little angry, but they added to the calamity.'
>
> "Therefore, this is what the LORD says: 'I will return to Jerusalem with mercy; and there my house will be rebuilt. And the measuring line will be stretched out over Jerusalem,' declares the LORD Almighty.
>
> "Proclaim further: This is what the LORD Almighty says: 'My towns will again overflow with prosperity, and the LORD will again comfort Zion and choose Jerusalem.'"

There are only two relationships described in the Bible where jealousy is a potentially appropriate reaction: the divine-human relationship and the marriage relationship.[29] These are the only two relationships that are considered exclusive. Humans can have only one God. If they worship another, it triggers God's jealousy. God's jealousy is an energy that tries to rescue the relationship. Similarly, a man and a woman can have only one spouse. If there is

---

27. See also Isa. 42:13; Ezek. 36:5-6; 38:19.

28. For the translation and commentary, see T. Longman III, "Nahum," in *The Minor Prophets: An Exegetical and Expository Commentary*, vol. 2 (Grand Rapids: Baker, 1993), pp. 787-89.

29. B. Webb ("The Song of Songs: A Love Poem and as Holy Scripture," *RTR* 49 [1990]: 98, n. 18) points out that Deut. 32:21-22 shares the distinctive vocabulary of 8:6 as it expresses the jealous love of God for Israel.

211

a threat to that relationship, then jealousy is a proper emotion.[30] All this is because so much hangs on the integrity of the relationship. It is so basic, so deep, that it stirs up strong emotions and passions.

In Song of Songs 8:6, the woman expresses her belief that her desire to hold on to the man and her desire to have him hold on to her will surpass even the power of the grave. The *grave* in Hebrew is *š^e'ôl*, a well-discussed term. It likely indicates "both the grave and the netherworld, particularly the latter."[31] It provides a suitable parallel to death in colon a. Like death, *š^e'ôl* too can be personified (2 Sam. 22:6 = Ps. 18:5 [English 18:4]; Job 24:19; Ps. 141:7).

The comparison between jealousy and the grave hinges on the word *qāšā,* which we have rendered *tenacious.* It could also be translated hard, difficult, or cruel. As noted above, the REB takes the word in the last-mentioned sense, perhaps generated by a negative view of jealousy. However, the idea in the context, particularly as implied by the parallel with *stronger ('azzâ),* is positive and basically means that it is tough or long lasting in spite of obstacles.

The last poetic line of the verse further describes the power and energy of love. It uses the image of a hotly burning *flame.* Literally, the first colon of this concluding parallel line is "Its flame is flames of fire"; the term *flame* translates the word *rešep,*[32] which is related to the Ugaritic god of plague, Resep, thus rendering even more likely that the earlier references to Death and Sheol are personifications. Indeed, this flame is so hot that the poet piles up words denoting fire and then concludes with the strongest of all superlatives, a *-yah* suffix on *lehābâ.* The *-yah* has been debated. It is the shortened form of the divine name, but the question is, Should it here be translated as God's personal name Yah (thus, "flame of Yah"), or should it be taken as the use of the divine name in the sense of a superlative?[33] We go for

---

30. Certainly even within the marriage relationship, this emotion can be seriously abused. For a fuller discussion, see D. B. Allender and T. Longman III, *Cry of the Soul* (Colorado Springs: NavPress, 1994), pp. 107-32.

31. *NIDOTTE,* vol. 4, p. 6. The author points out that it often occurs in parallelism with words like "pit" (*bor:* Isa. 14:15), "death" (*māwet:* Ps. 89:49 [English 89:48] and in the present context); "destruction" (*'^abaddôn:* Prov. 27:20).

32. Which Keel (*Song of Songs,* p. 275) takes, I think wrongly, as "arrow."

33. Keel, *Song of Songs,* p. 274: "Hebrew frequently combines a noun with Yah(weh) to build a superlative." We should note that there seems to be a disagreement going back to the Masoretes themselves. We have followed the Ben Asher tradition, as reflected in Leningradensis, whereas the Ben Naphtali tradition clearly understood the phrase as "flame of Yah." See M. Saebo, "On the Canonicity of the Song of Songs," in *Texts, Temples, and Traditions,* ed. M. V. Fox et al. (Winona Lake, IN: Eisenbrauns, 1996), p. 275.

the latter chiefly because God's name has not been mentioned; as a matter of fact, it has been avoided by circumlocutions in previous places (2:7; 3:5).[34] In either case, the force of the word is to say that it is a "god-awful" flame, i.e., burning hot. This flame represents the intensity of passion and perhaps hints again that there is potential danger involved. Care must be exercised around something as powerful as love.

This love is, of course, the erotic, sensual love that the poet has expressed throughout the Song. However, as we described in the Introduction, the love between a man and a woman is used to describe the love between God and his people. One thinks of the tenacious love of God for a recalcitrant Israel in Hosea 8:8-9:

> How can I give you up, Ephraim?
>   How can I hand you over, Israel?
> How can I treat you like Admah?
>   How can I make you like Zeboiim?
> My heart is changed within me;
>   all my compassion is aroused.
> I will not carry out my fierce anger,
>   nor will I turn and devastate Ephraim.
> For I am God, and not man —
>   the Holy One among you.
>   I will not come in wrath.

As we turn our attention to the New Testament a couple of passages that articulate the power of love come to mind. The entirety of 1 Corinthians 13 reflects on the nature of love, but, perhaps more than any other part of that passage, Song 8:5 brings to mind Paul's statement that "Love never fails" (1 Cor. 13:8). In Romans 8:38 Paul lists death as one of our enemies unable to separate us from Christ's love.

7   The woman continues her strong statement of love's intensity. Love is like a fire that cannot be put out. Even a surface reading of the first parallel line indicates this. An abundance of water is insufficient to handle this bright flame. The image clearly points to the endurance of love. Furthermore, the meanings of the poetic pair *many waters (mayîm rabbîm)* and *rivers (neharôt)* go well beyond their literal meaning. We must read this passage against a mythological background. One of the fundamental and most pervasive myths that we have from both Ugarit and Mesopotamia is the conflict between the God of order and personified chaos. In the Ugaritic text,

---

34. Tromp ("Wisdom and the Canticle," p. 95) counters by arguing that much of the vocabulary in this unit is new to the poem. However, again I would urge the consideration that there has been a conscious avoidance of specific reference to God in the Song.

which T. Jacobsen has argued is the primary myth,[35] the god Baal fights the god Yam (Sea) in order to assume the kingship of the pantheon.[36] It is interesting, and relevant to the present verse, that the phrase *many waters*[37] is also found in the context of the Ugaritic myth and, furthermore, that a second name for Yam is "Prince River," the Ugaritic word for river being cognate to the Hebrew *(nhr)*. The philological connections are not as close in the Mesopotamian (particularly Akkadian) myth, but the conceptual association is clear. The *Enuma Elish* is one of the primary cosmological myths from that part of the ancient world.[38] At the center of the *Enuma Elish* is the conflict between Marduk, the creator god, the god of order, and Tiamat, the goddess of the waters. Marduk defeats Tiamat and creates the universe out of her body.

It is highly likely that the *waters/rivers* of 8:7 intended to evoke these mythological overtones in the ancient reader.[39] The poet, thus, exclaims that not even these quasi-divine, superhuman forces are able to quench love — a strong statement of the power of love to endure, to be sure.

Similar language is used in Isaiah of mighty forces that strike such fear in Israel as to cast doubt on God's redemption:

> When you pass through the waters,
>   I will be with you;
> and when you pass through the rivers,
>   they will not sweep over you.
> When you walk through the fire,
>   you will not be burned;
>   the flames will not set you ablaze. (Isa. 43:2)

So far the woman has placed the power of death and even the power of the mythological waters against love, and has found the latter to be superior. Lastly, she pits love against another powerful force, money *(the wealth of his house),* with the same result. Money will bring many things, but not love. Love is not able to be bought. Even to try brings shame. All the money at one's possession will fail.

---

35. T. Jacobsen, "The Battle between Marduk and Tiamat," *JAOS* 88 (1968): 104-8.

36. For the text, see *ANET,* pp. 129-42, and CS, pp. 241-73.

37. This expression is unusual in English but is common in Hebrew poetry. It has the sense of waters that overwhelm their boundaries, for instance, a flood or a raging river.

38. See T. Lambert, "A New Look at the Babylonian Background of Genesis," *JTS* 16 (1965): 287-300, for the view that we should not reduce Mesopotamian thought by arguing that there is one and only one cosmology.

39. The phrase *mayîm rabbîm* occurs over twenty-five times in the Hebrew Bible (e.g., Ps. 74:13-14; Isa. 17:12-13), referring, as here, to the powers of chaos. The NRSV will sometimes translate this phrase "mighty waters"; cf. Jer. 51:13.

POEM TWENTY-ONE:
PROTECTING THE SISTER (8:8-10)

If the previous poem is the most profound of the Song, then poem twenty-one is one of the most playful, perhaps providing relief after the intensity of the previous poem. Here the brothers speak for the first time, although the woman mentions them in 1:5-6. As a matter of fact, the mention of the brothers in chapter 1 may well balance their role here in chapter 8. In any case, they, as in the earlier context, appear to be responsible for their sister and her sexuality. They query how best to protect her and prepare her for the "day she is spoken for," a presumed reference to her future wedding. In her response, for this is a dialogue, the tone is indignant, and she appears to set their misperception about her sexuality, both her maturity and her chastity, in proper place. The climax of the poem has her claiming that she is one who brings "peace" to another. We are likely to see here another of the plays on the root *šālôm* in the Song of Songs.

The Brothers
8. *Our sister is small,*
    and she has no breasts.
 What should we do for our sister
    on the day she is spoken for?
9. *If she is a wall, we will build a silver battlement for her.*
    But if she is a door, we will enclose[40] her with a cedar board.[41]

The Woman
10. *I am a wall, and my breasts are like towers.*
    Thus, I will be in his eyes like one who brings peace.

8 We encountered the brothers for the first time in 1:6. They were cast in the role of the woman's protector there as well, but her perspective was not totally affirming. They made her work the fields, and thus she became too dark and unattractive. In the present context, the brothers are again in the role of protector.[42] They address a question *(What should we do . . . ?)* to an unnamed audience. They want to know what they can do to take care of their

---

40. Taking the verb as related to *ṣwr* I (*NIDOTTE,* vol. 3, pp. 791-92) "to enclose, besiege, block," as opposed to the versions that take it from *ṣwr* III "to fashion or shape" (*NIDOTTE,* vol. 3, pp. 792-93).

41. *Lûaḥ* most often means writing tablet, but its meaning *board* may also be seen in Exod. 27:8 and Ezek. 27:5.

42. Gen. 24:29-60 and Judg. 21:22 make it clear that brothers played a role in the marriage of their sister.

sister (we will see by the end of the unit that the woman finds her brothers of dubious help). The brothers represent societal restraint on the woman's love, and the time appears to be right that that restraint be lifted. Ben Sira 26:10, 12 expresses well the sentiment felt by the brothers here:

> Keep watch over a headstrong daughter,
> For if allowed liberty, she will abuse it.
> Like a thirsty wayfarer who opens his mouth
> And drinks any water that is near,
> She will squat before every tent peg,
> And open her quiver to the arrow.

We can understand the speech pattern in the Song of Songs in one of two ways. Either the brothers are speaking for the first time in the poem, which is totally unexpected, or else the woman is quoting them. There is really nothing to indicate the former, so we have taken the verse in the latter sense. The meaning of the passage is not affected in either case, though we might imagine that the woman would deliver her brother's lines with a sarcastic tone.

The unit pivots around rival perspectives concerning the woman's maturity. The brothers speak first and suggest that the woman is not mature. They express this in terms of her physical maturity — *"her breasts are small."* They want to protect their immature sister *"for the day she is spoken for" (bayyôm šeyyᵉdubbar-bāh).* This circumlocution is somewhat vague but not completely ambiguous. In the context of sexuality and relationship, it is most probably that the day they have in mind is her future wedding day.[43] In essence, they are asking what strategy they should follow in order to prepare the woman for her future marriage. The interchange to follow will confirm this interpretation.

9 The brothers respond to their own question ("What should we do for our sister?"), though verse 8 is not obviously a rhetorical question. Their actions toward their sister will depend on her actions. They speak metaphorically of her as a *wall (ḥômâ)* and then as a *door (delet)*. This architectural imagery denotes her sexual activity or, so they hope, the lack of it. The image of a *door* is clearer, and so we will begin with that explanation. A door is an opening into a room, building, or city. The second colon describes the brothers intended reaction if the woman is (sexually) open to others, i.e., promiscuous. This use of the door image has an ancient Near Eastern background, as illustrated by the Gilgamesh Epic.[44] At a crucial point in that story, the

---

43. Indeed, in 1 Sam. 25:39 this expression *(dbr b-)* is used to describe David asking for Abigail's hand in marriage.

44. R. Lansing Hicks ("The Door of Love," in *Love and Death in the Ancient*

goddess of love, Ishtar, becomes enamored with the king's beauty. She wants to bed him. His response shows little respect for her and ultimately will lead to his friend Enkidu's death at the hand of Ishtar's father Anu. Gilgamesh insults her by reminding her of all her past lovers who suffered horrible fates, and he throws some unpleasant names at her. She is a:

> Brazier which goes out in the cold;
> A back door [which does not] keep out blast and wind-storm;
> A palace which [soils] its bearer. . . . (Gilgamesh, tablet VI, 33-35)

Thus, the best understanding of the door image is that of a sexually promiscuous woman. The opposite image is that of a *wall (ḥômâ).*[45] "Walls are upright structures erected to enclose, divide, support, or protect."[46] If the woman is a wall, then she is a virgin, she is chaste. Her sexuality has not and will not be penetrated.

Playing with these images of wall and door, the brothers speak to their response to either of these theoretical possibilities. If she is a wall, that is, chaste, they will build a *silver battlement (ṭîrā)* for her. A *ṭîrā* refers to either a "camp protected by a stone wall" or "a row of stones."[47] In other words, they will reinforce her will to be chaste by further protecting her. The fact that this *battlement (ṭîrā)* is *silver (kesep)* may be a way of indicating that they honor her for her decision.

However, if the woman proves to be a door, then they will watch over her with a *cedar board.* In other words, they will plug up her opening. They will force her to cease being sexually open. In the biblical world, the brothers often played the role of protector of their sister's sexuality. This likely lies behind the brothers' (over)reaction to the rape of Dinah in Genesis 34. In our present verse, the brothers do not use any old wood but rather *cedar ('erez),* of which "the timber is fragrant, valuable, rot resistant, and knot free. It can be quite hard, close grained, and full of resin."[48] It would, of course, be overreading the image to try to find analogs to all of its characteristics in the

---

Near East: Essays in Honor of Marvin H. Pope, ed. J. H. Marks and R. M. Good [Guilford, CT: Four Quarters, 1987], p. 153) adds examples from *Ludlul Bel Nemeqi* and elsewhere.

45. Keel (*Song of Songs,* pp. 278-79) argues against this view on the grounds that the passage does not specify an open *door* and that (this seems an odd argument) p^etāḥ is the word used for the door opening and *delet,* the word here, is used for the object that closes the opening. I do not agree that the words are used with this level of semantic precision.

46. *NIDOTTE,* vol. 2, p. 49.

47. So, according to *NIDOTTE,* vol. 2, p. 362, its other occurrences (i.e., Ezek. 46:23) as well as its cognates (Arab. *ṭawār* and Syriac t^eyārā').

48. *NIDOTTE,* vol. 1, p. 511.

woman, but I would focus in on the hardness and the fragrance of the wood to understand its use here.

10 Though they do not address themselves to her, the woman responds to the speech of her brothers. She disputes their perceptions of her maturity and asserts her chastity, a virtue prized greatly in women in the world of the Old Testament. She does the latter by simply saying, "I am a *wall*" (see the previous verse for the meaning of this image). She does the former by responding to their comment about her lack of breasts with *"my breasts are like towers."* She is sexually mature and has, until this point at least, kept herself from men. As a result, she is ready for an intimate and satisfying relationship with a man. The term *lord (ba'al)* could easily, and perhaps in this context should, be translated "husband."[49] It is because of her sexual maturity and exclusiveness that she will bring *peace (šālôm)* to her lord/husband. The term *šālôm* has a rich connotation, including not only the absence of strife but also fulfillment, contentment, satisfaction, and wholeness.

POEM TWENTY-TWO:
WHO OWNS THE VINEYARD? (8:11-12)

This poem is filled with enigmas, beginning with the question of who is the speaker. Nothing in the text clearly indicates the speaker,[50] although the speaker is certainly an individual (note the first-person singular suffix on vineyard in v. 12), and so the chorus is ruled out. But is it the man or the woman? If one believes that there are two characters in the Song, and one of them is Solomon, then the woman is the natural speaker. Others, however, detect a third speaker who is male, and understand this speech to be his effort to slap the lecherous Solomon in the face. While we see only one male speaker in the book, we don't identify that voice with Solomon, and so it is theoretically possible that this speech is still a speech about Solomon, who represents a person trying to buy love (see 8:10). More elegant perhaps is to hear the voice of the woman here as she proclaims her own independence from an oppressive male like Solomon. In her mouth, this poem becomes a boasting song.

---

49. *NIDOTTE,* vol. 1, pp. 681-83.

50. R. Alden ("Song of Songs 8:12a: Who Said It?" *JETS* 31 [1988]: 275) stated that "among the commentators there is no such unified opinion. In fact, of the more than twenty commentaries I consulted ten seem to credit the words to the maiden. Eight credited the words to a man. The rest did not discuss it or gave the speech to another party."

The Woman
11. *Solomon had a vineyard in Baal-hamon;*
      he entrusted the vineyard to guards,
         each one brings a thousand pieces of silver for his fruit.
12. *My vineyard is mine alone;*
      the thousand is for you, Solomon,
         and two hundred for the ones who guard its fruit.

11   This verse presents a narrative description about *Solomon* and his *vineyard*. Though the book as a whole is associated with Solomon in the first verse (1:1), this is only the second occasion where Solomon is mentioned by name in the poetry section proper (cf. 3:6-11). Both passages have their ambiguities, but for the most part Solomon appears in a positive light in chapter 3 and a negative one here.

The passage begins in a way similar to that of another vineyard passage, Isaiah's parable of the vineyard (*kerem hāyâ lᵉ-;* Isa. 5:1-7). However, this similarity does not make 8:11-12 a parable, like the Isaiah passage. It is certainly metaphorical, but the reference to *Baal-hamon* could conceivably be a place where the historical Solomon had vineyards. As pointed out by a number of commentators,[51] Judith 8:3 mentions a place called Balamon, possibly a Greek equivalent to Baal-hamon, which is near Dothan. In this regard, it is interesting that the Septuagint translates the Song of Songs' reference as *Beelamon*. However, it could also refer to an otherwise unknown location. From another angle, the meaning of its name is "lord/possessor of tumult/crowd," and the Vulgate translates it as *quae habet populos* ("which has people") rather than as a place-name. If so, such a translation might support the idea of the verse (described below) that Solomon had a mass of women, whereas the ideal couple of the Song have only each other. It would, thus, juxtapose (and implicitly favor) their monogamy over against his polygamy.

To begin to understand this rather opaque verse, we observe that throughout the Song the *vineyard* is used as an image of feminine sexuality or the place of lovemaking (1:6; 2:15; 7:9 [English 7:8]). The verse then describes Solomon's large holdings in vineyards. This vineyard is so large that he could not handle it on his own, but had to turn it over to subordinates *(guards)*. This vineyard is so large that it generated a huge income. Isaiah 7:23 describes a wealthy vineyard as one that generated a *thousand* pieces of silver, but for this one each person (*îš*), presumably the guards, paid a thousand. This may well describe the large stable of women that King Solomon had in his harem (1 Kings 11:3: "He had seven hundred wives and three hundred concubines"). The next verse makes the contrast with the couple at the center of the Song.

---

51. For instance, Snaith, *Song of Songs,* pp. 126-27.

12 As mentioned in the Introduction, it is unclear exactly who speaks here. Is the man boasting about his relationship with the woman or is the woman asserting her independence and, hence, her devotion as rooted in love, not profit? Both points are being made, perhaps with different levels of emphasis.

The speaker, whether the man or the woman, makes a contrast by picking up on the *vineyard* image of the previous verse. Solomon has his vineyard, and he can keep his thousand pieces of silver. The speaker seems to be saying in effect that Solomon can keep his harem. However, the speaker's vineyard is his or hers alone. It may not be so large as to need guards or to generate the abundance of income, but it is his or hers alone, freely given out of love, not sold for gain.

The nagging question of the section, though, is, Where do the *two hundred* pieces of silver for the guards come from if the one thousand are Solomon's? Perhaps I am being too much of a stickler on the mathematics. The guards certainly deserved their payment for their work, and that may be all that she is trying to say. Basically, everyone can keep what is due to them, but Solomon should not think that he can buy her vineyard. Murphy, in this case, would be correct to call the two hundred pieces of silver "a satirical panache."[52] In this sense, the thought of 8:11-12 is similar to that of 8:7b, which rails at the idea of purchasing love, and also 6:8-10, which contrasts the singleness of love between a man and a woman against the plurality of a harem. Thus, this poem, and indeed much of the Song, may be read as supportive of exclusive, devoted sexual love and against polygamy and promiscuity.

POEM TWENTY-THREE:
BE LIKE A GAZELLE (8:13-14)

The final poem is a short interchange between the man and the woman that expresses yearning for union. It honestly seems an odd way to end a poem; we might expect that the conclusion would bring complete and unbreakable intimacy. Perhaps, however, this better expresses love in the real world. We yearn and hope and occasionally get glimpses of a deep and satisfying relationship, but complete union is reserved not for this world but for the eschaton. If so, then we might use the term "consummation" in more than one sense to describe the world to come.

52. Murphy, *The Song of Songs*, p. 200.

The Man

13. *You who dwell in the gardens,*
    companions[53] are listening,
    let me hear your voice!

The Woman

14. *Sneak away, my lover, and be like a gazelle,*
    or a young stag on the mountains of spices.

13   The verse is very difficult to understand due to the grammar. It opens with a qal feminine participle of *yšb* "to dwell." Of course, this immediately signals to us that the man is speaking about the woman. That the woman is the object of the speech is confirmed by the second-person feminine pronominal suffix on *"voice."* The waters are muddied, however, by the reference to the *companions* (*ḥᵃbērîm*) and the fact that the hiphil participle of *qšb* that follows is also in the plural. In other words, it is difficult to describe the function of the male companions in this verse. Our approach is similar to the NLT ("O my beloved, lingering in the gardens, how wonderful that your companions can listen to your voice. Let me hear it, too!") and the NIV ("You who dwell in the gardens with friends in attendance, let me hear your voice!"). However, our literal translation preserves the terseness of the Hebrew.[54] The sense of the verse is that the woman is in the garden[55] but estranged from the man. He yearns to be in her close proximity; thus he asks that he might hear her voice. The male companions are either his companions who are aiding him in the search or else rivals who are also listening for her voice. We cannot be sure, but there have been no earlier references to male companions analogous to the female chorus, while there have been at least subtle allusions to rivals (2:15).

Our translation (as the others)[56] supposes a different division of the poetic line than that suggested by *BHS* (following the MT accentuation). We put the poetic pauses after each set of two Hebrew words. Thus, the prepositional phrase "to your voice" (*lᵉqôlēk*) is placed with the final verb *let me hear* (*hašmîʿînî*).

14   As the man expresses his desire for a relationship with the woman (he wants to hear her voice), so the woman, in language reminiscent of 2:17, expresses her wish to be with the man. The opening verb (the imper-

---

53. The other notable instance of the noun *companion* (*ḥābēr*) is found in 1:7.
54. This is supported by the Vulgate *fac me audire vocem tuam*, for the final colon.
55. We take the plural of *gardens* as a plural of generalization.
56. For instance, Murphy, *The Song of Songs*, p. 194.

ative of *brh*) denotes the idea of escape or flight, in this context perhaps *sneak away*.[57] The verb begs the question, "From where?" The answer, though, is really unimportant. The woman asks the man to extricate himself from wherever he finds himself and come swiftly to her. Thus, he is quickly to sneak away from anything and anyone that separates them from each other and come to her. She can hardly wait. The image of the lover as a *gazelle* and a *young stag* appears as early as 2:9 in the Song (for details of the vocabulary consult that verse). As there, the simile raises the issue of how the lover is like these animals. Swiftness is one characteristic of these animals that is surely in view here. She wants him to come to her with all speed. Gazelles are also beautiful animals. This, of course, is an obvious compliment. It may also be the case that the animal radiates a virility that is here imputed to the lover. Pope draws our attention to the fact that the gazelle is evoked in Mesopotamian love incantations to dispel impotence.[58]

The *mountains of spices*[59] is similar to other mountain imagery in the Song. In this context, it may have a double evocation. On the one hand, mountains are obstacles to travel. She may want him to be like an animal that bounds easily over these geographical obstacles to get to her. On the other hand, they may be an representative of her breasts, suggesting that she wants her lover to romp over her most sensitive and private parts.

The Song ends abruptly, leaving the reader begging for more. Again, that is the intention of the poet or the collector of the poems. His literary expression thus matches love itself, never satisfied with enough, but longing for more.

---

57. For a discussion of the root and the suggestion of this meaning for the present context, see *NIDOTTE*, vol. 1, pp. 743-45.

58. Pope, *Song of Songs*, p. 392.

59. Spices is from *bōśēm*, also found in 4:10 (see commentary).

INDEX OF SUBJECTS

223

Second Council of Constantinople, 39
Seek and (Not) Find Motif, 127-31, 160-76
Septuagint, 20, 22, 30, 90, 110, 111, 118, 128, 142, 152, 153, 164, 165, 185, 190
Songs of yearning, 49, 89
Spices, 156-58, 200, 201
Springtime, 117-26
Syriac, 20

Tamil, 18, 54
Tease, 99-100
Terseness, 9-10
Text criticism, 19-20

Theology: as divine-human relationship, 67-70; as love poetry, 58-62; as the story of sexuality redeemed, 63-67

Ugaritic, 18, 53, 90, 142

Vineyard, 117-26, 199-202, 218-20
Vulgate, 2, 31, 87, 96, 110, 153, 185

Wedding, 131-39
Waṣf, 12-13, 38, 49, 51-53, 140-59, 160, 164, 170-75, 177-83, 188-99
Westminster Assembly, 34
Wisdom, 49

INDEX OF AUTHORS

INDEX OF SCRIPTURE REFERENCES

INDEX OF FOREIGN WORDS

235

GREEK

apo	22
apeblepsen	165
archēs	22
daddēka	90
dōsō	184
euthetēs	90
ēgapēsen	90
ekei	184
ekalesa	128
eklektē	182
eudokia	179
thugatēr	190
kathēmenai	164

krinon	111
lelousin	164
mōmos	148
mastoi	90
mastous	184
orgaō	151
orgē	151
pallakē	182
paradromais	190
pisteos	22
sullabouses	205
tamieion	205
tryphon	190
phoreion	134
plerōmata	164

phuousai	164
hydatōn	164
hypēkousen	128

LATIN

canalibus	190
consitae a	164
electa	182
fluenta	164
juxta	164
plenissima	164
resident	164
sed	96